PERSPECTIVES
FEDERAL TRANSPORTATION
POLICY

A conference sponsored by
American Enterprise Institute
for Public Policy Research

PERSPECTIVES ON FEDERAL TRANSPORTATION POLICY

Edited by James C. Miller III

American Enterprise Institute for Public Policy Research
Washington, D.C.

ISBN 0-8447-2055-0 (Paper)
ISBN 0-8447-2056-9 (Cloth)

Library of Congress Catalog Card No. 74-29369

© 1975 by American Enterprise Institute for Public Policy Research
1150 17th Street, N.W., Washington, D.C. 20036

Printed in the United States of America

MAJOR CONTRIBUTORS

John W. Barnum
Under Secretary, U.S. Department of Transportation

Yale Brozen
Professor of Economics, University of Chicago

Arthur S. De Vany
Associate Professor of Economics, Texas A&M University

George W. Douglas
Associate Professor of Economics, University of North Carolina (Chapel Hill)

George C. Eads
Associate Professor of Economics, George Washington University

Ross D. Eckert
Assistant Professor of Economics, University of Southern California

George W. Hilton
Professor of Economics, University of California (Los Angeles)

William A. Jordan
Associate Professor of Administrative Studies, York University (Toronto)

Alan K. McAdams
Associate Professor of Managerial Economics, Cornell University

James C. Miller III
Associate Professor of Economics, Texas A&M University

Herbert Mohring
Professor of Economics, University of Minnesota

Alexander L. Morton
Assistant Professor of Economics, Harvard Business School

James C. Nelson
Professor of Economics, Washington State University

A. Daniel O'Neal
Commissioner, Interstate Commerce Commission

Roy Pulsifer
Assistant Director, Bureau of Operating Rights, Civil Aeronautics Board

Gary L. Seevers
Member, Council of Economic Advisers

John W. Snow
Deputy Assistant Secretary for Policy and International Affairs,
U.S. Department of Transportation

Robert D. Tollison
Associate Professor of Economics, Texas A&M University

FOREWORD

In February 1974, the American Enterprise Institute for Public Policy Research held a two-day conference in Washington, D.C., on Perspectives on Federal Transportation Policy. A group of about seventy academicians, transportation experts, and government policy makers were asked to appraise national policy as revealed in the effects of economic regulation of transportation. The group also addressed itself to an evaluation of experimental federal transportation projects. This volume contains the papers and proceedings of the conference.

At the time of the conference, transportation problems were in the news—President Nixon had just introduced an omnibus transportation regulatory bill, seven bankrupt railroads were being reorganized, and the energy crisis was again focusing public attention on mass transportation.

More and more economists who have studied the various modes of transportation have become increasingly critical of the effects of government regulation on the nation's transportation system. They have raised the question whether the consumer is better served with existing government regulation of the various modes of transportation than he would be with less regulation. But transportation specialists still maintain that government regulation of transportation is necessary for the public's interest to be safeguarded. The conference brought experts with these contrasting points of view together for discussion and debate.

The American Enterprise Institute hopes that the distribution of the proceedings of this conference will contribute to increased public understanding of some of the issues involved in transportation policy and that it will aid in the consideration of future policy alternatives.

The presentations made at the conference have been organized into six sections. The first two sections analyze government regulation of surface and air transportation. The third deals with different approaches to problem solving among economists and government officials. The fourth analyzes four federal transportation programs, and the fifth and sixth present the responses of transportation policy makers to the questions raised.

We are indebted to James C. Miller III, associate professor of economics at Texas A&M University, for helping to organize the conference, for editing the proceedings, and for providing introductions and summaries for the various sections.

THOMAS F. JOHNSON
Director of Research
American Enterprise Institute
for Public Policy Research

CONTENTS

PART THREE
Problems of Public Policy Reform

PART FOUR
Evaluations of Federal Transportation Programs

GENERAL INTRODUCTION

James C. Miller III

It has become fashionable in some circles to assert that there is a "crisis in transportation" or that "transportation is at a crossroads." Actually, both assertions are accurate. The reason lies partly in the fact that of all the large industries in the United States none is more influenced by government policy than the transportation industry. Not only does the government regulate the carriers and the services they offer, but it is deeply involved in financing and providing large-scale transportation projects and programs. Transportation is perennially in a "crisis" because of rising demands on the part of the public that the government "do something" about a perceived deteriorating state of affairs. Transportation is at a "crossroads" because the decisions that policy makers render will greatly affect the way in which the crisis is ultimately resolved.

It has been said that academic researchers, especially economists, have much to offer policy makers in the way of information and advice on how to improve transportation policy. But it would appear that there has been some inefficiency in the communication process. Transportation policy makers have often voiced the opinion that the work of economists "isn't relevant" to the set of feasible policy options open to the policy maker. Economists, on the other hand, have often expressed disappointment that their work "isn't taken seriously" by those in authority. There would seem to be a need to try bridging the apparent gulf between academic economists and transportation policy makers.

The spring of 1974 was a propitious time to bring academic economists and transportation policy makers together. Not only was the time ripe for investigating how economists might aid policy makers (and vice versa), but national policy appraisal was sorely needed both in economic regulation and in project evaluation. On the day before the conference opened, the Nixon administration sent to Congress its proposed Transportation Improvement Act (TIA), which called for less constraining regulation by the Interstate Commerce Commission (ICC). This, of course, led to the questions: What are the effects of ICC regulation, and how would the TIA alter the outcome? Moreover, on January 2, 1974, the President signed into law the Regional Rail Reorganization Act, setting up a United States Railway Association to reorganize the seven bankrupt Northeast railroads and turn them over to a semipublic and nonprofit Consolidated Railroad Corporation. It may be asked: How would this agency operate? What pitfalls should it avoid?

1

How would it be affected by ICC regulation? And in air transportation, the Civil Aeronautics Board (CAB) was just finishing its lengthy Domestic Passenger Fare Investigation (DPFI) and was beginning to review the possible use of intercarrier agreements to limit capacity as a "regulatory device." This suggests the questions: Are the policies being developed in the DPFI consistent with economic efficiency? What would be the public interest ramifications of capacity agreements?

The federal government's involvement in transportation also extends to the public provision of private and public goods. Several government programs in these areas are in great need of review. For example, the airport/airway development program, established in 1970, has been spending huge sums to expand our capacity to accommodate air travel. Are these funds being allocated efficiently? The Urban Mass Transit Administration has been providing sizable subsidies to local governments for the development of mass transit systems. Is this program successful? What are the alternatives? Amtrak, begun in 1971, is now at the end of its formal "experimental" period. Has this program succeeded or failed? Why? The Interstate Highway System, begun in 1958, will shortly be completed. Have funds under this program been used wisely and effectively? Where do we go from here?

On February 14 and 15, 1974, the American Enterprise Institute assembled in Washington a group of some seventy academicians and government policy makers to address questions of regulation, government projects, and the relationship between the academic community and government officials. This volume contains all the formal presentations made at that conference. Versions of the papers in Parts I through IV were circulated to conference participants in advance. The responses of policy makers, contained in Part V, were given at the conference's final session. Under Secretary of Transportation Barnum's presentation, comprising Part VI, was given as a luncheon address on the first day of the conference.

For each section (except Parts IV and VI),[1] the editor has provided a brief introduction. Also, he has attempted to report the major topics in the discussion that followed the formal presentations. These summaries, compiled from notes, undoubtedly fail to do justice to the depth and breadth of the interchanges that took place. Moreover, because of the likelihood of error, he has chosen not to attribute comments to those who made them, unless the comments were made by one of the panelists.

The editor wishes to express his gratitude to the major contributors to this volume for assuring the conference's success. He also wishes to thank the other conference participants for their cogent commentary during the discussion sessions. A special thanks is due Robert D. Tollison for helpful suggestions on many facets of the program. Finally, to Thomas F. Johnson and the American Enterprise Institute, we all express our sincere appreciation for orchestrating the conference and for making both the conference and this volume possible.

---

[1] The introduction to Part IV has been provided by Professor Yale Brozen.

PART ONE

SURFACE TRANSPORTATION REGULATION

INTRODUCTION

The Interstate Commerce Act, its essential elements having been enacted in 1887, is the nation's oldest statute authorizing direct federal regulation of industry. For the first few decades of its existence, the Interstate Commerce Commission (ICC) played a decidedly minor role in determining the character of rail service. Of much more importance in determining rates and service was the behavioral chemistry of shippers on the one side and the railroads and their cartels on the other. By the Great Depression, however, the ICC was firmly in command. Rather than seeing the increasing competition that trucks were providing as evidence of a diminishing need for transport regulation, the ICC (and Congress) chose to *increase* regulation by bringing the truckers under the regulatory umbrella. Later, in 1940, regulation was extended to inland water carriers.

During the period when the ICC's regulation was fairly innocuous, it received little attention from the professional economist. However, beginning in the 1930s, the ICC came under increasingly close and critical scrutiny by the economics profession. This scrutiny has continued to this day, with academic economists being practically unanimous in their view that the ICC perpetrates enormous economic efficiency costs through its constraints on pricing, entry, and exit. As there has been a secular rise in real national income, so there has been a secular rise in the cost of inefficiencies attributed to the ICC. Barring fundamental institutional reform, it is likely that such criticism of the commission will continue unabated.

Prompted to some extent by these criticisms, various proposals have been put forward to reform ICC regulation. For example, a major force behind the Transportation Act of 1958 was a move to prohibit the ICC from holding up rate decreases on grounds of protecting competing carriers. As it turned out, a last-minute change in the legislation, making reference to the national transportation policy set forth in the preamble to the Interstate Commerce Act, essentially gutted this provision. Another case was the "Kennedy message" of 1962, wherein President Kennedy proposed to eliminate the ICC's power to disapprove rate decreases. This proposal was not brought to fruition. A third example was the Nixon administration's proposed Transportation Regulatory Modernization Act of 1971 (TRMA), which would have restrained (to some extent) the commission's power to control rates, railroad abandonments, and trucking entry. Although congressional hearings were held, no affirmative action was taken. A final example is the

Nixon administration's proposed Transportation Improvement Act (TIA), sent to Congress the day before this conference began. This proposal is the topic of considerable discussion in the session from which the papers in this section come.

In the first paper, Professor James C. Nelson outlines the history of the ICC and its regulation. He gives special attention to the forces and conditions which brought on and supported the regulation of the railroads and to the reasons for including the other modes in regulation during the 1930s and 1940s. Professor Nelson then outlines his assessment of the costly effects of ICC regulation and ends by calling for substantial deregulation in all areas (except possibly certain provisions dealing with railroads), stating that conditions today are "vastly different" from the conditions which may have justified regulation at the turn of the century.

Professor Morton, who, like Professors Tollison and McAdams, served on the recent Task Force on Railroad Productivity, reports that the chief argument advanced against deregulation of the surface freight industry is that competition among carriers will not adequately police the market. He suggests that a restructuring of the railroad industry into four or five continental systems would greatly heighten competition in the freight market, thereby enhancing the feasibility of deregulation.

Professors Tollison and McAdams focus attention on recently enacted and proposed legislation. In his paper, Professor Tollison suggests that the Regional Rail Reorganization Act of 1973 (RRRA) provides far too much money for the ailing railroads in exchange for little substantive reform. Moreover, he suggests that only lip service is being paid to the goal of economic efficiency and that one should not be optimistic about the new corporation's ultimate success. Tollison also takes on the Department of Transportation's TIA. He states that the ill-fated TRMA at least had solid theoretical underpinnings: whereas the TRMA set rules for ICC decisions and limits thereon, the TIA would allow the commission a great deal too much discretion. Also, he argues, it is inexcusable that (unlike the TRMA) the TIA would do nothing about the wasteful inefficiencies in ICC-regulated trucking.

In a similar vein, Professor McAdams criticizes the RRRA for not addressing the root causes of the Northeast rail problem. Instead, according to him, the bill is directed toward treating symptoms. The problems involved have demand aspects, supply aspects, and organizational aspects. The solution to the problems requires the design and implementation of a national, truly competitive, intermodal rail service, free of debilitating regulatory constraints. Under such a solution the various modes would specialize where they realized a comparative advantage and would provide improved service at lower cost. Instead of this approach, however, the recent legislation provides extensive public funding and public management, with little substantive change in the causes of the present rail problems.

6

THE CHANGING ECONOMIC CASE FOR SURFACE TRANSPORT REGULATION

James C. Nelson

Special economic regulation of the railroads in the United States is now a century old, if one dates its birth to the Granger state regulation in the early 1870s. During that long period, the federal government has achieved ascendency in the exercise of regulatory powers; economic regulation has been extended to include other modes of transportation (although large proportions of interstate passenger and freight transport are exempt from economic regulation); the scope of regulatory powers and the essential tasks of economic regulation have changed drastically; and public criticism of the Interstate Commerce Act and the Interstate Commerce Commission has become severe, persistent and widespread except in regulatory circles and among the regulated carriers. Increasingly, the critics claim that in the pervasively competitive transport of recent decades there is less public need for regulation of carriers, including the railroads; that under today's conditions in transport markets regulation of the present variety and scope is for the benefit of the regulated, not of the general public; and that such regulation is in fact a hindrance to technological progress in surface transport and a misallocator of traffic and resources among surface modes and between transport and the rest of the economy. How did all this come about? Why did we regulate the railroads and some other modal carriers? How has regulation changed? What have been its economic effects? And are the conditions in transport markets today similar to or different from those in 1871, 1887, 1903, 1906, 1910 and even 1920? If they are different, what should be done about regulation of surface carriers in the future?

The Forces in Support of Economic Regulation, 1887 to 1920

Dominant and well-established railroads early sought to organize traffic associations that could agree on rates, and traffic and revenue pools that could attain rate stability and that higher profitability coming from higher rate levels and from allocation of market shares among the cartel members. This happened in the 1870s, 1880s and 1890s, when new and extended railway lines and great excess capacity were creating substantial rate competition among railroads and even ruinous or

7

cutthroat competition in some instances.[1] Nevertheless, the major forces bringing about government regulation of the railroads and the oil pipelines during those periods and up to World War I were shipper groups and intermediate-territory communities. These groups and communities initiated political action to subject to government control the market power of individual railroads and groups of railroads. This was particularly true of Granger state regulation and only somewhat less true of federal regulation by the ICC. By the time passage of the Act to Regulate Commerce was seriously considered, the railroads—which had fought the legality of Granger state regulation through the courts and had lost in *Munn* v. *Illinois* and other decisions by the Supreme Court and which had obstructed regulation from the start—saw advantages in moving the public regulatory power to the federal government. They believed they could make early federal control largely ineffective for protection of its primary sponsors, the shipping and consumer groups, and include some provisions which, in addition to the presence of sympathetic members on the regulatory body, would be helpful in stabilizing competitive rates through action of their cartels and rate agreements.[2]

The shipper motivation for early regulation can be seen in the nature of the controls established in the Act to Regulate Commerce in 1887, and particularly in those controls not granted to the commission until more than thirty years thereafter. The controls granted were few but were all necessary for the ICC to regulate railroads in the shipper and consumer interest. They consisted of the requirements that common carrier rates be filed and kept open to the public, that there be a period of notice before changes in rates could become legally effective, and that common carrier rates be just and reasonable. There were also three sections for the control of discriminatory rates: one prohibiting personal discriminations, one prohibiting unjust discrimination with respect to commodities and locations, and one conditionally prohibiting long-haul/short-haul discrimination. Significant 1906 and 1910 amendments gave the ICC power to set maximum rates, to suspend filed rate increases for ICC investigation as to lawfulness under the act's standards (with the burden of proof placed on the carriers), and to eliminate the most objectionable

---

[1] See Paul W. MacAvoy, *The Economic Effects of Regulation: The Trunk-Line Railroad Cartels and the Interstate Commerce Commission Before 1900* (Cambridge, Mass.: The M.I.T. Press, 1965).

[2] See Gabriel Kolko, *Railroads and Regulation, 1877-1916* (Princeton, N.J.: Princeton University Press, 1965), for a revisionist view of the forces in support of federal regulation of the railroads—a view that overemphasizes the railroads' role in bringing about that regulation and mistakes the interest of the railroads in obtaining the appointment of sympathetic persons to the Interstate Commerce Commission with active sponsorship of the regulation actually enacted. Even Kolko at various points admits that shipper groups and disagreements among the railroads over regulation were significant forces in determining regulatory legislation. (For example, see pp. 5, 21-24 and 31-34.) What the railroads really wanted—legalization of pooling, explicit consideration of railroad welfare as a goal for federal regulation, and statutory recognition of rate agreements as lawful—they did not obtain in the Act to Regulate Commerce and its amendments. Only in 1920 in the first two instances and in 1948 in the last instance were these things accomplished.

long-haul/short-haul discrimination. These added powers strengthened ICC regulation of monopolistic rate practices obnoxious to shippers in general, and were strongly advocated by shipper groups.[3] The ICC was established to carry out those controls for the protection of the public and only incidentally to assist the railroads in stabilizing their competitive rates, even though the railroads sponsored the Elkins Act (1903) to limit departures from filed rates resulting in revenue losses and to fix liability and make penalties more certain for unlawful rebating and personal discriminations.[4]

The powers and mandates that would have made the railroad rate cartels truly effective for the railroads as perfect cartels but that were not granted to the fledgling ICC are significant. Pooling of traffic and revenues was specifically forbidden, and although rate agreements through traffic associations were not, neither were they approved by the Act to Regulate Commerce (1887) nor by any subsequent enactments until the Reed-Bulwinkle Act of 1948. Until 1920 there were no franchise or certificate provisions to limit development of new railroads or extension of existing ones into new territories in competition with existing railroads—an important factor in the competitive rate cutting which dominant railroads tried to curb by cartel action. No minimum-rate provision was enacted until 1920, although the ICC early asked for it and there was some railroad support for it.[5] Moreover, until 1920 there was no regulatory prescription for the ICC to encourage combination of railroads, although combination would have lessened rate instability under conditions of increased duplicate rail capacity and high excess capacity. Finally, all suggestions that the goal of railroad welfare,[6] as well as that of shipper and public welfare, be written into the Act to Regulate Commerce were rejected by Congress until the Transportation Act of 1920 and the World War I recognition that the earnings of regulated carriers, too, were factors in the public interest in adequate and efficient transport.

Not to be overlooked in their influence on the character of early federal regulation of the railroads were the antitrust laws. Foremost among these was the Sherman Antitrust Act of 1890, which did not exempt the already regulated railroads from its ban on conspiracies in restraint of trade. This was confirmed by the Supreme Court in 1897 and 1898 when it upheld two antitrust actions finding rate fixing by railroad traffic associations unlawful under that act.[7] Next to be mentioned are several antitrust cases against the attempts by major railroads and financial

---

[3] Ibid, pp. 102-6, 110, 118-20, 123-24, 131-32, 164-69, 177-79, 182, 187 and 193-94.

[4] Ibid., pp. 94-101.

[5] Ibid., p. 131. The ICC recommended that it be empowered to set minimum rates as early as 1893, but discontinued that recommendation from 1904 until 1919.

[6] James C. Nelson, "New Concepts in Transportation Regulation," *Transportation and National Policy,* National Resources Planning Board (Washington, D.C.: U.S. Government Printing Office, 1942), pp. 198-99.

[7] United States v. Trans-Missouri Freight Association, 166 U.S. 290 (1897); and United States v. Joint Traffic Association, 171 U.S. 505 (1898).

interests to monopolize the markets for rail service by combination or acquisition of control of competing railroads after the traffic associations proved to have limited success in stabilizing competitive rates and were found to be unlawful.[8] Finally, Congress passed the Panama Canal Act in 1912 which forbade rail ownership or control of vessels or ship lines using the Panama Canal and almost did the same for rail ownership of shipping on domestic routes. All of those actions outside or auxiliary to the Act to Regulate Commerce show a clear intent by Congress not to promote a monopoly organization of rail transport or even to promote cartel functioning of the railroads.

Rather, so far as possible, Congress sought to make the railroad industry and all intercity transport conform to competitive organization of the American economy. Certainly, the section 5 ban on pooling in the 1887 act intentionally prevented operation of perfect railroad cartels, with division of markets as well as agreement on rates. Only the Elkins Act, which forbade departures from filed rail rates and increased penalties in order to limit rate rebating to large shippers, can be cited as supporting rail rate stabilization, along with the original requirements in the 1887 act for the filing and changing of rates. Though these provisions had railroad support because they were deemed helpful to private rate stabilization activities, they were essential to the shippers' gains from limitation of secret rates, rebating, and other rate discriminations favoring large and powerful shippers. To say that Congress intended to promote monopoly firms in railroad markets or the perfection of rate cartels requires a highly strained interpretation of the ban on pooling, of the regulatory tools not granted, and of the application of the antitrust laws to the railroads. A far less strained explanation is that Congress, in sponsoring the competitive organization of rail transport among major terminals and regions, merely did not ban the industry rate fixing long known to have existed, nor impose effective regulation against such railroad activities. No doubt, many congressmen, several Presidents, and some early members of the ICC believed that, without some industry stabilization of rates, ruinous competition would prevent the earning levels required for the continued flow of capital into the railroad industry.

The Economic Case for Early Regulation of the Railroads

The railroads were regulated, after several decades of widespread public and governmental sponsorship of their free-entry development, fundamentally because their economic characteristics in the late nineteenth and early twentieth centuries required a wide exercise of price discrimination for them to be profitable, for them to operate with efficient levels of traffic, and for them to offer service to all

---

[8] Northern Securities case, 193 U.S. 197 (1904); Union Pacific-Southern Pacific case, 226 U.S. 61 (1912); and Central Pacific-Southern Pacific case, 259 U.S. 215 (1922). See Eliot Jones, *Principles of Railway Transportation* (New York: Macmillan, 1929), pp. 345-51.

shippers and regions, no matter how remote from the large markets or how undeveloped.

These economic characteristics were well known. First, the number of competing railroads in each region was always limited, although the number of competitive routes, including very circuitous ones, between large centers or traffic territories were far more numerous and much market competition existed. Second, each railroad had many intermediate points or territories for which a firm possessed a monopoly of rail service. Third, during the 1870s and 1880s, or even later, the railroad rate agreements were effective for varying periods, during which times railroads priced much traffic as a group monopoly.[9] Fourth, alternative modes of comparable low cost and speed were unavailable, except where canals and deep water courses existed for alternative low-cost transport. Fifth, railroads had a large ratio of fixed and common costs and by nature their capital could not be expanded or curtailed in close alignment with traffic variations. Finally, there was great or substantial excess capacity in railroad plant, owing to the building of railroads in advance of traffic demand, some overbuilding, and the large minimum capacity of a single-track railroad. Together with some initial railroad system economies of scale, the decreasing average costs of the railroad with greater utilization made knowledgeable people, including railroad men and economists, skeptical of the efficacy of complete reliance on price competition. And with their numerous monopoly traffic and locational areas and their recurring rate agreements, the railroads were able to engage in widespread monopoly discrimination, with high rates assessed on commodities and at points having a low demand elasticity for rail service and low rates assessed on commodities and at points having high demand elasticity.

With some exceptions, the shipping groups, communities and territories objecting to railroad rates and demanding governmental intervention in their behalf did not object to rate discrimination per se. Rather, they objected to the rate preferences (including rebates) that large shippers could make carriers give them by their power to assign large traffic volumes among competing railroads. They also objected strenuously to being assessed higher rates for short hauls to and from points in intermediate territory than for the longer hauls to and from the terminal cities located on water courses and enjoying rail-water competition. Communities, regions, and shipping groups not enjoying alternative railroads or not producing large traffic volumes objected to the fact that they were assessed rates higher than the rates between large centers or territories enjoying both several alternative railroads and active rate competition for large traffic flows. In short, the excesses of the monopoly and discriminating pricing of the railroads, springing from both monopolistic and competitive forces in the markets, stimulated the political

---

[9] MacAvoy, *Economic Effects of Regulation,* pp. 13-14, 25-27, 39-41, 50-62, 79-106, 125-35, 144-50, 157-61, 164-79, and 187-91.

demands that led to state and early federal regulation. Early regulation was a shipper-motivated response to imperfectly competitive markets for railroad service, not a planned governmental device for perfecting the railroad rate and pooling agreements. To the extent that it was at times supported by some or all railroads, it was supported because of the railroads' realization that regulation was inevitable because of public demands and that some aspects of regulation might be useful to the railroads in their attempts to stabilize competitive areas of rail pricing to increase profitability. The hope existed, too, that rate cartels would be recognized as lawful, but it took many decades before Congress was willing to exempt ICC-supervised rate bureaus from the antitrust laws.[10]

An alternative case could have been made for another kind of regulation, aimed directly at perfecting the rate and market-sharing cartels of the railroads or at organizing the railroads of each region into single-firm monopolies. If there had been known large economies of scale in size of railroads—economies of scale sufficient to warrant monopoly firms—this organization would eventually have come about without the necessity of regulation as it often did in the public utility industries. Since monopoly firms did not emerge under free-entry conditions but competitive railways did, it might have been argued that restraints, including governmental restraints, on price competition were necessary because of tendencies toward ruinous competition in a high fixed-cost and excess-capacity industry. Such a view would suggest the type of government regulation that would have perfected the railroad cartels and would have provided the minimum rate power instead of the ban on pooling enacted in 1887. Obviously, railroad cartels were not perfected by regulatory legislation until six decades later, and entry and consolidation policies have not been provided by Congress to reorganize the nation's railroads into single-firm monopolies in each region, even in the 1920 act.[11] It can only be concluded, therefore, that the policy of Congress was not pro-monopoly, but rather pro-competition, looking at the economic structure of the railroads, and that regulation up to 1920 was principally designed to bring about greater equality of treatment of shippers and communities. Moreover, except for the Panama Canal Act's divorcement of railroads from ownership or control of water carriers and except

---

[10] Accomplished by provision of section 5a of the Interstate Commerce Act by enactment of the Reed-Bulwinkle Act, 62 Stat. 472 (1948).

[11] The Regional Rail Reorganization Act of 1973 (P.L. 93-236), enacted January 2, 1974, for the purpose of restructuring bankrupt Northeastern railroads in the hope of avoiding nationalization, might prove to be a step toward eventual regional monopoly organization of the railroads, though elimination of some excess branch and main lines in the Northeast appears a more likely result. See U.S. Department of Transportation, *Rail Service in the Midwest and Northeast Region,* A Report by the Secretary of Transportation (Washington, D.C.: U.S. Government Printing Office, 1974), vols. 1 and 2. Also, see the case made for a limited number of transcontinental railroads, largely on service and competitive grounds rather than on anticipated economies of scale in size of firm, in *Improving Railroad Productivity,* Final Report of the Task Force on Railroad Productivity to the National Commission on Productivity and the Council of Economic Advisers (Washington, D.C.: U.S. Government Printing Office, 1973), pp. 231-81.

for regulatory provisions enforcing rail connections and joint rates with water carriers, the original scheme of regulation did not attempt to allocate traffic between modes. Rather, it sought to maintain rail-water competition as well as rail-rail competition.

Changes in Transport Regulation in 1920

The Transportation Act of 1920 restored railroads to private ownership and changed strongly negative ICC regulation to affirmative regulation to promote an adequate supply of rail facilities and more efficient rail transport. Some of the act's provisions can be taken as suggesting that Congress had at last decided to promote monopoly organization and to perfect the rate agreements that had continued through reorganized rate bureaus after the 1897 and 1898 antitrust decisions of the Supreme Court. The consolidation plan and adoption of certificates of public convenience and necessity for new or extended railways suggest the former interpretation, while relaxation of the ban on pooling and enactment of the minimum rate power suggest the latter. The newly introduced rule of rate making, following the fair-return-on-a-fair-valuation standard applicable in public utility regulation, for the first time wrote into the Interstate Commerce Act a necessity for regulators to give attention to the earning levels that were essential if the carriers were to attract capital. This rule can best be regarded as neutral in relation to the economic organization of the railroads. But it was a change toward considering all economic aspects of rate control, long-run as well as short-run, and overall effects as well as effects on shippers and regions in particular markets.

Clearly, however, Congress did not legislate a monopoly organization for railroads. Rather, it sought to continue competitive railroads where traffic justified competition. Consolidations were sponsored primarily in order to solve the problem of weak railroads and secondarily to gain economies by reducing the number of competitive railroads. Both objectives, if they had been attainable, would have been in the interest of many shippers and many producing areas. Likewise, given the run-down character of the railroad plant at the end of World War I, shipper and consumer interests required higher rate levels and rates of return to attract capital into freight cars and road improvement. On the other hand, the minimum rate power and certificate entry control introduced could in theory have supported railroad rate stabilization activities, although in practice minimum rates were seldom set until after passage of the 1935 act to regulate motor carriers. Entry control by itself could not have much effect in limiting price competition from new railroads or extensions into new traffic territories: the peak of railroad development had already taken place. In fact, some noteworthy rail line extensions did take place and did increase rail-to-rail competition—for example, the Bieber extensions of the Great Northern and the Western Pacific in the early 1930s, undertaken to

13

form a competitive route along the Pacific Coast.[12] The certificate provision, however, has primarily been invoked to delay or stop abandonment of branch and other low-density rail lines. Its exercise has been a barrier to removal of redundancy in the railroad plant brought about by the development of highways and inland waterways. Though it has aided some shipping interests, it has injured railroad profitability and most shippers.

Changes in Transport Regulation in 1935, 1940, 1942 and 1958

The 1920 act changed the original scheme of surface transport regulation only in detail: it did not sponsor monopoly railroads, it did not perfect rail cartels, and it merely completed the partial regulation of rates in the shipper and consumer interest. It did not undertake regulatory allocation of traffic between modes except through some further promotion of rail-water competition. The one desirable thing it accomplished was to make it necessary for regulators to take into account earning levels essential to support adequate capacity and technological innovation. Curtailment of carrier competition through entry control and minimum rate control, regulation to establish rate cartels that had not existed previously, and actions to monopolize and fragmentize transport markets and to "fair-share" traffic between competing modes—these were not to become a deliberate and prominent feature of surface transport regulation until the essentially competitive motor and domestic water modes of transport were subjected to economic regulation in 1935 and 1940.

The Forces in Support of the Extended Regulation. The railroads, the state commissions, the federal coordinator of transportation, and the ICC were the strongest forces for extension of regulation to the motor carriers. The larger for-hire truckers, who participated in creating a national association of trucking with NRA financial support and under NRA regulation, including the establishment of some rate committees, became prominent among the supporters of extending regulation after the National Industrial Recovery Act was declared unlawful by the Supreme Court in 1935. Carrier groups and regulators were the primary sponsors of extending regulation which was not the case in 1887. Conspicuous by their absence in support of the new regulation of competitive transport industries were the agricultural and industrial shipper groups, although in 1934 the National Industrial Traffic League, by a closely divided vote, promised support for motor carrier regulation, with important qualifications. Without carrier and regulatory advocacy, it is doubtful that the railroad pattern of federal regulatory controls would have been extended to motor and water carriers.[13]

---

[12] Great Northern Ry. Co. Construction, 166 I.C.C. 3 (1930), 170 I.C.C. 399 (1931), 175 I.C.C. 367 (1931), and 175 I.C.C. 513 (1931); and Western Pacific C.R. Co. Construction, 170 I.C.C. 183 (1931).
[13] Nelson, "New Concepts in Transportation Regulation," pp. 201-4.

14

The Economic Rationale of Motor Carrier Regulation. Federal motor carrier regulation was a product of the Great Depression—of numerous railroad bankruptcies, low rates of rail utilization and return, and general disparagement of price competition during that period. Actually, the so-called destructive or savage competition deplored by regulators, railroads and some motor carriers represented only excessive competition in an easy-entry field during a long period of high unemployment. It was argued that transport was in oversupply, that intermodal and intramodal competition was wasteful and financially demoralizing, and that many truckers were unstable, not financially responsible, and not capable of rendering high standards of service. Hence, both restrictive regulation of entry and rate stabilization through minimum-rate regulation were thought to be essential in limiting excessive competition, in making carriers responsible and stable, and in equalizing competitive conditions for rail and motor carriers. Responsible and larger carriers under controlled competition were to be substituted for the many small carriers and free but chaotic competition under depression conditions. An incidental effect of such extended regulation might be the safeguarding of the low value-of-service rail rates on which long-distance shippers of agricultural and extractive products had long depended, but this was not a major explicit factor in the rationale given for motor carrier regulation.[14] And, it must be added, it is doubtful that anyone, even Federal Coordinator Joseph B. Eastman, foresaw the ultimate market structural effects of the new regulation or the misallocation of traffic, revenues and resources it would produce.

The economic characteristics of motor transport before federal regulation were far different from those of the railroads in the 1871-1920 period. Costs were almost all variable and average costs declined little, if at all, with scale except when operations were over dense-traffic routes where high average load factors could be achieved. Barriers to entry were minimal—operations could be started with one second-hand truck-trailer, and no investment in ways or terminals was necessary. Consequently, what was not true with the railroad industry, there were no monopoly areas in intercity motor freight transport except on rural routes of little traffic significance. In large markets, typically, there were many special-commodity and general-commodity truckers of varying sizes competing for traffic. Firms were free to adopt regular route service or anywhere-for-hire service, or both. Rate bureaus were nonexistent except for some rate committees established under the NRA code of fair competition. Rates were set by demand and supply, and the hearings before congressional committees revealed no shipper or regulatory complaints of rate discriminations burdensome to shippers or communities. Generally, shippers were well satisfied with the low competitive rates and services offered,

---

[14] Ibid., pp. 211-12. Compare Ann F. Friedlaender, *The Dilemma of Freight Transport Regulation* (Washington, D.C.: The Brookings Institution, 1969), pp. 21-23, where the author has overemphasized the maintenance of the rail value-of-service rate structure and low rail rates on agricultural products as congressional motives for extending regulation in 1935 and 1940.

though they often had to exert themselves to check financial responsibility or to arrange inland marine insurance. The motor carrier industry did not demonstrate the natural monopoly or cartel characteristics of decreasing cost to scale or utilization and ruinous competition that inevitably substitutes monopoly or group monopoly for competition. All that could be said was that truck intramodal competition was excessive under Great Depression conditions and that intermodal competition was shifting traffic and revenues from the hard-pressed railroads or forcing them to quote low competitive rates where truck competition affected their markets.

Nevertheless, carrier and regulatory concerns, along with labor union pressures, eventually had sufficient weight in Congress to bring about enactment of the Motor Carrier Act of 1935, with vast exemptions for for-hire carriers specializing in agricultural products, private carriers, and local carriers in urban areas. This was done either without shipper advocacy or, for the most part, with unenthusiastic and divided shipper support, as in the case of the National Industrial Traffic League.[15]

A major change in the character of transport regulation took place with the passage of this act. The principal regulatory tools became entry controls and minimum-rate regulation rather than maximum-rate and discrimination controls. The dominant political support for regulation came from the regulated carriers and the regulators, not from the shippers. Regulation was to curtail intramodal competition rather than to extend or preserve existing competition. Regulation was supposed to reorganize the market structure of regulated modes rather than to accept the competitive ones developed under free-entry conditions. Rate cartels, both railroad cartels and those newly established by the motor carriers with strong ICC encouragement,[16] were to be implemented by exercise of the minimum-rate power and suspension of lower competitive rates, with the burden of proof on the carrier proposing to engage in price competition. Within the motor carrier industry, further reinforcement was to come from entry denials and certificate restrictions fragmentizing markets in a manner conducive to limiting the number of effective competitors in many markets.[17] Since no natural monopoly rationale could be found for the establishment of monopoly firms or even rate cartels, emphasis was placed on the belief that there were too many truckers and firm turnovers, too much irresponsibility in service and instability of rates, too low wages and carrier profits, as well as on the dubious theory that regulation is required for competitive transport as much as for natural monopoly or oligopoly transport. It is doubtful

---

[15] Nelson, "New Concepts in Transportation Regulation," p. 202 and footnote 25.

[16] Ibid., pp. 219-24.

[17] James C. Nelson, "The Effects of Entry Control in Surface Transport," *Transportation Economics* (New York: National Bureau of Economic Research, distributed by Columbia University Press, 1965), pp. 381-422; and Board of Investigation and Research, *Federal Regulatory Restrictions upon Motor and Water Carriers,* Senate Document 78, 79th Congress, 1st session (1945), directed and largely written by the author.

that anyone forecast the drastic reduction in the number of truckers competing in relevant markets or the reduction in total numbers, the gigantic size of many truckers under entry restrictions and the numerous authorized mergers. Nor did anyone predict the tremendous lift that the adoption of rail value-of-service rates for the relevant commodities and services and truck-rail rate parity supported by minimum-rate regulation would give to misallocating traffic from the railroads to regulated truckers under "fair-sharing" regulatory rules.[18]

Extension of Regulation to Other Modes and the National Transportation Policy. Though there were fewer firms in inland waterway markets than in the trucking industry, about the same forces and rationale were advanced for the extension of ICC regulation to the domestic water carriers by the Transportation Act of 1940 as had been advanced for the extension of ICC regulation to the truckers. Water carriers were not high fixed-cost firms experiencing decreasing costs to scale or utilization: they did not invest in waterways and locks, and often not in terminals. They were an essentially competitive mode on the principal waterways. But they competed with railroads for bulk commodities and heavy industrial goods without payment of tolls; and though the Interstate Commerce Act and the Panama Canal Act had long protected their independence from railroad control, in the Great Depression their competition was regarded as a considerable factor in railroad difficulties. Hence, their regulation was strongly advocated by the railroads, regulators, and by water common carriers of manufactured products. Again, strong shipper opposition was in evidence and bulk-commodity water carriers demanded exemptions from regulation. The exemptions granted by Congress for petroleum carriage and carriage of not more than three bulk commodities exempted 90 percent or more of the industry from regulation. For the remainder, the pattern of controls adopted was similar to the pattern of controls adopted for motor carriers. Carrier welfare dominated the legislative decision to regulate, and controlled competition was substituted for free competition. Entry control has been less restrictive for water carriers than for motor carriers, though minimum rates restricting competition have frequently been set for rail carriers competing with water carriers.

Though it had been forecast by similar terms in the policy statement (section 202) in the Motor Carrier Act, a far more important part of the 1940 act was the declaration of national transportation policy which was made substantive law for the ICC. That policy generally specified that the ICC was to engage in fair and impartial regulation of the rail, motor and water modes with regard to the inherent advantages of each. But this economic directive to allow each mode to develop and share markets on the basis of its relative costs and services was hedged by other directives to rule out "unfair or destructive competitive practices"

---

[18] James C. Nelson, "A Critique of Governmental Intervention in Transport," in Joseph S. DeSalvo, ed., *Perspectives on Regional Transportation Planning* (Lexington, Mass.: D.C. Heath and Co., 1973), pp. 229-90, particularly pp. 236-43.

and to foster "sound economic conditions" in the regulated modes. Those elements in the national transportation policy could be, and were, interpreted by the ICC to justify both frequent entry denials and highly restrictive certificate limitations for motor carriers and the setting of minimum rates to prevent so-called destructive competition. Under the full-cost standard often adopted for regulated carrier competition and for finding the low-cost carrier, the effects of ICC minimum-rate regulation were to keep all regulated carriers in the market, including the high-cost carriers; to foster service competition rather than price competition to the advantage of the service-intensive truckers and the disadvantage of the railroads; often to deny railroads the privilege of reducing their competitive rates to levels below average costs but above variable costs when they operated with excess capacity; and to "fair-share" high-revenue traffic to regulated motor carriers on the basis of service and high motor-rail rates in parity relationship, and low-grade traffic to water carriers by holding them to be the low-cost carrier on fully allocated costs and without consideration of public waterway costs, even though the relevant marginal costs of the rails were less than those of the water carriers.[19]

An attempt was made by President Eisenhower's cabinet committee and the railroads in the middle 1950s, with considerable shipper support, to get Congress to substitute a completely pro-competitive national policy for the existing one. However, strong opposition from regulated motor and water carriers prevented any changes in the 1940 policy statement when the Transportation Act of 1958 was passed. In addition, those carriers succeeded in getting a change legislated in the rule for rate making from being effective to the present day—a change legislated (section 15a[3]) to forbid the ICC from holding the rates of a low-cost carrier to the level of the rates of a high-cost mode—by the simple device of getting Congress to insert a clause that requires the ICC to observe the national transportation policy's ban on destructive competitive practices. The result was little real change in ICC minimum-rate regulation that "fair-shares" competitive traffic, though recently the ICC has moved, after years of delay, toward eventual adoption of the variable cost standard for minimum competitive rates.[20]

Extension of regulation to freight forwarders came in the 1942 Freight Forwarder Act. As the permits required for entry and operating authority were not conditioned according to the effects on competing carriers, this regulation for some years had very little effect on intramodal competition. However, forwarders obtained an amendment from Congress in the 1950s to condition entries and extensions according to the effects on competing carriers, with the result that forwarder

---

[19] Ibid., pp. 239-40 and footnotes 26, 27 and 28.

[20] See James C. Nelson, "Revision of National Transport Regulatory Policy," *American Economic Review,* December 1955, pp. 910-18; George W. Hilton, *The Transportation Act of 1958* (Bloomington, Ind.: Indiana University Press, 1969); and the Initial Decision of Administrative Law Judge Daniel J. Davidson, *Cost Standards in Intermodal Rate Proceedings,* ICC Docket No. 34013 (Sub.-No. 1), May 7, 1973.

regulation, too, has restricted competition. Entry control came in spite of the for-warders' small fixed investments. Forwarders limit their activities to gathering and distribution and to consolidation of small shipments for shipment over railroads and other carriers at low-quantity rates.

Since 1970, the tide has turned toward proposals to deregulate surface trans-port, though the rail and regulated motor and water carriers have continued attempts to convince Congress that restrictive regulation should be extended to exempt motor and water carriers. Though the proposal to do this has encountered too much shipper and unregulated carrier opposition to win enactment to date, the regulated carriers have succeeded in preventing passage of the proposed liberal Transportation Regulatory Modernization Act of 1971. This bill would provide commercial freedom to the rail carriers as in Canada and several European coun-tries, would legislate the variable cost standard for minimum rates now applicable in Canada, and would gradually free motor carriers of wasteful certificate and permit restrictions and lessen the occasions for barring new entries or extensions of operating authority on the ground that existing regulated carriers would be sub-jected to increased competition. An interesting feature is the support of powerful industrial shippers for much of the DOT-proposed deregulation except for the wide zone in which railroads could adjust their rates without being subject to the maximum-rate power. Today, the agricultural and bulk-commodity shippers and many large industrial shippers are supporting less rather than more regulation of surface transport and support the limitation of the ICC to regulating the few monopoly and naturally discriminating areas left in surface transport.[21]

The Economic Effects of Surface Transport Regulation

In view of the long history of ICC regulation and the strong support originally given by shipper groups and regions to the idea of economic regulation of common carriers, what accounts for this turn toward freeing for-hire carriers from regula-tion? Several factors can be mentioned. First, the original tasks for ICC regulation, control over the excesses of rate and service discrimination and rebating, have either largely been accomplished to the extent desirable, or could be accomplished without the comprehensive regulation of the entire market that has gone on since 1935 and 1940. Second, the basic economic characteristics of the transport indus-try have changed with the technological revolution and public investment in (and operation of) airways and airports, highways and inland waterways, and with higher utilization of the main railroad lines. Third, as a result of these changes

---

[21] See U.S. Department of Transportation, *Executive Briefing, Transportation Regulatory Modernization and Assistance Legislation,* January 1972; and U.S. Congress, House of Repre-sentatives, Subcommittee on Transportation and Aeronautics of the House Committee on Interstate and Foreign Commerce, *Transportation Act of 1972,* Hearings on H.R. 11824, and other bills, 92d Congress, 2d session (March 27-May 12, 1972), parts 1-4.

and of traffic growth, transport no longer is a one-mode affair with few firms in the important markets. Transport has become instead a multi-modal and a many-firm industry, and there are (or would be under free-entry conditions) many firms in the significant intramodal markets including all modes except the railroads and the oil pipelines. Fourth, since the services of two or more modes are substitutable, though their services are not strictly homogeneous, and there are (or would be) many competing carriers in most markets, transport has become pervasively competitive or could attain that condition without today's regulatory restrictions. Fifth, shippers and travelers have found that by providing their own motor-vehicle or barge transport they can improve the services available to them and transport themselves or their goods at lower costs than are required by regulated common-carrier rates. Sixth, there is far greater faith in the efficacy of competition in markets for goods and services today than there was during the long depression of the 1930s. Seventh, studies by economists have found that up to $10 billion each year is wastefully spent on freight transport services because of misallocation of resources heavily influenced by ICC regulation. Eighth, the low and variable earnings of the railroads and the bankruptcy crisis of the eastern railroads in times of prosperity and high traffic volumes have prompted many to conclude that regulation has retarded technological progress in the railroad industry, stimulated nonenterprising management and traditional pricing by railroad firms, influenced the diversion of high-value traffic from the railroads to the truckers, and prevented sufficient inflows of capital into the railroad industry. Finally, Australia, Canada, Great Britain, the Netherlands, Sweden, and Switzerland have completely or materially deregulated surface transport in recent years.[22]

The effects of early railroad regulation are not easy to discern without detailed examination of thousands of regulatory decisions. The discriminating rate structure, designed by the railroads long before regulation came, facilitated the economic integration of the continental United States. It fostered regional specialization, afforded wide markets for both extractive and manufactured products, and stimulated large-scale production in industry. The ICC generally accepted that rate structure as fitting the economic characteristics of the railroads, and changed it only in details. By limiting personal, long-haul/short-haul, commodity and place discrimination in many cases in which railroad practices were questionable, the ICC widened the competitive opportunities for particular shippers, communities, and regions—especially for shippers at intermediate locations and shippers of agricultural and extractive products located far from their markets. Regulation was thus a force in the initial development of the South, Southwest and West as agri-

---

[22] See "Reply Statement of James C. Nelson," in *Railroads' Reply to Submission of Other Parties,* ICC Docket No. 34013 (Sub.-No. 1), *Cost Standards in Intermodal Rate Proceedings,* April 30, 1970, Appendix C; and James C. Nelson, "Implications of Evolving Entry and Licensing Policies in Road Freight Transport," in *Proceedings of the First International Conference on Transportation Research* (Chicago: Transportation Research Forum, 1974).

cultural and extractive regions, and the Northeast as the primary industrial, commercial and financial region of the United States. By limiting rebating and rate and service preferences to large and powerful shippers, regulation probably also promoted more competitive structures in industry. Finally, by requiring rates to be filed by making departures from filed rates illegal and subject to penalties, the ICC may have contributed somewhat to the profitability of the railroads participating in rate agreements that curbed what might have become ruinous competition between railroads. On the other hand, the ICC's hesitation to allow the railroads to raise their rate levels before World War I contributed to reduction of their profitability and to the inadequacy of freight-car supply during that war. No doubt, the ICC has equalized car supply among shippers and industries by its car-service regulations during periods of freight-car shortages. ICC regulation and the Panama Canal Act promoted rail-water competition by ending railroad control of water carriers and by compelling physical connections and joint rates.

One thing that the ICC did not accomplish, however, was the rationalization of the nation's railroads. Nor has the ICC exercised its power to grant or deny voluntary railroad mergers in the 1950s and 1960s in such a way as to make the eastern railroads more profitable, more efficient, or more capable of solving their intermodal competitive problem and their capital and maintenance improvement problem.[23]

Continuing shipper support for ICC regulation of maximum and discriminating rail rates and for control of freight-car allocation suggests that such regulation has benefited the users, though perhaps less in recent decades than formerly because of the growth of competitive alternatives. In periods of inflation, shippers temporarily gain from delays in raising rates occasioned by the ICC's investigating applications for general rate increases. However, there can be offsetting service disadvantages from lower profitability and lower capital investment in equipment by the railroads.

The benefits of motor and water carrier regulation to the users are not so visible, although the smaller number of larger firms that have been encouraged by regulation may be more convenient for many shippers and more financially responsible than the greater number of smaller firms would be in the absence of regulation. Moreover, service competition has been encouraged by regulation. However, the growth of private carriage suggests that the service standards encouraged by regulation have often come at too high a price, that regulated rates under

---

[23] See *The Penn Central and Other Railroads,* A Report to the Senate Committee on Commerce, 92d Congress, 2d session (December 1972), pp. 186-87 and 198-202. On p. 186 it was stated: "The Penn Central case is a docket of dismal failure by the Interstate Commerce Commission. The Interstate Commerce Commission was the principle [sic] governmental body charged with overseeing the operation of the rail industry and with protection of the public interests. Other government entities failed to recognize a problem and to obtain authority to deal with it; the Interstate Commerce Commission failed to use the authority it had."

restricted entry, rate agreements and minimum-rate orders are higher than private carrier costs. As negligible economies of scale in size of firm are realized in trucking, it is unlikely that the large firms encouraged by entry restrictions have reduced unit costs and rate levels. On the contrary, the evidence indicates that regulation has raised truck rates and returns above competitive levels. It has also introduced numerous service inflexibilities and the wastes of excessive empty hauls and circuitous mileage from commodity, gateway and return-haul restrictions. The satisfaction of agricultural shippers with the rates and services of the exempt carriers and their long-standing opposition to proposals to regulate exempt truckers, and the growing lack of enthusiasm of industrial shippers for entry, operating-authority, and minimum-rate regulation, all suggest that shippers find the economic benefits from truck regulation extremely doubtful. Where the economic case for restrictive regulation is weak as it is for the essentially competitive modes with constant rather than decreasing costs, limited shipper and consumer gains from regulation could reasonably be predicted. The gains to be realized are almost solely in the form of higher incomes for regulated carriers and for their labor, given protection from economic and active competition.[24]

The economic costs of today's comprehensive regulation are far more prominent than the economic gains it gives society. First, the costs of administering detailed entry and rate regulation and the costs for carriers and shippers involved in ICC procedures, appearing in regulatory hearings, preparing and filing testimony and briefs, and keeping up on regulatory policies and decisions, are enormous, probably several hundred million dollars each year. Second, monopoly increments in cartelized truck rates add to the cost of transport service and limit use of transport, a dead loss to society. Third, regulatory policies in minimum-rate cases have inefficiently shifted traffic from low-cost carriers to high-cost carriers, a shift involving misallocation of high-value traffic and resources in large annual amounts. This misallocation comes about from the regulatory support of rate parity policies and the encouragement of service competition between the rail and truck modes rather than price competition.[25] Fourth, regulatory restrictions on rate competition have impeded technological change in railroading because the introduction of large modern freight cars, multiple-car shipments, and unit trains cannot be profitably

[24] Friedlaender, *The Dilemma of Freight Transport Regulation,* pp. 148, 153-55, 164-66, and 173-74; James C. Nelson, "Toward an Efficient Role for Transport Regulation," *1970 Conference on Mass Transportation* (Popular Library Edition), United Transportation Union, University of Chicago Center for Continuing Education, April 23-25, 1970, pp. 291-304; and Larry J. Dobesh, "Earnings Control Standards for Regulated Motor Carriers" (Ph.D. diss., Washington State University, Department of Economics, 1973).

[25] *The Penn Central and Other Railroads,* pp. 10, 87-91, 199-200, 206-7, and in part II, Richard J. Barber, "The American Railroads: Posture, Problems, Prospects," pp. 214-15, 217-18, 269, 276-79, and 280-83. Also see James C. Nelson, "Toward Rational Price Policies," in Ernest W. Williams, Jr., ed., *The Future of American Transportation* (Englewood Cliffs, N.J.: Prentice-Hall, 1971), pp. 122-24.

and quickly accomplished because the lower rates justified by cost savings which make them attractive to shippers are held up by regulatory delays or by the objections of carriers opposed to increased railroad competition. Finally, restrictive regulation has maintained or increased the excess capacity on the railroads, not only through service-compelled traffic diversions but also through restraint on the abandonment of unprofitable lines and facilities.[26] It has also created excess capacity in regulated and unregulated trucking, even when lessening the number of regulated firms—a result of the ICC's highly restrictive limitations on the commodities that can be carried, the points and territories that can be served, return hauls, and the gateway restriction that requires carriers serving two end points to do so over circuitous highway routes instead of over the direct ones—all in the interest of protecting some regulated carriers from the competition of other regulated carriers or the competition of new or exempt carriers eager to interpenetrate their markets.[27]

After reviewing various studies by economists of the economic cost of surface transport regulation, the Task Force on Railroad Productivity confirmed the growing suspicion that present regulation has retarded railroad and other carrier productivity and has proved costly to the American economy. The task force conclusions on the social costs of regulation were as follows:

> An attempt has recently been undertaken to make a net evaluation of the cost to society of ICC regulation. These total costs . . . are placed in a range between $3.8 billion and $8.9 billion. An intermediate estimate, which may be taken as the best single "guess," is $5.6 billion per year. The estimates, incidentally, include nothing for the misallocation of traffic between railroads and barges. Accordingly, if the estimates err, they probably err on the side of understatement. Indeed, simply the idleness in railroad plant and in trucking might justify an estimate almost as high as $5.6 billion. The author of the estimates [Thomas Gale Moore], recognizing their incomplete character, has suggested that including costs which he was unable to quantify, the actual total excess cost was probably between $4 billion and $10 billion per year.
>
> In sum, the present organization of intercity transportation creates an implicit tax on consumers and shippers of perhaps some $4 to $10 billion per year. The Federal government should attempt to relieve society of this tax. The question necessarily arises whether it is institutionally feasible to do so as distinct from the question whether the political interests which the present organization engenders can be overcome.[28]

---

[26] Ann F. Friedlaender, "The Social Costs of Regulating the Railroads," *American Economic Review,* May 1971, pp. 226-34.

[27] Nelson, "Effects of Entry Control," pp. 408-12; and Thomas Gale Moore, *Freight Transportation Regulation* (Washington, D.C.: American Enterprise Institute, 1972), pp. 41-48 and 79-81.

[28] *Improving Railroad Productivity,* Final Report, p. 197.

Conditions in Transport Vastly Different than in 1887-1920

From the analysis given here, several things are abundantly clear. First, the market structures and conditions in transport during the 1935-1940 period of extension of regulation were basically different from those in the 1887-1920 period. Second, the transport market structures, conditions in transport, and general economic conditions today are radically different from those in the Great Depression and the earlier period of regulation. Third, the present-day economic structures, transport conditions, and general economic conditions no longer provide a logical or rational economic case for the greater part of the Interstate Commerce Act or for ICC regulation. Fourth, if any economic regulation is still called for in the public interest, it consists of the regulation of maximum rates, of undue and uneconomic rate and service discrimination, and of mergers and unifications of carriers and modes, largely or wholly of the railroads and the oil pipelines. Fifth, entry controls in the workably competitive trucking and domestic water carrier industries and minimum-rate regulation could be abandoned or greatly curtailed without social loss and with large economic gains. If minimum-rate control were continued it should be strictly limited to the variable cost standard and should not be used for a regulatory allocation of traffic between carriers and modes. Sixth, the relevant antitrust laws should be restored to apply to regulated carriers except to the extent essential for them to reach agreements for establishing through-services and joint rates. Finally, the size and functions of the ICC could be curtailed greatly: its major functions, largely unnecessary under competitive transport, could be dispensed with without injury to the economy.

The deregulation of carriers is a rational economic policy under present-day conditions in surface transport. And it would have been rational during the 1930s, if some erroneous economic ideas concerning competitive markets in that period had not dominated policy decisions or if a longer view had been taken of the economic effects of regulation contrasted with those of competition. Free competition is not an unstable or chaotic condition for the competitive modes except perhaps temporarily under conditions of great general unemployment or during rapid transitions from regulated to free market conditions. Free competition would be highly workable in eliminating regulation-induced rate discrimination, in fixing rates at marginal costs and average costs at efficient rates of output, in promoting the actual service standards demanded by shippers, and in limiting carrier returns to normal competitive returns sufficient for the attraction of necessary capital.

Railroads, like trucks and water carriers, operate in a competitive intermodal environment except for some transcontinental and other long-distance commodity traffic for which trucking costs are too high for effective intermodal competition and competitive water channels do not exist. Since railroads are still competitively organized but with fewer competitors on dense-traffic routes than formerly because of the many authorized mergers since 1950 and since, in spite of vast intermodal competition, they still retain some monopoly traffic areas and must discriminate in rates, some regulation of maximum rates and of unjust and uneconomic rate and service discrimination could be retained, along with minimum-rate regulation limited by the relevant marginal cost of the rail competitors. Merger supervision, too, should continue to be exercised, but with far more attention than in the past to economies or diseconomies of scale and to the requirements of competitive and efficient services. Even without railroad rate bureaus (except for through-services and joint rates) and with reapplication of the relevant antitrust laws, rail-to-rail competition is unlikely to be ruinous or cutthroat today, given the vast size of the key railroads and the higher rates of utilization of fixed facilities today and in the future than in the 1871-1913 era. Retention of certificate control of new entries and expansion or abandonment of railroad lines—under economic standards not preventing efficient entrance into markets and not preventing abandonment of seriously unprofitable and redundant railway lines—would also be tenable.

25

IS THERE AN ALTERNATIVE TO REGULATION FOR THE RAILROADS?

Alexander L. Morton

Even those who are impressed by the waste and inequity caused by ICC regulation of the freight market may lose their resolve to change things when they are pressed to propose and defend an alternative. The obvious alternative is, of course, free competition. But competition is widely believed to be less workable in transportation than in other industries. If indeed this is true, it may be asked why this is so, and whether anything can be done to improve the workability of competition.

The Role of Competition in Transportation

Curiously, deregulation is attacked as producing too much competition—"chaos" and "jungle" are words often used—and as producing, at the same time, too little competition—the shippers and the public will be "victimized" by rail monopolies. There was in 1887 and there continues to be some merit in both these seemingly contradictory objections to deregulation—largely for geographical reasons. Locations served by two or more railroads enjoy active competition for their traffic. For shippers situated at these locations competition tends to drive down rates to variable or out-of-pocket costs. Because of fixed overhead and joint costs in railroading, variable costs tend to be below average total costs. The railroads try to recover their overhead and joint costs from shippers located where competition is lacking—that is, from shippers served by a single railroad. Over the years, the railroads have shown themselves to be quite willing to compete aggressively both by rates and by service for the business of larger shippers served by competing roads and to exploit smaller shippers without transport alternatives. Since rail costs are often believed to be more "fixed" or "joint" than they may actually be, the degree of rate discrimination (both by place and by commodity) is often substantial.

 The emergence of trucking—both for-hire and private—greatly increased the ubiquity of competition in the freight market and reduced the latitude for rate and service discrimination by railroads. The public roads and highways are open to all, so that even shippers having access to but a single railroad now find themselves with a broadened choice of transport alternatives. Lest it be thought that the truck is at best marginal competition to the railroads, one has only to note that truck freight revenues have grown to roughly five times rail freight revenues. The potency of truck competition for the railroads is easily underestimated.

The ICC could have taken the opportunity to relax regulation when trucking introduced widespread competition for freight, but in fact the commission has by various policies actually repressed competition in the freight market. There is a historical explanation for this. The Interstate Commerce Commission was created in part to prevent the rate and service discrimination generated by geographically differentiated inter-railroad competition. During succeeding decades the railroad rate structure grew more complex and internal cross-subsidies were built up as various social, economic and regional objectives were built into it by Congress and the ICC. The advent of truck competition in the 1920s and 1930s threatened to collapse this highly cross-subsidized and politically sensitive rate structure. The trucks readily captured that rail traffic for which high rates had been maintained in order to subsidize other traffic. The response of Congress and the ICC was to regulate trucking in order to preserve the rate structure and to protect the railroads from losing the traffic that provided the subsidizing. Hence the evolution of policies whose effect is to repress some aspects of truck-rail competition. Minimum-rate controls, restrictions on railroad diversification into trucking and on the use of trucks for pickup and delivery of containers, and commodity and route restrictions on motor carriers are examples of such protective regulation.

While the emergence of trucking stimulated competition for the traffic of shippers for whom trucks are a viable alternative to rail transport—and these are numerous—there remain some industries (notably movers of bulk commodities) that are still dependent on rail service or water transport. Even after one excludes shippers for whom truck, barge or pipeline is an option, there remain firms for whom competition—if it is to exist—must come from within the railroad industry. It is the absence of rail competition for their traffic that is one of the chief remaining arguments against deregulation. Can competition among railroads be made effective and ubiquitous?

Factors Currently Restraining Inter-Railroad Competition

Two factors are principally responsible for the subdued and incomplete character of inter-railroad competition. Geographic limits on competition have already been noted. Inter-railroad competition may thrive at locations served by two or more railroads, while it necessarily languishes at locations served by a single railroad. The fact that use of each railroad right-of-way is reserved to the owning carrier is the basis for the oft-cited argument by Michael Conant that inter-railroad competition is a myth or impossibility. A shipper, Conant argues, is for practical purposes captive to the railroad that serves his siding. By controlling the switching of cars in and out of a plant, that railroad for practical purposes controls the level of service, the routing, and hence the rate that the shipper pays.[1]

This geographic argument against the possibility of inter-railroad competition is easily overstated and is progressively less true as time passes. First, very large factories such as steel and automobile plants tend to be switched by two or more railroads. Roughly one-fifth of all rail carloads originates at plants served by more than one railroad. Another sizable fraction of industrial traffic is switched by terminal railroads that serve two or more trunklines. Second, plant mobility provides a company with a countermeasure to its subservience to direct rail connections. And the mobility of American industry is surprisingly great. A count based on Dun and Bradstreet data on manufacturing plant locations reveals that during recent years jobs in manufacturing have been relocated at the rate of about 5 percent a year.[2] If the relocation of jobs through building and closing of plants is added, the rate of annual relocation is doubled. If one includes the relocation occurring as a result of differential rates of plant expansion, the rate of geographical mobility is driven still higher. Multiplant firms dissatisfied with the service or rates offered by one rail carrier may shift production to plants where transport service is better. By threatening to move or to expand facilities along the line of another carrier, a shipper is able to exert sufficient pressure on a railroad to prevent some of the abuses of rail monopoly. This ability to exert pressure suggests the importance of preserving several competing railroads within each region, so that the threat of relocation may continue to be a real one.

Finally, the growth of piggybacking lessens the dependence of shippers on the particular carrier that switches them. With piggyback, a shipper can deliver his cargo to whichever railroad within reach promises the best service. Pickup and delivery by truck are both more economical and more prompt than all-rail (switching and local-train) service, so that having to rely on truck pickup and delivery to reach a noncontiguous railroad is no real disadvantage. To promote the inter-railroad competition that piggybacking encourages, it is necessary, of course, for several railroads serving each market area to be preserved.

The other principal factor that currently decreases inter-railroad competition is the degree of interdependence among railroads, given the present corporate structure of the industry. Some 50 percent of all rail shipments (accounting for about 70 percent of rail ton-miles) are interlined—that is, must travel over two or more railroads to reach their destination. Interline traffic is therefore an essential part of the business of almost every individual railroad. In order to obtain a share of this interline traffic and in order to handle this traffic efficiently, a railroad is

---

[1] Michael Conant, "The Myth of Inter-railroad Competition," *Railroad Mergers and Abandonments* (Berkeley, Calif.: University of California Press, 1964), chapter 2, reprinted from *Stanford Law Review*.

[2] See Robert A. Leone, *Location of Manufacturing Activity in the New York Metropolitan Area* (New York: National Bureau of Economic Research, forthcoming), chapter 1.

29

obliged to cooperate with connecting roads. Inasmuch as a railroad's competitors are also often its connections, competition among railroads tends to be conditioned by this mutual interdependence. For instance, if one carrier pursues the traffic currently moving by another railroad, the first railroad may face a loss of interline traffic whose routing the second carrier controls. Again, if one carrier seeks to win traffic away from another carrier by instituting a new service or rate structure, the affected carrier will respond as likely as not by seeking to have the new service disapproved by a rate bureau or suspended by the ICC rather than by offering an improved service itself. If inter-railroad competition is to be effective as a substitute for detailed regulation, then the industry must be restructured in such a way that individual railroads can act more independently of one another than they can at present.

Restructuring the Railroads to Promote Competition

There does exist a means of restructuring the railroad industry so as to promote inter-railroad competition, thus paving the way for deregulation. The plan is to consolidate the remaining thirty-eight independent Class I railroad systems so as to form four or five continental systems.[3] Each of these systems would serve most or all of the major regions and metropolitan markets in the United States. Correspondingly, each of the major regions and large metropolitan markets would be served by two, three or four rail systems. Each system would have the ability to carry any shipper's freight to virtually any of a varied set of destinations, using piggyback service for pickup and delivery as necessary. The formation of these continental systems should not prove difficult. What is chiefly required is that the trend toward parallel mergers and the formation of regional rail monopolies be arrested and that end-to-end mergers be encouraged instead.

Note that this restructuring meets both of the criteria discussed above for making inter-railroad competition more effective. First, by the creation of four or five continental systems it is made certain that each market area will be served by at least two, three or four rail systems, each capable of carrying traffic to a wide variety of destinations. Greater use of piggybacking in the years ahead will assure that each of the carriers serving a market can compete for most of the traffic in that market on a more or less equal footing. Beyond that, the natural location mobility of industrial production will assure continued competition among rail carriers. Thus inter-railroad competition will become nearly as geographically

[3] The plan to form continental railroad systems has lately been attracting increased attention. See *Improving Railroad Productivity,* Final Report of the Task Force on Railroad Productivity to the National Commission on Productivity and the Council of Economic Advisers (Washington, D.C.: U.S. Government Printing Office, 1973), chapter 8, on which this paper draws heavily. [Editor's note: Professor Morton was a major author of that report.] Also see Henry Livingston and Nancy Ford, "A Plan for Tomorrow," *Modern Railroads,* vol. 28, no. 9 (September 1973).

pervasive as truck-rail competition is at present. Second, since each of the continental systems will serve most of the major regions and markets of the United States (using trucks for more and more of the pickup and delivery operations), the volume of interlined rail shipments should diminish drastically—from 50 percent of rail shipment at present to less than 5 or 10 percent. Individual railroads will manage deliveries from origin to destination. As a result, the mutual interdependence of railroads will be attenuated, and competition will not be so muted and qualified as it is under the present structure.

There are other advantages to such a restructuring that are perhaps equally compelling. First, the fact that this restructuring enhances inter-railroad competition diminishes the necessity of continued regulation of the industry. Second, the percentage of traffic interlined will diminish, as noted above. The process of transforming a shipment from one railroad to another is itself costly in switching expense and clerical and administrative expense, as well as in delay. In the trucking industry, where interchange tends to be less complex than it is in railroading, it is a rule of thumb that a full day is lost in transferring shipments between carriers. Moreover, interlining causes one railroad to be highly dependent on the train operations of others. One less-than-cooperative railroad can destroy the ability of the railroads to perform as a system. It takes only one railroad participating in a movement to cause late or damaged delivery. One railroad in a joint movement can in various ways throw costs onto connecting carriers, and a substantial amount of such suboptimizing behavior occurs in the railroad industry. The continental rail systems envisioned here would largely be freed from this dependence on the cooperation of other railroads. Each railroad would have more or less complete control over its own shipments, and be able to manage its operations, assets, and marketing independently of other railroads. This new independence of individual railroads together with the heightened competition among railroads should go a long way toward improving the service and attention shippers receive from railroads—one of the great shortcomings of the railroad industry at present.

The other additional benefit from the proposed restructuring is that it offers an attractive solution to the rail crisis in the Northeast. Essentially, the bankrupt properties in the Northeast would be absorbed by profitable Western and Southern trunklines in the process of forming continental systems. The formation of balanced, competitive systems virtually necessitates that the Penn Central be dismembered into at least two pieces, roughly resembling the former New York Central and the former Pennsylvania, and sold off to Western or Southern connections. Bankrupt roads seldom have an abundance of management talent on hand, so that disposing of the bankrupts in this manner would also provide for an infusion of management talent into the Northeast.

In sum, highly effective intermodal or intramodal competition—as a potential substitute for detailed ICC regulation—exists in most segments of the intercity freight market. The only major category of traffic that currently lacks such competition is traffic in bulk commodities dependent on rail transport. The absence of inter-railroad competition is no longer so much a function of railroad technology as of the corporate structure of the railroad industry. The formation of four or five competing, independent continental railroad systems would greatly enhance competition among railroads, thereby filling in this missing piece in freight transport competition.

ECONOMIC OBJECTIONS TO THE PRESENT APPROACH TO PUBLIC POLICY ON SURFACE FREIGHT TRANSPORTATION

Robert D. Tollison

In recent years the reform of regulatory policy governing surface freight transportation has been a topic of considerable interest to economists.[1] This interest played a significant role in the development of a 1971 Nixon administration proposal, the Transportation Regulatory Modernization Act (TRMA). This act would have instituted a series of mild regulatory changes designed to foster a more competitive and presumably more efficient surface freight transportation sector. As events unfolded, however, political opposition easily overtook the idea of regulatory reform, and the administration seemed to back away from suggesting even mild doses of regulatory reform. This is best illustrated in the recent Nixon administration proposals to deal with the Northeast railroads and regulatory reforms for railroads.

Since the present legislative strategy is divided into two parts—one addressed to the short-run adjustment problems of the Northeast railroads and the other to general regulatory reform for railroads—the discussion here will follow this division. The first section evaluates the Nixon administration proposals for dealing with bankrupt railroads in the Northeast, and a second evaluates the regulatory reform measures proposed by the Department of Transportation (DOT). The last section contains comments on the validity of this general legislative strategy of separating the problems of the Northeast railroads from the problems of regulatory reform for all modes of surface freight transportation.

Nixon Administration Policy toward the Bankrupt Northeast Railroads

The policy approach to the Northeast rail problem that should be evaluated here is given in the DOT proposals made before the recent enactment of a money bill

Without implicating him, the author would like to thank James C. Miller III for helpful comments on an earlier version of this paper.

[1] See, for example, John R. Meyer, Merton J. Peck, John Stenason, and Charles Zwick, *The Economics of Competition in the Transportation Industries* (Cambridge, Mass.: Harvard University Press, 1959); Ann F. Friedlaender, *The Dilemma of Freight Transportation Regulation* (Washington, D.C.: The Brookings Institution, 1969); Thomas Gale Moore, *Freight Transportation Regulation* (Washington, D.C.: American Enterprise Institute, 1972); and *Improving Rail Productivity,* Final Report of the Task Force on Railroad Productivity to the National Commission on Productivity and the Council of Economic Advisers (Washington, D.C.: U.S. Government Printing Office, 1973).

33

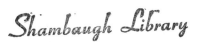

for railroads (the Regional Rail Reorganization Act of 1973), since these are the proposals DOT would presumably have liked to see enacted. The first part of the Nixon administration proposals addresses the problem of restructuring the Northeast rail system. Policy planners in DOT seem to have had three operating principles on this issue.

> Confronted with the railroad bankruptcies in the northeast area, Secretary Brinegar determined that the only meaningful answer to the problem must have three essential characteristics:
>
> (1) The restructured system should make the most efficient use of all resources;
>
> (2) The core rail system chosen to serve the northeast should be made up of economically viable services which constituted the most efficient form of transportation; and,
>
> (3) That service be supplied to the largest part of the dependent population with the least amount of Federal funding, and within the broad framework of the private sector.[2]

The mode of determining the core rail system was "design testing" by departmental analysts. The means of achieving these objectives were to be $40 million for planning the restructuring and $80 million for payments to the railroads for cash needs during the restructuring period. (The actual amounts turned out to be $43.5 million and $85 million, respectively.) However, DOT had more concrete legislative objectives for the Northeast railroads.

> (1) The legislation must protect the public interest in seeing that adequate rail service is provided where warranted;
>
> (2) It must provide for a restructuring that involves the six bankrupt carriers as a group;
>
> (3) In order to avoid a repeat of the present crisis, the restructured system must be economically viable in the long run; and
>
> (4) Federal financial assistance should be coupled with private sector involvement—a joint effort, not a Federal bail-out with a heavy burden on the general taxpayers.[3]

There is a hint that further aid for railroads could be forthcoming if the rebuilt system cannot stand on its own feet.[4]

---

[2] This and subsequent quotations in the text outlining the Department of Transportation's approach to the Northeast rail problem and regulatory reform are taken from a speech given by John W. Snow, deputy assistant secretary of transportation for policy, plans and international affairs, before the annual meeting of the Accounting Division, Association of American Railroads, Phoenix, Arizona, October 26, 1973. The criticisms in the text of these proposals are not directed personally at Dr. Snow. Rather, his speech was used as a source because it provided a readily available version of the proposals DOT presumably wished to have enacted.

[3] Ibid.

[4] Ibid.

In many respects this plan was not a particularly bad one from an economist's point of view. But if one reads the plan closely, it is apparent that there are some serious problems. One problem is raised by the (as it turns out) false stress on efficiency in resource allocation as the primary objective for a restructured Northeast system. This stress on economic efficiency seems somewhat odd since it only refers to the operation of the restructured rail system and not to the restructuring itself. The problem of minimizing the cost of the allocative adjustment in this sector is also important. But it is not really the critical problem since in the DOT legislative objectives the idea of efficiency seems to have been displaced in favor of some principle of "warranted" rail service. What seems to be behind this change is a vague notion of non-market-determined "essential" rail services—services presumably to be decided upon by departmental analysts with the use of simulation techniques ("design testing").

What can one say about this approach to economic efficiency? On the one hand, if the talk about economic efficiency is serious, there is reason to believe that it would be appropriate to allow the market to adjust resource allocation in this sector. Deregulation and private financing of adjustment costs would promote an efficient allocation of resources among Northeast railroads. A simulation study of essential rail services would be somewhat beside the point in this setting inasmuch as market actors possess the information necessary for efficient resource allocation.[5]

The notion of essential rail service and the use of a simulation study by DOT to define essential rail services suggest that economic efficiency is not the only DOT objective. Some non-market criterion is being applied to define essential rail service, although the criterion is never explicitly defined. A simulation study might be useful if there were some well-defined criterion to be used in determining whether the market for rail services is misallocating resources. In the absence of such a criterion, simulation studies can only give the appearance of defining an "essential" rail network.

These points are obvious, though not so obvious to economists before Hayek's seminal paper on knowledge,[6] and the conclusion to be drawn on the basis of this discussion is that (contrary to the language of "efficiency" used by DOT), there must always have been an implicit non-market criterion involved in planning for the Northeast roads. This is not surprising. What is hard to discover, however, is exactly what this criterion is. At one extreme, it could be ventured that the criterion would be defined by the fact that congressmen object to the abandonment of transportation services in their districts. In this case essential rail services would predictably turn out to encompass a larger Northeast rail system than the market

---

5 J. M. Buchanan, *Cost and Choice* (Chicago: Markham, 1969).

6 F. A. Hayek, "Economics and Knowledge," *Economica*, vol. 4 (1937), pp. 33-54.

would produce. At another extreme, simulators might overzealously prune more trackage from the Northeast rail system than a market adjustment would prune.

A main problem in this case is that the simulators may view the competition of competing mainlines as costly and therefore proceed to streamline the Northeast rail system into one or a series of monopoly lines. In other words, the simulators may forget that there are important costs of avoiding competition in this way. There is, for example, the cost involved in the continued regulation of these railroads by the Interstate Commerce Commission (ICC) on the ground that monopoly power would otherwise prevail in this sector. A related and severe problem lies in the danger of trying to simulate what the market would produce when the simulation must by and large accept the present technology of railroading as given. Simulation cannot sensibly take into account the fact that, under open competition and free from regulatory and labor constraints, railroads might be able to serve many now unprofitable branch lines profitably with one-man trains. Finally, if one wanted to seek culprits elsewhere, it could also be observed that bureaucracies like to control things, and bureaucrats often think themselves smarter than those they control, in this case railroad managers.[7] While it is interesting to know why bureacracies behave as they do, there would appear to be justifiable concern that this approach and attitude would result in a considerable misallocation of railroad resources.

A second major problem in the DOT approach to restructuring the Northeast rail system lies in the proposed procedures for conveying the assets of the bankrupt roads. The following view on conveyance procedures has been stressed by the Department of Transportation:

> We believe it essential that the transfer of assets from the bankrupt companies to the new system be arranged through negotiation. We are opposed to the provisions of the bill which would mandate any direct or indirect Federal taking. As noted earlier, we feel that a mandatory taking could lead to excessive values being placed upon the transferred assets. We believe the proper way to establish equitable value is by negotiation, not legislation.[8]

While this recommendation does not necessarily imply a large gift to claimants in the bankrupt estates, it does imply some federal gift to these individuals beyond what their assets would bring in a pure auction. This does not seem a wise policy to follow. Perhaps the best analogy to such a procedure is that of subsidizing flood insurance for those who build on a flood plain. The cost of making bad decisions is thereby lowered and, at the margin, entry into counterproductive activity promoted.

---

[7] While at present railroad managers survive who play the regulatory game well, this is merely a form of maximizing behavior within the relevant constraint set. It carries no implication at all about how "smart" railroad managers are or how they would respond to an altered constraint set, such as deregulation.

[8] Snow, speech, October 26, 1973.

A final problem remains to be noted in the government's approach to the short-run adjustment of the Northeast roads. Government officials appear to believe that the economic adjustment required will not be painful or severe. Of course, one can see why it would be advertised that an interim private-public body and a little (lots of?) money can make required economic and social adjustments less painful. But this sort of advertising usually turns out to be like patent medicine, and when the economic adjustments do come, no one seems prepared for their severity. Would it not be better to address the issue more frankly?

DOT's Proposals for Regulatory Reform

It is difficult to discern the problems in DOT's present regulatory reform initiatives for railroads simply by reading their list of proposals. An understanding of the problems in this area requires considerable reading between the lines in the present proposals. The discussion in this section is addressed to this reading between the lines.[9]

An initial problem in the DOT approach to regulatory reform for railroads is the department's implicit assumption that the ICC is a group of "good guys" who can be counted on to apply considerable discretion in implementing the various regulatory changes proposed—all the discretion being exercised in a manner that will help achieve economic efficiency. As an example, let us suppose that railroads are to be provided with an expedited procedure for abandoning service. Under the new procedure there would continue to be considerable ICC discretion in the process of abandonment. Indeed, it is hard to determine by reading the DOT proposal whether abandonment would be speeded up at all. And the proposal for abandonment is just one example. The same point applies to all the substantive regulatory reforms for railroads—abandonment, rate making, and so on. To allow the ICC to continue to exercise this sort of power amounts to a wish (a death wish?) that the ICC will regulate in the interest of economic common sense. But surely enough evidence has been gathered in the past to lead one not to trust such wishes.

In this respect the contrast with the TRMA is startling. Rather than leave the ICC discretion to operate regulatory controls, the TRMA set forth rules which bounded the domain of regulatory power. The "zone of reasonableness" proposed for rate-making freedom is perhaps the best example of this approach. Admittedly, the ICC's power was not bounded entirely, but TRMA was surely a step in the right direction. The drafters of TRMA made no assumptions about the good intentions of the ICC. The analogy of rules against discretion in the conduct of monetary policy is too strong to miss here.

---

[9] For the DOT proposals, see the Transportation Improvement Act sent to Congress by the Nixon administration on February 13, 1974.

A second problem in the DOT package of regulatory reforms is the absence of any attempt to foster a more competitive trucking sector. It is noted that "the Department has underway a major research program designed to identify the need for regulatory change in the trucking and water carrier industry." [10] This appears to be another example of an escape route enabling the bureaucrats to avoid confrontation with special interests. However, the department could advance several (false) justifications for failing to suggest regulatory reforms for trucking. For example, the department could argue that not enough is known about the "need" for such reforms. But this is pure evasion, since there are ample existing studies demonstrating the allocative and distributive economic costs of ICC controls over trucking.[11] Furthermore, one would not ordinarily expect more knowledge about monopoly rents to change anyone's views on whether there should be unrestricted entry into trucking. Indeed, the department may argue that trucking does not present a public policy issue in the same sense as railroads since it is a "healthy" industry (indeed!) by the usual standards. But of course the establishment of monopoly power through regulation is just as serious a "public problem" as a declining industry in which disinvestment is being systematically hampered by public policy (indeed, disinvestment caused by public policy in some areas, for example, boxcars).

Finally, in considering the DOT proposals, it should be recalled that the provisions in TRMA were by and large formulated for clear analytical reasons.[12] The major studies of the effects of regulation on surface freight transportation suggest that certain welfare gains could be realized by easing certain regulatory constraints. The TRMA attempted to achieve these gains in an orderly fashion and on the basis of sound economic theory. The current DOT approach shows anything but a well-founded basis in economic theory. The proposals have no special rationale except perhaps that they are those that will generate the least political opposition from special interests.

Going a little further in the same vein, it is useful to examine the often-heard objection that public policy cannot be made on the basis of "economic theory." Of course, welfare loss measures are sensitive to specification and data problems, and, indeed, the dollar amounts involved usually strike one as trivial (not counting the questionable redistribution of income from consumers to special interests). But several points should be noted here. First, there are a number of reasons to suspect that published estimates of welfare losses from regulation of surface freight

---

[10] Snow, speech, October 26, 1973.

[11] See footnote 1 above. Perhaps the department wished to have its own study of trucking. This is fine, but at the margin seems to be a waste of paper and time, given that there have already been a number of competent and thorough inside and outside studies addressed to the deregulation issues presented by trucking.

[12] See *Economic Report of the President* (Washington, D.C.: U.S. Government Printing Office, 1970, 1971, and 1972).

38

transportation are biased on the low side.[13] Second, the fact that any given measure of welfare loss is small relative, say, to GNP is little comfort when government does many things to misallocate resources.[14] Third, welfare loss measures do not account for the transfer of rents from consumers to shareholders in firms sheltered from competition by government. While this is an income transfer and not an allocative loss, most equity criteria would weigh against the distributional consequences of economic regulation. Fourth, on the view that one cannot make policy based on economic theory, it is useful to reiterate the simple point that everyone operates according to some theory or model when dealing with a policy problem (or any problem). The relevant issue is whether the model is internally consistent and related to the real world. It seems clear that in the regulatory reform of surface freight transportation, the economists are the only ones to have offered an explicit, consistent, and empirically relevant model. While one may object to the economists' approach, it seems a little silly to object to it on the grounds that it is "unrealistic." Translated properly, "unrealistic" usually means that a proposal has not taken account of political income transfers. But even on this count, the DOT proposals seem overall to amount to a subsidy to the railroads in exchange for virtually no regulatory medicine—some deal.

This sort of analysis could be prolonged by an examination of each detailed proposal listed by the department. (For example, why does there have to be a publicly financed study of means to improve control over rolling stock?) However, enough has been said to give the general flavor of an economic criticism of the DOT approach, or non-approach, to regulatory reform.

Separating the Northeast Rail Problem from Regulatory Reform

A final point that seems worth emphasizing is that the legislative strategy of separating the present problems of the Northeast roads from general regulatory reform measures seems unwise. In the first place, the regulatory reforms, since they affect all railroads, are really the crux of the matter. Without some sort of sensible regulatory reform, one shudders to think of the future of private railroading in the United States. In an economic sense the problems facing the Northeast roads and the issues of regulatory reform are not really distinct. The central problem is to promote an efficient surface freight transportation sector over the long run, and the answer lies in practically complete deregulation. But the first half of the Nixon administration proposals have led to a massive handout to the industry. It is incredibly hard to understand why the railroads continue to get those doses of public income free of charge.

---

13 See the relevant discussion in the sources cited in footnote 1 above.

14 See L. Yeager and D. Tuerck, *Trade Policy and the Price System* (Scranton, Pa.: International Textbook Co., 1966), p. 60, for the attribution of this point to Ronald Coase.

THE PENN CENTRAL CRISIS, A FAIRY TALE, AND THE NORTHEAST RAIL BILL

Alan K. McAdams

The transportation system of this country or of any industrialized country is extremely complex. Few in this room can claim to understand our transportation system fully, yet most of us know more (almost infinitely more) about it than the "intelligent layman"—a category into which most members of Congress outside the relevant committees must fall on an issue such as this. The U.S. transportation system is larger and more difficult to comprehend than the proverbial elephant explored by the blind men. Reports from persons experienced in various aspects of the transportation system filter in to the layman in a manner more confusing than the reports attributed to those blind men. Yet some things are "known" today about the system, its workings, and its failings.

Professor Nelson's paper reaffirms one thing we do know: at least from the 1930s on, the railroads have been in a competitively structured industry. A second thing we know from experience is that railroads—and the Penn Central in particular—are an essential part of the transportation system of the country. This has been brought home by each cessation of service, no matter how brief. It takes a perverse sort of genius for a country "committed" to a market economy to arrange for an essential economic activity carried on through an inherently competitive structure to be delivered without profit. Yet this is what we as a nation have achieved.

In this paper I wish to raise several questions. First, have we, through the Northeast rail bill (that is, the Regional Rail Reorganization Act of 1972), exercised ingenuity of a similar quality to resolve the railroad crisis? Second, what would be required for a full resolution of railroad problems of the nation? Third, if the federal actions to date do not represent a full resolution of the railroad problems, how effective are they likely to be?

In its final report in November 1973, the Federal Task Force on Railroad Productivity states unequivocally that the Northeast rail crisis is merely the forerunner of the nationwide rail crisis which has been simultaneously in the making. This evaluation appears not to have gained much attention in the reactions to the report, but it lends urgency to an analysis of the Northeast rail bill and the further

The author wishes to express appreciation to George Hilton, Marvin Kosters, and James C. Miller III for their comments on the original draft of this paper.

proposals by the executive and legislative branches of government for resolving the problems of the railroads in the Northeast.

Let me not keep you in suspense. Some aspects of the bill can be evaluated immediately and without a detailed analysis of the legislation in question—because the most important features of the Northeast rail bill are those which are absent. One major conclusion of this paper is that the Northeast rail bill represents an enormous opportunity lost. It and the subsequent proposals before Congress imply a continuing deterioration of rail freight service in the U.S. and the emergence of new rail crises in the future—very likely the not too distant future.

Some persons in Congress appear to have recognized this at least on an intuitive level. For example, Senator J. Glenn Beall of Maryland expressed his disquietude on the floor of the Senate during debate on the final version of the legislation: "This is the last step, in my opinion, before nationalization of the railroads of the Northeastern section of the country." Though he did go on to soften his remarks a bit in his next sentences, it appears that he may have been quite correct in what he said. The parallel of the current situation in the U.S. to an earlier stage in British rail history (as well as to the recent record of Amtrak) are a bit unsettling.

Background

The symptoms of the railroad problem have been around for some time: (1) bankruptcy and near bankruptcy of major carriers, (2) decreasing service levels from the system as a whole, (3) recurring freight car shortages, (4) threatened labor strife, and so on. These symptoms have occurred despite facts which would apparently imply improvement in the condition of railroads: (1) continuing major gains in productivity per man-hour over many years, (2) a recent boom in rail traffic growth, (3) apparently harmonious achievement of a 61 percent decrease in the railroad work force over the past quarter century, and (4) virtually complete removal of the passenger service deficit through Amtrak.

An observation that must be made by even the complete layman is that the negatives in the first grouping have persisted despite the presence of the positives in the second list. One hears vague statements in explanation of this, attributing the fact to "inefficient management." The task force report presents the problem more concretely in pointing out that no one person, and no one group, is in a position to manage a given railroad, and this in face of one of the most demanding sets of circumstances facing management anywhere. Managers cannot appropriately be held responsible for something over which they do not have power or authority. The manager's lack of power to manage is in fact one of the key problems of the railroads. What are others?

The Problems

The problems of the railroads in the U.S. involve factors of demand, factors of supply, and factors of organization.

Since 1910, when the U.S. rail network was essentially in place, a number of fundamental changes have occurred to influence the demand for rail services. First, the price elasticity of demand for railroad services has increased enormously through the availability of alternate modes of transport—autos, airplanes, and buses for passengers, trucks and air freight for high-value manufactured goods, barge lines and ships for some bulk cargoes, pipelines for petroleum and other fluid or fluidized products, and high-voltage transmission lines to substitute for the rail shipment of coal. Second, the income elasticity of demand for railroad services has decreased sharply as we have become more affluent—the United States now has a service-based economy with more than half of GNP originating in the service sector, light-weight, high-technology goods are being substituted for heavier manufactured products, and foodstuffs and other bulk commodities are becoming less prominent in the economy.

Many of the changes on the supply side of the picture have already been catalogued for their impact on demand elasticities. Other fundamental changes have also occurred, some in response to demand changes. The output mix has changed substantially—mainly toward bulk commodities and heavy low-value manufactured goods. The input mix has shifted—a slowly rising level of output has been supplied with a roughly constant level of plant and equipment and a rapidly declining labor force. Service has declined both absolutely and relatively—delivery times are less certain and generally longer, breakage is excessive, and freight car "shortages" recur time after time.

Organizational difficulties on various levels have also contributed significantly to the problems of the railroads. First, the railroad plant has remained essentially static in the face of significant population shifts. For example, at the turn of the century the population was largely rural, with centers located along rail lines; today, however, the population is predominantly urban and suburban and scattered broadly. Second, there are sixty-eight Class I railroads in the country which must cooperate to perform as a system, and yet must compete with each other to gain the patronage of shippers. Being required to do both, they neither cooperate nor compete effectively. Third, a large portion of total commerce in the U.S. today is carried on in self-sufficient regions of approximately 200 miles' radius (the megalopolies). Fourth, today's railroad managers do not control their own destinies. The ICC controls the rate of exit from markets. It also controls the price charged for freight, and other railroads and even truck lines and barge lines are able to intervene in rate setting through rate bureaus. Railroads must negotiate with each other over the division of revenues from interline shipments (and 50 percent of shipments for a total of 70 percent of revenues go over two or more lines). Revenues are essentially unrelated to costs, and thus many railroad managers do not know their costs. Rail cars move freely over the full railroad system, so that no railroad can control its own fleet. Per diems, demurrage, and mileage charges for the use of cars of other lines are set arbitrarily by regulators. Up to $5 billion worth of rail cars are not even owned by railroads, but by shippers or financial institutions. Finally, work rules and manning requirements negotiated over a long history and reflecting the balkanized past dictate train size, crew size, and arbitrary change points.

The impact of these factors has been felt not only in the Northeast, but throughout the system as a whole. The impact on the Northeast has been more profound because of the relative decline of that sector of the economy along with the presence there of the most elaborated (and overbuilt) portion of the rail network. But there is something more. The U.S. railroads have not achieved a rationalization or adaptation of their physical plant to the changed conditions of their markets. Rather they have been forced to operate with redundant lines, or unprofitable lines, or both. The heavy hand of federal and state regulation has assured this.

The apparently favorable factors melt under scrutiny. The rail task force report shows that the productivity criterion of "ton-miles per man-hour" proved to be unadjusted for shifts in output mix and inappropriately adjusted for shifts in input mix. Rough adjustments for these factors caused the apparent 5 to 6 percent annual productivity rate per man-hour to shrink to a total-factor productivity gain of 1 to 2 percent (while that for the overall economy has been 2.5 percent annually). The large decrease in the railroad work force was achieved with the negative legacy of work rules and manning requirements already referred to. The remaining work force has—as it should have—maintained a growth in wages at the average for the economy as a whole. After analysis, productivity and wage rates confirm the observed substantial and continuing decline in the profitability and general financial condition of all railroads of this country. Further, the recent boom in rail traffic has revealed weaknesses in the system coming from periods of neglect of investment and maintenance of ways, structures, and rolling stock. Rail passenger deficits continue—they have merely been transferred from private rail financial statements to the federal budget.

Solutions

A natural question arises: Is there any way out of the current situation? After many months, the task force came to the conclusion that indeed there is. You have heard from Sandy Morton already. He has eloquently explicated the case for truly national, competitive, private rail systems actually operating intermodally. This approach combines the natural advantages of each mode: trucks for low-cost, short-haul pickup and delivery (retail shipment) and rail for low-cost, long-distance line-haul service (wholesale shipment). The intermodal operation requires a major shift to the technology of containerized freight for manufactured goods to facilitate quick, economical transfer of a given shipment between modes.

These changes cannot be achieved without substantial changes in the physical plant of today's operating railroads. To be efficient the changed plant must be responsive to the demands of the market for intermodal service offered competitively. This implies the abandonment of some feeder lines, entirely new strategies for terminal location, layout, and equipage, and perhaps the enhancement of other feeder lines. Today, intermodal operation is illegal and the proposed program thus would require legislative change. Wide-ranging mergers would also be required, as would great flexibility in procedures for abandonment of old lines and services, and flexibility in the pricing and introduction of new services, with prices reflecting costs.

The emergence of competitive intermodal transportation networks would make possible the removal of virtually all of the economic restraints now embodied in ICC regulation. But we have already observed that the emergence of competitive intermodal transportation networks requires the removal of most of the restraints of economic regulation. We could be caught in a chicken-and-egg problem. But the logic of the situation suggests the existence of reinforcement mechanisms, and the history of movements toward deregulation in other countries shows that each move generates new momentum toward further deregulation. This could happen here also.

Abandonment of existing redundant trackage would be made easier by the availability of new service—intermodal containerized shipments—which should relieve the dependence of shippers on given spur or feeder lines. (It should be recognized that already efficient unit trains remain appropriate for bulk cargo. But even here a modified form of containerization might prove useful on some branches of the currently overextended feeder lines in Granger territory.)

Relaxation of work rules and manning requirements could have profound impact on the organization, structure, and profitability of the railroads even with existing technology. Old railroad hands have traced for us the implications of the four-man crew size for a freight train. The "high" wages of the crew suggest the need to spread the cost over as many ton-miles as feasible. In U.S. practice this has led to train lengths of 120 cars, even 180 cars (a phenomenon common only in the U.S.). Assembly of such monsters requires huge marshaling yards, complex procedures, much switching, and so on. It also requires time. How long does it take before it is possible for one of the 68 Class I railroads to assemble 120 freight cars in a given marshaling yard and head them out in a given direction?

The impact of the fixed work crew has implications for car construction, breakage of freight, and overall costs. The braking system on U.S. trains stops the engine and the lead cars before the braking impulse reaches the rear cars. In a long train this can lead to impacts on the lead cars equivalent to that from hitting a stationary barrier at fourteen miles per hour (recall your Allstate ads on auto impacts). The lead car can be beefed up to withstand such impacts—for a price. But it is not known in advance which car will be the lead car, so that all cars must be beefed up—at very great cost. But it does not pay to beef up the packing of all shipments as if they would be in the lead car. Those that are are subject to unusual breakage rates.

The work-crew problem has implications for the frequency of service. If one monster train has been assembled and shipped, how soon will traffic levels require another? And there are further indirect implications. Intermediate and interline interchanges and switching (with their attendant clerical and paper work) become more complex and costly. In sum, the entire operation becomes less predictable, more cumbersome, more costly.

This catalogue of interrelated misallocations shows the price that must be paid when the legitimate interests of workers are inappropriately tied to specific operations of the firms involved. The costs that technological change imply for employees cannot and should not be ignored. But they should not be built into the system in a way that continues to distort incentives and resource allocation through their impact on the marginal costs of operating.

What could happen if the requirement for a four-man crew were relaxed, even with existing technology? Small crews would permit shorter trains (with perhaps as few as twenty cars). These could easily be assembled. There are many through-routes which require twenty cars delivered with relative frequency. Through-trains imply less switching. There is less braking and thus the breakage problem is greatly ameliorated. Regular and frequently scheduled trains appear possible. Assured delivery times become feasible. Good service could attract new customers, requiring more trains, more workers, perhaps even permitting electrification of routes (should that prove desirable). In turn, this could imply new flexibility in energy sources for the railroads. If all this were combined with competitive national networks of intermodal lines, low-cost pickup and delivery at modern terminal points would become possible. All facets of the operation would be more efficient.

Intermodal service becomes harder and harder to beat in the marketplace. No regulators are required. Truckers too can be freed of regulation, freed also to compete to supply railroads with pickup-and-delivery service or to purchase a rail line to provide long-haul wholesale transportation to complement their own skills and economic advantages. Technological innovation could be focused on making the system as a whole more efficient.

It all sounds like a fairy tale. Why, in such a world it might even pay the railroad to use only equipment which it owned, and to own only equipment which it used. Then the real economic impact of the equipment would become internalized with both the costs and benefits from its use accruing to the decision maker (something like what happens today in trucking). Then the manager, facing competition in each major market from similarly skilled, equipped and motivated intermodal lines, might find it useful to know how much equipment he has, where it is located at a given moment, and the relationship of its cycle time to the profitability of his own road (something like what happens today in trucking). Shippers might be discouraged from using rail equipment as temporary (or mobile) storage (somewhat as they are discouraged from doing in trucking today). Equipment shortages might disappear (since managers of competing lines might interpret them either as indicators of underpricing or as profit opportunities—in either case, the "shortage" would be overcome).

To sum up, rail efficiency could be enhanced, with enormous benefits to society, through intermodalism, containerization, national private networks, roadbeds everywhere but only where profitable, real competition, small crews, short trains (where the market dictates), frequent, predictable service (whatever the length of the train), adequate and properly priced capacity, technology appropriate to the real economic situation, profitable companies, and growing revenues. Yes, it must be a fairy tale.

This catalogue should also be read in a direct and positive sense to suggest those ways in which we could move from where we are today to achieve real solutions to our transportation problems. All moves need not be made at once. Some movement is preferable to none—if it is in the right direction. An explicit analysis of feasible moves from where we are today is a topic of great interest—but one which requires a separate paper for effective presentation.

Notice that in this fairyland there are still many actors. There are many happy, profitable truckers doing that which markets impersonally reward them for doing, but there are no independent long-haul truckers striking (they are free to price their services in response to changes in their costs). There are many railroad engineers, but no firemen. There are happy shippers availing themselves of the multiple freight transport options that are competitively offered to them. There are happy consumers who now find "windfall" gains in real income in excess of $10 billion annually (because there now is no loss from waste). Also, all former regulators have gone into business for themselves. They have chosen various niches of the transportation industry and their expertise has allowed them to capture great economic rents in the marketplace. Everyone is fulfilled and happy. Even the former administration and congressional statesmen, now retired, rock a bit and smile contentedly. It was through their foresight, wisdom and initiative that the nation and its transportation network have been brought to this state of bliss.

The Northeast Rail Bill

As stated at the outset, the trends in motion before we move into our fairyland in which markets control resource allocation with such salubrious results are still in motion for all railroads in the country. And what of the railroads in the Northeast after the Northeast rail bill? [1] We all know that the bill involves creation of new not-for-profit and for-profit rail corporations, that it provides up to $250 million for dislocation of workers, $500 million in loan guarantees to build high-speed rail lines in the Northeast corridor for passenger traffic, $500 million, at least, to rebuild ways and structures of the bankrupt roads and $500 million for purchase of assets, with various millions for working capital, studies, and the like. But what about the fairy tale of efficient transportation?

Does the Northeast rail bill deal with intermodalism? *No,* that's illegal.

Does it deal with containerization? *No,* it's silent on that.

Does it deal with nationwide private rail networks? *No,* at least not positively. If it is successfully implemented it would imply the creation of a single Northeast rail company to emerge from the bankrupt roads with no end-to-end mergers.

Does it deal with roadbeds only where they are profitable? *Yes and no.* No in the fairy tale sense, because the fairy tale was based on intermodal operations whose roadbeds were responsive to competitive needs. The Northeast plan comes from a simulation of boxcar traffic flows under ICC pricing, monster trains, and today's conditions of competition (or the lack thereof).

Does it deal with real competition? *No.* It envisions competition only as currently restrained and inhibited by the ICC, balkanized railroads, rate bureaus and the like.

Does it somehow provide for small train crews or changes in work rules? *No, it does nothing there.*

Does it encourage short trains under existing technology? *No.*

Does it deal with frequent, predictable service? *No,* that grows out of the other factors not dealt with.

Does it encourage new technology appropriate to the 1970s and 1980s? *No.*

Does it deal with profitable companies? *No.* It deals with companies set forth to operate in a system essentially unchanged from that which we face today.

Does it promise growing revenues and happy people everywhere? *No.* The current system is winding down everywhere. It does wind up the Northeast a bit, but the same old springs are in the system. It will wind down again after a time. But also for displaced permanent workers who are guaranteed up to $30,000 per year for life.

---

[1] The analysis applies with equal effectiveness to the Nixon administration's proposed new Transportation Improvement Act, especially that portion calling for $2 billion in additional federal subsidies for freight cars, ways and structures. This latter set of provisions would further deepen the commitment of the railroads to their existing outmoded technology and methods of doing business. But most telling of the criticism to be leveled against the proposal is that it deals only with the railroads and not with the transportation system as a whole. If enacted, however, it might prove marginally beneficial.

48

Concluding Remarks

Only in a crisis democracies move toward the solution of problems that differentially affect powerful groups with apparently opposing interests. It appears that only then can political leaders take the gamble that the cost of change might be outweighed by the cost of standing pat. Today we are in the midst of a full-fledged crisis in transportation whose importance is magnified by the energy situation. Congress and the Nixon administration have acted, the tab to the federal government for its actions runs into billions of dollars, but what real progress has been made to move the nation out of this crisis? What do we get for our money? Were it possible for Pogo to respond, he might say, "We get the chance to pay double for nothing."

SUMMARY OF DISCUSSION

These four papers elicited some lively discussion from the audience. One noted economist disagreed with Professor Nelson's interpretation of the origins of ICC regulation, preferring instead the theory that regulation was enacted more to assure the stability of railroad cartels than to protect the shipper. A railroad expert also argued that it is erroneous to presume that railroad cartels are necessarily anathema to shipper interests. He said that some shippers actually prefer the continuation of railroad cartels (reasons not specified). There was also some discussion over what course regulation might have taken had Congress set up independent regulatory agencies for each surface mode.

In response to Professor Morton's paper, one member of the audience was struck by the difference in approaches represented by the Task Force on Railroad Productivity and by the Nixon administration's policy toward the energy industry. Whereas in the energy area the administration looks toward disintegration as a means of preserving competition, the task force proposes railroad integration as a means of enhancing competition. In answer, Morton and others reiterated that the rail restructuring they are proposing is necessary to make rail competition truly viable. Along the same lines, however, one economist in the audience pointed out that the task force's major justification for rail restructuring hinges on there being large transaction costs among carriers. He argued that the evidence shows that this is not the case, that railroads can be competitive even without integration.

The main point of contention in the responses to the papers of Professors Tollison and McAdams was whether DOT had gone "far enough" in its proposed TIA. Several in the audience defended the TIA as being a pragmatic approach to the need for regulatory reform and suggested that Tollison and McAdams were unduly harsh in their criticisms. An industry representative even branded the task force report an example of "academic arrogance." In the main, all conceded that DOT was moving in the same direction as Tollison and McAdams would have them move—that the essential conflict is over the rate of movement, not the amount. In short, the strategy problem devolved, arguably, into a choice between a "high" probability of gaining some significant change which would set the stage for more later (DOT) versus some "lower" probability of gaining truly fundamental reform (Tollison and McAdams).

PART
TWO

AIR TRANSPORTATION REGULATION

INTRODUCTION

In 1938 Congress enacted the Civil Aeronautics Act, bringing the U.S. airlines under regulation by the Civil Aeronautics Board (CAB). It is worth noting that Congress chose not to bring the airlines under ICC control. The reason both for regulation and for the creation of a separate agency had to do with "promotion." During the 1920s and 1930s, the U.S. government actively encouraged the development of civil aviation, primarily through the awarding of lucrative airmail contracts. By the latter part of the 1930s, however, this scheme appeared to many to be "unworkable" without direct federal control over entry, exit, and fares. On the other hand, the ICC had no historical role in promotion and thus it was decided to commission a new regulatory agency with a promotional role as well as a regulatory role.

As the industry "matured" over the postwar period, two events brought about a fundamental change in the nature of regulation. First, during the 1950s, the trunk carriers became self-sufficient and no longer required subsidy. Second, during the late 1950s and early 1960s, the CAB allowed entry of existing carriers into new city-pair competition at such a rate that the proportion of "monopoly" service fell from over 50 percent to less than 25 percent. This changed the CAB's role from that of regulating monopolists, providing subsidy as needed, to that of regulating a group of self-sufficient competitors.

The papers in this part seek to explain the nature of airline competition under the present regime and to characterize the current objectives of CAB regulation. The opening paper by Professor Jordan looks primarily at the latter point. In Professor Jordan's view, the CAB is not in the business of protecting consumers from producers; rather, it is in the business of allocating the benefits of air service among many different groups. These include consumers of air services, airline stockholders and management, airline employees, aircraft manufacturers and their employees, lawyers and other regulatory practitioners, government agencies supplying the supporting infrastructure, and so forth. On the basis of the implied objective, Professor Jordan outlines several measures the CAB could take to increase the total benefits to be allocated. These measures relate mainly to streamlining the regulatory process and making regulation more effective.

The papers by Professors Douglas and De Vany deal essentially with the nature of airline competition in the existing regulatory environment. Although they use different approaches in their analyses, each sees that the CAB is presiding over a non-price competing cartel. In essence, the CAB establishes the fares charged in various markets, and then the carriers treat these prices as parameters and tend to compete away excess profits through changes in scheduling.

Professor Douglas notes that an important corollary of this model is that the CAB controls the quality of service implicit in the regulated equilibrium. That is, *ceteris paribus,* higher fares bring on greater excess capacity, greater frequency of service, lower load factors, and thus greater service convenience. Depending on the characteristics of the market (distance, density, value of passengers' waiting time), there is an optimal load factor/fare combination. This may or may not comport with the regulated outcome. Moreover, Professor Douglas argues that because non-price competition tends to "regulate" airline profits, attempts by the CAB to ensure a specified "reasonable" rate of return on investment will be self-defeating and can set up a destabilizing process which takes the regulated equilibrium farther away from the efficient ideal.

Professor De Vany also models airline competition and tests the effects of flight scheduling by comparing the social value of an extra flight with its social cost. He finds in general that, in markets served by only one or two carriers, flight frequency falls short of eliminating excess profits, whereas in markets served by three or more airlines excess profits tend to disappear. Moreover, on an overall basis, Professor De Vany finds that the CAB-established fares are too high inasmuch as in competitive markets the value of an additional flight is less than its additional cost. The evidence also leads Professor De Vany to conclude that the CAB has chosen an overall fare level which tends to maximize total scheduling rather than total traffic. This result is of special interest, given the CAB's congressional mandate to "promote" civil aviation.

IF WE'RE GOING TO REGULATE THE AIRLINES, LET'S DO IT RIGHT

William A. Jordan

Introduction

There is every indication that government regulation will be with us for many years to come. Despite accumulating evidence that regulation greatly increases operating costs, despite assertions that regulatory commissions have been perverted from their alleged purpose of promoting consumer benefits, and despite frequent statements from academicians that regulation should be substantially changed, reduced, or even abolished, it seems highly likely that regulation will continue in essentially its present form. Given this likelihood, it it worthwhile to investigate how regulation might be operated more effectively under existing laws. This investigation will be carried out in this paper, with emphasis being placed on how the CAB's regulation of the airline industry might be improved. Much of this analysis, however, is also applicable to other regulatory commissions.

Normative Considerations

Implicit in the title of this paper is the normative consideration of what comprises "proper" regulation—that is, when do we know that regulation is indeed being done "right"? Is the proper purpose of regulation the achievement of economic efficiency (both in production and exchange)?[1] Is it to protect defenseless consumers from the economic power of large impersonal corporations?[2] Is it to protect hard-working producers from capricious consumers?[3] Is it to provide goods and services in a politically popular manner with little drain on tax revenues, thereby helping to keep politicians in office?[4] Or is it some poorly defined combination of these and still other aims?

---

[1] See George W. Douglas and James C. Miller III, *Economic Regulation of Domestic Air Transport: Theory and Policy* (Washington, D.C.: The Brookings Institution, 1974), pp. 1-3, 61-62 and 182.

[2] See Marver Bernstein, *Regulating Business by Independent Commissions* (Princeton, N.J.: Princeton University Press, 1955), chapter 3.

[3] See William A. Jordan, "Producer Protection, Prior Market Structure and the Effects of Government Regulation," *Journal of Law and Economics,* vol. 15, no. 1 (April 1972), pp. 151-76.

[4] See George J. Stigler, "The Theory of Economic Regulation," and Richard A. Posner, "Taxation by Regulation," *Bell Journal of Economics and Management Science,* vol. 2, no. 1 (Spring 1971), pp. 3-21 and 22-50.

It is often said that the proper role of regulation is to serve the "public interest," but this raises the twin problems of defining just what comprises the "public," and identifying just what is in their best "interest." Happily, air transportation (in common with most economic activity) is a positive-sum game where, through specialization and exchange in production and consumption, essentially all members of society are benefited by its existence. While some of these beneficiaries might prefer to have their local airport located farther away from their homes, almost no knowledgeable person would seriously propose abolishing air transportation.

Given air transportation's enhancement of social benefits, the twin problems regarding the "public interest" are reduced to specifying the relative portions of increased benefits to be received by various groups of individuals within the total "public," and to determining the forms of such benefits. Even these simpler problems, however, yield much controversy. It is politically popular to exclude every-one living in other countries from consideration, but even defining the total "public" as all residents of a particular country does not prevent arguments arising when the consumers of that country receive fewer benefits than the producers, or vice versa. Arguments also arise if all the residents of a country are benefited in one way while those directly concerned with air transportation lose in some other way. For example, the provision of reserve airlift for national defense serves to protect all residents in general while reducing airline profits and yielding higher prices for the actual consumers of airline services (who also benefit from the increased protection).

The resolution of these arguments is a normative matter in which one's opinion is heavily influenced by his position in the economy. University professors, whether because of their search for the general welfare or because they are frequent consumers of airline services, often say that consumers should be the primary beneficiaries of air transportation. Airline executives say that airline shareholders should be given a "fair" return on their investment which, of course, means that the executives keep their jobs and enjoy this same return on their own stock holdings. Airline employees argue (directly and through their unions) that without their services the airlines could not operate and that, therefore, they should receive ever higher incomes and shorter working hours to reflect their constantly increasing productivity. Suppliers of aircraft, fuel, airports, airways, and all the many goods and services required to provide air transportation similarly seek to obtain more benefits from this tremendous positive-sum game. Operators of rival transport modes complain that airline fares and rates should reflect the full costs of air services and should not be "unfairly" subsidized by the public purse. And there, in the middle, is the CAB charged with promoting the interest of this diverse "public." How do CAB members know when a decision they make is "right"? What are they supposed to maximize? Until these questions are answered the basis for evaluating the effectiveness of regulation will be lacking.

58

Insights from Economic Theory

Let us turn to economic theory on nonregulated industries to get some idea how the question of what to maximize is resolved in our economy in the absence of regulation. Economic theory assumes that producers endeavor to maximize profits (by operating where marginal costs equal marginal revenues), with profits serving as a proxy for the utilities of individual decision makers whose interests are, implicitly, thought to be identified with those of the owners of the firm. We all know that this is an extreme assumption, but it does yield hypotheses and predictions that are supported by evidence from actual experience. Note the simplicity and unambiguity of the assumption that the goal is profit maximization. There is no concern about what comprises the diverse "public interest." Quite the contrary, the decision-making question is "what's in it for me?"

While this decision-making rule is simple and unambiguous, the solution to the profit-maximizing problem is difficult and complex. It happens that in a private-property market-exchange system, firms cannot tax or otherwise compel consumers to buy their goods and services. In order to maximize profits, firms must provide goods that consumers value at prices (exchange ratios with other goods) equal to or less than the values consumers place on other goods. As a result, we find that "business firms have two roles: (1) a *purposive* role to increase the wealth of the members of the firm and (2) a resultant *functional* role to produce goods in response to market demands." [5] It is through this second role that firms serve the "public interest." The first role provides the motivation for these actions. The key problems are how to identify and how to respond to the multitude of diverse and changeable market demands.

Firms operating in the private-property market-exchange system have generally been able to identify market demand and to achieve profits. In the absence of legal barriers to entry, however, successful firms face still another problem. Their economic profits attract other firms to the industry. These new firms endeavor to obtain a share of the profits by providing the same goods at lower prices, improved goods at the same prices, or some combination of the two. Furthermore, should the industry have the productive characteristics that allow a competitive market structure to be approximated, the marginal cost of production will eventually equal the price of each good, thereby yielding economic efficiency in production and exchange. Note that under the original situation, consumers are better off with the existence of the monopoly firm than they are without it (they voluntarily purchase the goods at the original prices), but under the final, multi-firm situation they are even better off since they can get the same (or improved) goods at lower prices. A firm, on the other hand, is better off if it is the sole supplier of a good, and worse off when new firms enter and reduce profits through inter-firm rivalry.

---

[5] Armen A. Alchian and William R. Allen, *University Economics,* 2d ed. (Belmont, Calif.: Wadsworth Publishing Co., 1967), p. 274.

Clearly, the traditional *open-entry,* private-property model is a "consumer-protection" model, even though owners of surviving firms benefit by earning the market rate of return on their investments and are in a position at least equal to what they would be in if their firms were producing their next highest valued alternative product.

What happens, however, when entry is not open—that is, when the original firm is protected from the entry of other firms by ownership of a key input, social customs, legal prohibitions, or what have you? The decision rule is the same—profit maximization—but when new firms are not allowed to enter in response to economic profits the owners of the original firms enjoy relatively more benefits than they would under conditions of open entry, while consumers benefit less from their voluntary exchange with these firms. Furthermore, if we make the extreme assumption that a single price is charged by the producer, the negatively sloped market demand curve results in price being greater than marginal revenue so that when profits are maximized the value of the good to the consumer (the price) is greater than the marginal cost of producing the last unit of output, thereby yielding inefficiency in exchange. Happily, for those who prefer efficiency, this inefficiency in exchange can be reduced or eliminated by the producer's adopting a discriminatory multipart pricing structure similar to that used by electric utilities.[6] In this situation, various consumers pay a series of sequentially decreasing prices for increasing quantities of the good until the price paid for the last unit of output bought by the last consumer indeed equals the marginal cost of producing the marginal output.

The major difference between the discriminatory multipart pricing result and the competitive market structure result is that firm owners enjoy greater benefits (capture more of the consumer surplus) under this pricing technique, while consumers enjoy greater benefits under the open-entry, competitive market structure. Both results can be economically efficient in production and exchange. Obviously, the *closed-entry,* private-property, market-exchange model is a "producer-protection" model, even though consumers are better off than if the good were not produced at all.

There is abundant evidence that air transportation is not a natural monopoly —that is, that there are few, if any, economies of scale available in nonregulated airline operations.[7] This and other data provide good reason to believe that the nonregulated, open-entry airline market structure would approach a competitive market structure, thereby maximizing overall consumer benefits while yielding efficiency in production and exchange.[8] It follows that if Congress believed the public interest should be equated with consumer benefit, Congress would have

---

[6] Ibid., pp. 113-17.

[7] William A. Jordan, *Airline Regulation in America: Effects and Imperfections* (Baltimore, Md.: The Johns Hopkins University Press, 1970), pp. 191-94.

[8] Ibid., pp. 24-32, 255-57 and 233-36.

adopted a policy of nonregulated open entry for the airlines. But instead Congress enacted the Civil Aeronautics Act of 1938,[9] and then, after observing twenty years of CAB performance during which entry was largely closed, it left the CAB's economic regulatory powers essentially unchanged when enacting the Federal Aviation Act of 1958.[10] This demonstrated that Congress believed the CAB's performance to have been appropriate and believed that the public interest included more than consumer benefit. The question is what could Congress want besides consumer benefits?

For one thing, the policy statements of both acts specify that the "encouragement and development of an air-transportation system properly adapted to the present and future needs of . . . the national defense" shall be considered in the public interest.[11] This shows that Congress has wished the transport airlift capacity for national defense to be increased without direct payments being made to the airlines for providing this public good. In an open-entry, private-property, market-exchange system, any carrier independently providing national defense services without payment from the government would shortly be out of business as its costs increased and its rate of return fell below the market level. This factor alone means that the CAB cannot allow open entry into the airline industry.

Both acts also direct that air transportation be regulated so as to "assure the highest degree of safety in . . . [air] transportation."[12] There is good reason to expect that a nonregulated market structure would provide the optimal level of safety, but probably not the highest level of safety.[13] Thus, Congress has decided that more than optimal levels of safety are worth the higher prices required.

The two acts further admonish the board to "foster sound economic conditions" in air transportation, and "to improve the relations between . . . air carriers."[14] Given the economic environment of the 1930s (not to mention the present Penn Central problems), one doubts if Congress would believe that airline bankruptcies are consistent with "sound economic conditions," and there is every reason to think that open-entry rivalry between carriers would not "improve their relations." The lack of bankruptcies among the certificated airlines (in contrast to the occurrence of bankruptcies among nonregulated airlines)[15] and the CAB's prohibition against the entry of new carriers into each subgroup in the industry (trunk, local service, all-cargo, supplemental, and so on) provide evidence that the protection of existing producers is considered to be in the public interest.

---

9 52 Stat. 973.

10 72 Stat. 731.

11 49 U.S.C. 402 and 49 U.S.C. 1302, subsection (a).

12 Ibid., subsection (b).

13 At the same time, however, it can also be argued that CAB regulation fails to provide the greatest incentive to operate safely. See Jordan, *Airline Regulation,* pp. 49-53.

14 49 U.S.C. 402 and 49 U.S.C. 1302, subsection (b).

15 Jordan, *Airline Regulation,* pp. 23-24.

Other departures from the equation of consumer benefit with the public interest can be found in the act,[16] but what has been said above should suffice to demonstrate that Congress does not accept this equation as its sole consideration. To hold to the contrary would require the assertion that Congress does not know what it is doing despite its extensive experience with regulation since 1887. Thus, given the CAB's responsibility to Congress, it would be surprising if the CAB acted to maximize consumer benefits when acting in this way would be contrary to repeatedly demonstrated congressional policy. Maximizing consumer benefits is not what the CAB is supposed to do, even though it would be equally incorrect to say that the CAB is to ignore consumer benefits or to do everything possible to decrease them. Actually, CAB members must operate in a complex environment where, in order to make specific decisions, they have to evaluate ambiguous estimates of costs and benefits according to general and sometimes changing congressional policies, legal constraints and precedents, arguments and pressures from various interest groups, and their own differing personal views of what is desirable. An ill-defined balance between the benefits of consumers and other groups appears to comprise the "public interest"—all within the general environment of a positive-sum game in which almost everyone is better off with air transportation than they would be without it.

Which Other Groups?

One way to obtain a partial solution to the problem of determining when regulation is being done "right" is to focus on the negative—that is, to ask when regulation is being done "wrong." Since the evidence is that Congress does not consider consumer benefit to be identical with the public interest, we know that the CAB's promotion of consumer interest alone would be incorrect. From this touchstone it can be seen that the proper role of CAB regulation (as perceived by Congress) is to transfer benefits initially from consumers to the airlines (producers). Then, in order for still other nonconsumer groups in society to be benefited by regulation, the CAB must adopt policies which will motivate the airlines to act in ways that will reallocate some or all of the transferred benefits to these other groups. Some examples of nonconsumer beneficiaries (in addition to airline shareholders) are: airline employees, aircraft and engine manufacturers (their shareholders, employees, and so on), lawyers and other regulatory practitioners, government agencies supplying airport and airway facilities, communication carriers, petroleum companies, construction companies and landlords, catering firms, farmers and food/beverage processors, wholesalers and retailers, and public bodies such as the Department of Defense and city governments. Clearly, benefiting individuals in any one or in several of these groups could be interpreted as being in the public

---

[16] See, for example, sections 412 and 414 of the act, 49 U.S.C. 1382 and 49 U.S.C. 1384.

interest since they are all members of the public. This all-inclusiveness of the idea of the "public interest" is, of course, one of its fundamental deficiencies in providing guidelines for decision making.

Professor McKean introduces another facet to the problem of specifying an operational definition of the public interest. He argues that ". . . there is no ultimately correct criterion of the public interest. Even if I believe in absolute rather than relative values, and believe that there is a test for these on which people ought to agree, some persons will *not* agree with my values. There is then no demonstrably correct or universally agreed-upon criterion." [17] The actual or potential divergencies in values among individuals within one group (à la McKean), together with the more obvious differences in viewpoints between individuals in different groups, provide good reason to conclude that there are no objective criteria for defining the "public interest." Operationally this would mean that the "public interest" is essentially what Congress and others in power believe it to be. The efficient achievement of their goals would probably also be in the "public interest," even though the goals themselves might be economically inefficient.

The transfer of benefits from consumers to producers is what supports the producer-protection hypothesis on the actual effects of government regulation.[18] However, the subsequent reallocation of large amounts of these benefits to airline employees, aircraft and engine manufacturers and other airline suppliers, and various government bodies implies imperfection in CAB regulation to the extent that it does not maximize airline profits despite the inherent cartelizing nature of regulation.[19] But even though CAB regulation has been imperfect so far as maximizing airline benefits is concerned, it may be considered to have been relatively effective if the producer sector is defined as consisting of the airlines and their employees and their suppliers and government agencies—that is, the entire nonconsumer sector. For example, excessive purchases of aircraft have been detrimental to the airlines, but they have enhanced the national defense by providing a larger airlift reserve and by allowing aircraft manufacturers to maintain a larger production base capable of relatively rapid conversion to military output. Similarly, CAB regulation has not prevented airline failures, but the failures have been limited in number and those firms that have left the industry have done so through acquisition by other certificated carriers with a minimum of disruption in service to consumers, with shareholders receiving some payment for their stock holdings, and with employees retaining their jobs under protective clauses specified by the CAB. Things could have been worse from the viewpoints of many senators and congressmen.

---

[17] Roland N. McKean, *Public Spending* (New York: McGraw-Hill, 1968), p. vii.

[18] Jordan, "Producer Protection," pp. 174-76.

[19] A cartel is defined as a group of producers who form an agreement to act together. See George J. Stigler, *The Theory of Price*, 3d ed. (New York: Macmillan, 1966), p. 230. Also see Jordan, *Airline Regulation*, pp. 226-33.

Ways to Improve CAB Regulation

So far there has been nothing in this paper as to the ways CAB regulation might be improved in some normative (and thus debatable) sense. The thrust has been to explain why it is unrealistic to expect the CAB to act primarily to benefit consumers. Once this crucial point has been accepted, it becomes possible to consider ways to improve CAB regulation. The next matter to be resolved is whether the primary purpose of CAB regulation is to transfer benefits from consumers to the airlines alone or whether other nonconsumer groups should also benefit. If the airlines are indeed to be the primary beneficiaries of regulation, then the CAB's performance will be improved if its actions serve to make the airline cartel more effective and efficient. Specifically, more decision-making power should be transferred to the airlines themselves working together through an expanded Air Transport Association (with its several conferences and committees), various ad hoc groups such as those authorized since 1968 to organize capacity agreements, and so on. The ultimate aim of such a scheme would be to achieve full pooling of traffic and profits, with the CAB having its responsibilities limited to the following:

(1) Prohibiting new entry into the industry and controlling exit.
(2) Arbitrating disputes among individual airlines and groups of airlines.
(3) Policing and enforcing agreements to ensure compliance at low cost to the airlines.
(4) Facilitating airline cooperation in opposing demands by labor unions, aircraft manufacturers, fuel suppliers, airport authorities, and so on.
(5) Providing exemption from the antitrust laws.
(6) Collecting data from and disseminating it to the airlines.
(7) Conducting studies to help the airlines operate more efficiently and respond appropriately to changing economic and technological conditions.
(8) Occasionally modifying airline decisions should they be considered politically detrimental to the airlines' long-run interests.

In this model of benevolent CAB regulation, the guiding philosophy would be that something is desirable if it helps the airlines and their shareholders. Furthermore, those best qualified to decide what promotes their own interests would be the airlines themselves.

This model of CAB regulation is probably unrealistic. In a democracy there are just too many other claimants on government largess for one group to obtain unqualified government support. Thus, it seems reasonable to believe that the CAB's primary purpose is the much more difficult one of transferring substantial (but not all) benefits from consumers to the airlines and then on to other nonconsumer groups. This purpose, of course, imposes heavy responsibilities on the CAB and requires it to adopt normative criteria on what comprises a "proper" allocation of benefits among the various groups. In this complex situation, how might the CAB's regulatory procedures and decisions be made more effective in discharging its responsibilities? There seem to be two areas in which improvements could be made: (1) the speed and responsiveness of CAB procedures could be increased with the allocative aspects of decisions being made more explicit, and (2) the CAB could act to increase the efficiency of the airlines, thereby increasing the benefits available for sharing by the various nonconsumer groups at a given cost to society. Some suggestions on these two areas are proposed below.

Procedures and Decisions. Any changes in CAB procedures and decision making can easily run afoul of the Administrative Procedures Act [20] or of long-established legal precedents. However, with the necessary adjustments to accommodate these important considerations, the following could be ways to improve procedures and decision making:

(1) Announce a proposed decision at the start of each major proceeding. This decision would have been prepared by the CAB staff for review and prior approval by the board. It would identify the major groups in society that are directly influenced by the proceeding and make explicit estimates of the effects that the decision would have on each group. In the case of route proceedings it would specify the number of carriers warranted by economic considerations, national defense factors and previous CAB policies, and it would indicate (without recommending) which of the existing certificated carriers could feasibly be extended into the new route(s). For fare investigations, the proposed decision would outline revisions of the fare level and structure and would make explicit estimates of their effects on traffic volumes, carrier revenues and profits. The use of show-cause orders is an example of how this revised procedure might be implemented.

(2) In formal hearings, administrative law judges would require each party and intervenor (a) to criticize the CAB staff's estimates of benefit allocations among various groups; and, if it wished, (b) to recommend a revised CAB decision and make its own estimate of the benefit allocation such a decision would have on various groups as well as on itself. The resulting information would aid the administrative law judges and board members in implementing their perceptions of congressional, presidential and their own preferences.

(3) Given a decision on the preferred allocation of benefits among various groups, there remains the matter of carrying out the decision. Where possible, objective criteria should be used to do this. For example, in the case of route authorizations, the selection of carriers to implement the decision might be based on such criteria as (a) safety in operations, (b) operating costs, and (c) commitments of aircraft and personnel to national defense airlift reserves.[21] If one or

---

[20] 60 Stat. 237.

[21] Since safety and airlift reserves increase operating costs, tradeoffs would need to be established between these two factors and low-cost operations. One way to do this would be to rank the carriers in each factor and then apply weights to the resulting ranks (for example, a weight of .4 to safety, .25 to airlift reserves, and .35 to operating costs).

more carriers were not clearly superior on these criteria, the CAB should use some "fair" lottery system to select the recipient carrier(s). This would decrease decision-making delays and any errors (as perceived by the carriers) could be corrected through intercarrier route exchanges (see below). Note that whatever implementation criteria the CAB adopts will motivate the airlines to attempt to excel in these factors.

These changes would allow the CAB to provide more direction and structure to proceedings and would limit the areas of time-consuming, subjective argument as to which carriers should benefit from specific decisions. More responsibility would be placed on the CAB and its staff while inputs from carriers and various interested groups would be confined to establishing how benefits would be allocated and to summarizing performance levels. It would seem reasonable to expect opposition to these suggestions by lawyers, consultants, airline regulatory personnel and lobbyists since the demand for their services would be reduced.

Airline Efficiency. A comparison of CAB-regulated airlines with the nonregulated California intrastate carriers has indicated that real output per employee of the most successful California airline exceeded the average for all trunk carriers by more than 100 percent, and exceeded that of Western Air Lines (one of the more efficient trunk carriers) by over 60 percent.[22] It is certainly possible to debate the precise extent to which nonregulated airlines are more productive than regulated airlines, but the fact remains that there have been significant differences in efficiency in the production of basic transportation services.[23] Thus, if CAB members desire increased airline efficiency, they should adopt policies that will achieve this objective. Three examples of such policies are:

(1) The promotion of discriminatory multipart pricing to increase efficiency in exchange.

(2) The reduction of service-quality rivalry between carriers to increase efficiency in production.

(3) Allowing the buying and selling of operating rights by certificated carriers—essentially without regulatory interference.[24]

---

[22] Jordan, *Airline Regulation,* pp. 210-22.

[23] The relative efficiency of CAB-regulated airlines would probably be greater if their output were defined to include the benefits resulting from superior quality of service and contributions to national defense.

[24] In an October 1969 speech, F. D. Hall, then president of Eastern Air Lines, proposed "that airlines be permitted by the Civil Aeronautics Board to swap routes to achieve greater efficiency." *Wall Street Journal,* Midwest edition (October 3, 1969), p. 2. It is doubtful that limiting exchanges to a barter basis would increase efficiency as much as outright money sales. It would, however, tend to hide the true value of routes. A recent application by American and Frontier provides an example of a route exchange (CAB Order No. 73-6-106, June 27, 1973). It should be recognized that in some cases one carrier could pay another to take over a loss route. Furthermore, though this would require congressional authorization, it might be useful to allow airlines to pay the CAB to take back a loss route with the funds used to subsidize a lower-cost carrier to provide the service.

Because explicit price agreements are reached and enforced through the regulatory mechanism, the airline industry as a whole faces a downward-sloping market demand curve. Furthermore, a comparison of the coach fares charged by the essentially nonregulated California intrastate carriers with the coach fares that would have existed in major California city pairs under CAB regulation demonstrates that the nonregulated fares were much lower (32 to 47 percent lower during 1965).[25] These facts, plus standard economic theory, suggest that regulated coach and first-class fares are above the marginal costs of efficient operations and, therefore, if used alone, these fares will result in inefficiency in exchange. This inefficiency can be decreased by the adoption of multipart pricing in which lower prices can be enjoyed by consumers after they purchase initial quantities at higher prices (family plan fares, for example), or if they agree to purchase a large minimum quantity at one time (such as group tour and charter fares).[26] Inefficiency can be further decreased by the adoption of discriminatory pricing in which those with more elastic demand for air transportation pay lower fares than those with less elastic demand. Thus, if the CAB desires efficiency in exchange, it should encourage the full development of a discriminatory multipart pricing structure. This, of course, would benefit the airlines (which would capture more consumer surplus), those consumers who travel under the lower fares, and airline suppliers to the extent they could charge higher prices to the more profitable carriers.

Service-quality rivalry among the airlines has been a major source of inefficiency and an important means by which aircraft and engine manufacturers, other airline suppliers, airline employees, and the Department of Defense have benefited from CAB regulation. This is the fundamental imperfection of CAB regulation *if* the primary purpose of such regulation is to transfer benefits from consumers to the airlines alone rather than on to other nonconsumer recipients.[27] It is crucially important for Congress and the CAB to decide in general terms the extent to which regulation is to benefit the airlines relative to their employees, suppliers, and governmental agencies. If the airlines are to be the main beneficiaries of CAB regulation, an appropriate set of policies would reduce service-quality rivalry by promoting airline capacity agreements and (ideally) traffic and profit pooling, as outlined above. Such developments would motivate the airlines to decrease aircraft purchases, increase the utilization of these fewer aircraft, raise load factors, reduce the use of other resources such as labor and fuel, decrease the quality of inflight services, and provide relatively Spartan ground services.[28] All this, of course, would greatly increase airline efficiency in production.

[25] Jordan, *Airline Regulation,* pp. 109-13. Note the consistency between these price differences and the productivity differences mentioned above.

[26] Alchian and Allen, *University Economics,* p. 117.

[27] William A. Jordan, "Airline Capacity Agreements: Correcting a Regulatory Imperfection," *Journal of Air Law and Commerce,* vol. 39, no. 2 (Spring 1973), pp. 181-83.

[28] Ibid., pp. 193-210.

In contrast, should the aircraft-engine manufacturers and airline employees be the favored beneficiaries of CAB regulation, a continuation of traditional CAB policies promoting service-quality rivalry would be called for. The tremendous amounts of excess capacity resulting from the three major postwar aircraft replacement cycles,[29] and from the underutilization of aircraft,[30] would seem to be of great benefit to the manufacturers while serving to decrease airline efficiency. Indeed, the key role of the aircraft manufacturers in the airline industry during the 1930s, and their importance to the nation since World War II, make it quite reasonable to hypothesize that this apparent defect in CAB regulation was intentional. It is difficult to imagine legislative provisions (outside of direct subsidies or permission to cartelize) that could have been more beneficial to the manufacturers. If Congress wants aircraft manufacturers to continue to benefit from CAB regulation, one would expect the development of widespread congressional opposition to airline capacity agreements and pooling since these undertakings substantially reduce the flow of benefits through the airlines on to the manufacturers.[31] Similarly, such congressional opposition would also benefit airline employees, since capacity agreements and pooling reduce excessive flight schedules, service quality in general and, therefore, employment.[32]

Policies designed to increase the contributions of the regulated airlines to the national defense would require some changes in the CAB's traditional policies. Rather than the historical emphasis on passenger aircraft (which have limited military use), the modified policies should serve to encourage the purchase of excessive numbers of convertible or all-cargo aircraft. The failure of the present regulatory scheme to provide suitable aircraft types for airlift reserves is indicated by the fact that out of the 338 wide-body jets ordered by U.S. airlines through November 1973, only twenty are to be convertible to cargo use.[33] The Military Airlift Command's recent proposal that Congress enact a Federal Airlift Expansion Act to provide direct incentives to the airlines to purchase cargo-capable aircraft is further evidence of the ineffectiveness of present CAB regulation in enhancing national defense.[34]

The final recommendation—to allow carriers to buy and sell operating rights —would also increase airline efficiency. Information available to the CAB when it makes its decisions is imperfect and incomplete, and new economic developments occur continually. To allow the buying and selling of operating rights

---

[29] The pressurized aircraft, turbine-powered aircraft, and wide-body aircraft cycles. See Jordan, *Airline Regulation,* pp. 36-44, for a description of the first two of these cycles.

[30] Ibid., pp. 197-210.

[31] Jordan, "Airline Capacity Agreements," pp. 209-10.

[32] Ibid., pp. 202-209.

[33] David A. Brown, "MAC Plans to Aid Purchases of Airliners," *Aviation Week and Space Technology,* December 3, 1973, p. 24.

[34] Ibid., p. 25.

would make it possible for carriers to respond to changing developments or to correct any CAB errors in route awards by exchanging routes. The CAB's initial route allocations affect the relative wealth of various carriers, but once this allocation is made why should the recipient of the award be required to operate over the route in order to capture this wealth increase? This is especially true if some other carrier values the route more highly. The CAB would doubtless want to limit exchanges to existing certificated carriers and would probably limit them to carriers in each carrier class (trunks, local service, and so on). To do otherwise would allow open entry to develop—something the CAB has consistently opposed. Furthermore, should the CAB desire to retain intercarrier rivalry, it could prohibit the sale of operating rights which reduced the number of carriers allowed to serve any city pair. Beyond this, given the fact that every existing carrier has been approved by the CAB many times, there seems to be little reason to require further approval of the sales of individual operating rights.[35] Mergers and acquisitions of entire airlines would be a different matter since this would result in a reduction in the number of carriers in existence with significant impact on intercarrier rivalry.

Summary. These suggestions on how to improve CAB procedures and decision making are based on two premises. The first premise is that it is indeed desirable to shorten the procedures, make them more flexible, and reduce the resources required to undertake them. The second premise is that it is desirable to identify the various beneficiaries of CAB decisions explicitly. If these premises are generally accepted, it follows that the CAB and its staff should provide more direction and play a more active role in regulatory procedures. Furthermore, emphasis should be placed on the allocation of benefits among various groups while leaving the internal allocation of benefits within the airline group mainly to such objective criteria as low operating costs, high safety performance, and contributions to national defense. Should it be decided that the airlines are to be the main beneficiaries of CAB regulation, then a fully effective airline cartel should be promoted. If something less than this is desired, discriminatory multipart pricing, the reduction of service-quality rivalry, and the exchange of operating rights would be desirable. But it is not clear whether the airlines, out of all the nonconsumer groups, are to be the main beneficiaries of regulation.

Conclusion

When we investigate what the CAB should do in order to regulate correctly, we keep coming back to the necessarily normative question of what indeed is "right"?

---

[35] The CAB's consistent refusal to grant domestic routes to Pan American indicates that there may well be important reasons why the board wants to pass on the sale of each route. Doing so would, of course, open the way for substantial procedural delays and the use of regulatory resources in such proceedings that could otherwise be used in other activities.

The major theme of this paper has been that CAB regulation was not designed by Congress primarily to benefit consumers. If it were, the goal could be achieved quite simply by promoting the private-property, market-exchange system with open entry. The California experience demonstrates that regulation is not needed for such a system to operate effectively in the airline industry, and that such a system does benefit consumers. The fact that we do have airline regulation means that the "public interest" is not meant to be equated with consumer benefit or protection.

If consumers are not meant to be the beneficiaries of regulation, what group or groups are to be benefited and to what extent is each to benefit? In order to determine whether or not CAB regulation is being done "right," it is essential that some explicit decisions be made as to how benefits are to be allocated among and within these groups. This is a fundamental responsibility of the CAB (under the general mandate and review of Congress) and the CAB members would be wise to devote considerable energies and resources to making these decisions.

Historically, CAB regulation can be judged relatively effective if the important beneficiaries are supposed to include airline employees, aircraft and engine manufacturers, and, to a lesser extent, the Department of Defense. If, however, the original trunk carriers were to have been the prime beneficiaries, then CAB regulation has been quite imperfect. The recent development of airline capacity agreements is a step towards benefiting the trunk carriers, and explicit traffic and profit pooling agreements would yield further benefits, providing these agreements can be made flexible enough to adjust to underlying changes in economic and technological environments in contrast to the ICC's inability to provide such flexibility in railroad regulation.[36] One advantage of a truly effective airline cartel *might* be that decreased costs would result in lower profit-maximizing price levels and structures so that some consumers could also benefit while the airlines' position improved. It should be remembered, however, that these benefits would be gained at the expense of the aircraft and engine manufacturers and some airline employees. The political implications of this are great.

Obviously this paper has not explicitly answered the question implied in its title—how can regulation be done right? What it has done, hopefully, is to point out the essentially normative nature of any answer to this question, while indicating how the adoption of certain policies could result in substantial changes in CAB regulation which some might consider to be improvements over present practices.

---

[36] George W. Hilton, "The Consistency of the Interstate Commerce Act," *Journal of Law and Economics,* vol. 9 (October 1966), pp. 111-12.

REGULATION OF THE U.S. AIRLINE INDUSTRY: AN INTERPRETATION

George W. Douglas

Introduction

In examining the market structure, regulation and performance of the domestic airline industry, one is struck by a number of paradoxes. Although the natural advantages of air transport have caused it to grow at a rate more than double that of the GNP, thereby becoming the dominant mode of intercity travel by common carrier, and though it has been sheltered and nourished by the regulator, it has not rewarded its investors with exceptional profits. Rather, as is so often emphasized by the carriers' trade organization, the average return on investment has reached the CAB-defined "fair return" in only five of the past twenty years. While the absence of excess profits or rents in regulated air transport might conceivably be interpreted as the result of successful stewardship of the public interest by the regulator, closer inspection reveals a number of embarrassing incongruities. It is, of course, no surprise to most economists that the absence of monopoly profits is not in itself a sufficient condition for the existence of an economically efficient outcome. In the case of the airline industry, several critics have pointed out that excessive costs of production and inefficient service levels have resulted in regulated prices which greatly exceed the estimated prices of an efficiently configured air transport system.[1]

Perhaps the greatest source of frustration facing an economist who would seek to influence regulatory policy is the powerfully held belief of the regulator and the public that "fair price" and "fair profit" are equivalent. This belief is thoroughly institutionalized in regulatory proceedings, and even inculcated in some textbooks. In essence, this sets the economic cart before the horse: total operating expenditures and fair profits are estimated and summed to determine the "revenue need"; prices are then set so as to generate total revenues equal to that sum. Price struc-

---

Parts of this paper are based on joint research conducted with Professor James C. Miller III. The interpretations drawn here, however, are the author's own.

[1] See William A. Jordan, *Airline Regulation in America: Effects and Imperfections* (Baltimore: The Johns Hopkins University Press, 1970); Theodore Keeler, "Airline Regulation and Market Performance," *Bell Journal of Economics and Management Science,* Autumn 1972; and George W. Douglas and James C. Miller III, "Quality Competition, Industry Equilibrium, and Efficiency in the Price-Constrained Airline Market," *American Economic Review,* September 1974.

ture, in this format, usually places subjective notions of fairness or equity above costs. The outcome is typified by third-degree discrimination (value-of-service pricing) and a melange of cross-subsidies resulting from design or happenstance. I would suggest that this naive misperception of the public interest by regulators is largely responsible for the existence and perpetuation of inefficient regulation. I will here describe airline regulation and the industry's performance, and interpret both in this vein.

Characteristics of Regulation

The salient characteristics of CAB regulation of the domestic airlines may be summarized as follows:

Entry. In order to provide scheduled air service in any domestic market, the air carrier firm must obtain approval of the CAB, which may grant a certificate explicitly setting out the terminal and intermediate points which are to be served and other conditions of service.[2] The CAB is not directed by statute as to what specific criteria are to be followed in restraining entry, except for the usual admonitions concerning "public convenience and necessity."

The board's entry policy has been exceedingly restrictive on the entry of new firms into the industry, and has not in fact allowed the entry of a new trunk carrier since the CAB was set up in 1938. Its policies regarding entry by existing carriers into specific markets, however, have gone through phases of relative ease and tightness. By 1971, markets generating 76 percent of the total traffic were served by two or more competing carriers.[3] Similarly, market exit requires CAB approval— a fact which in practice serves as a constraint principally on the subsidized services of the smaller "local service" carriers.

Price. Although technically price adjustments originate in filings by the airlines with the regulator, those of any consequence engender regulatory proceedings wherein they may be contested by other parties. The CAB exercises considerable latitude in modifying, rejecting or granting the fares, and for all practical purposes can be considered the central force in setting fares. Most significant fare changes have been across-the-board adjustments, made with the adjustment of carrier profits as an explicit goal.

---

[2] Several exceptions might be noted: An airline which does not provide interstate service does not come under CAB economic regulation, though it still must abide by the safety and operational regulations of the Federal Aviation Administration. Also, the CAB further exempts operations of any carrier which uses aircraft with net weight of less than 7,500 pounds (which corresponds to about thirty passenger seats).

[3] George W. Douglas and James C. Miller III, *Economic Regulation of Domestic Air Transport: Theory and Policy* (Washington, D.C.: The Brookings Institution, 1974).

72

The structure of fares, market by market, reflects almost exclusively the relation of distance to cost. Other factors which affect unit costs, in particular, demand density, are not appropriately reflected and in some sense the fare structure represents a deliberate policy of cross-subsidizing small markets by large ones. (One of the ironies noted below, however, is that the effective cross-subsidy in practice may be just the reverse.) The price structure, by category of traveler, service and trip, has evolved in a classic pattern of third-degree price discrimination. The class of travel with the most inelastic demand is business travel; hence the various "discounts" which have prevailed have been aimed quite accurately at excluding business travelers, focusing on groups whose demand elasticity is higher.[4] The regulated prices, moreover, significantly exceed those arising in a few intrastate markets (not under CAB regulation) which are characterized by price competition. As reported by Jordan, these fares range from 30 to 50 percent less per passenger-mile than those in similar CAB regulated markets.[5] I will discuss the structure and level of fares in greater detail in a following section.

Flight Frequency and Service Quality. The CAB exercises pervasive control over seat size and spacing, food and beverages, movies, lounges, and other service amenities. The supervision of these characteristics (through requiring or not requiring extra charges) has to some extent served to limit competition by the carriers in these areas. However, the board is proscribed by statute from fixing schedules. Since the frequency of flights offered to a given destination has a significant effect on a traveler's choice of airline, this has become a principal arena for competition among the carriers.

Regulatory policies in this industry bear a remarkable similarity to those that would be pursued by a cartel. That is, entry barriers are erected and enforced by legal sanction, the market is divided formally among participants, internal price rivalry is discouraged, the price level is high, and third-degree discrimination is pervasive. It is understandable that at least one observer characterizes the industry as a legal cartel, albeit an imperfect one.[6] That "imperfection," however, lies in the fact that the firms have not earned better than competitive profits (though under other regulatory policies they could), and this makes such a label inappropriate and unnecessarily emotive. I will consider the development of these policies in a later section.

---

[4] For example, travel for pleasure is separated from travel for business purposes by the length of time of the overall trip (that is, the various "excursion" fares) and by type of traveler, with discounts for accompanying family members, youth, military, clergy, and so on. In the recent domestic passenger fare investigation, the CAB did, however, find many of these practices discriminatory and unlawful. See George W. Douglas and James C. Miller III, "The CAB's Domestic Passenger Fare Investigation," *Bell Journal of Economics and Management Science,* Spring 1974.

[5] Jordan, *Airline Regulation,* p. 226.

[6] Ibid., p. 227.

Market Dynamics and Equilibrium under Regulation

Market equilibrium in the regulated industry has recently been described in similar ways by a number of writers.[7] In essence, the firms regard price as a "given" (determined through regulation), leaving flight schedules (timing and frequency) as the principal strategic variable in attracting customers and determining costs. The description of a firm's profit-maximizing equilibrium is straightforward: the firm schedules flights to the point at which the marginal revenue for the last flight added equals the marginal cost of the flight. In a monopoly market the equilibrium is unique; in a competitive (really oligopolistic) market it depends on the anticipated response of other firms to the changes in the flight schedules of one firm. If the firm takes its rivals' schedules as "given," its perceived marginal revenue of an added flight exceeds that of the monopolist, since the added flight can be expected to divert some existing passengers from its rivals' flights. The result of this frequency competition is an increase in the total number of flights, and, since for the market as a whole added flights increase the total number of air travelers with diminishing returns, the average cost per passenger increases. Stated quite simply, the average cost per passenger is "bid up" to the given price.

This equilibrium may be conveniently described in terms of the number of travelers per flight divided by the number of seats per flight, which gives the average load factor. The cost of an air trip can be thought of as composed of two parts: (a) the cost of providing the aircraft flight itself, and (b) the cost of providing services to the travelers. The cost of providing the flight is defined as independent of the number of passengers carried, while the cost of providing services is, of course, directly related to the number of passengers carried.

The average cost per passenger carried depends on the number of travelers per flight. Thus, the average cost per passenger trip is inversely related to the average load factor, as shown in Figure 1. For any given price, P*, we may also define a break-even load factor as that average load factor at which the average cost per passenger is equal to P*. ("Fair profit" of course is included as a cost when the average cost curve is defined.) We would expect to find that equilibrium in airline markets to cause the realized average load factor to approach the break-even load factor in markets with active frequency competition. We would expect, moreover, that the degree of active frequency competition (and the perception of interdependence in scheduling) would be related to the number of firms sharing a market. A cross-section analysis of average load factors in 350 markets in 1969, reported in Table 1, found this to be the case.

---

[7] A limited sampling might include Arthur S. De Vany, "The Economics of Quality Competition: Theory and Evidence on Airline Flight Scheduling," processed, 1969; James C. Miller III, "Scheduling and Airline Efficiency" (Ph.D. diss., University of Virginia, 1969); and Joseph V. Yance, "Nonprice Competition in Jet Aircraft Capacity," *Journal of Industrial Economics,* November 1972. A more formal expression of the equilibrium and its efficiency may be found in Douglas and Miller, *Economic Regulation* and "Quality Competition."

Figure 1

AVERAGE COST PER PASSENGER VERSUS AVERAGE LOAD FACTOR

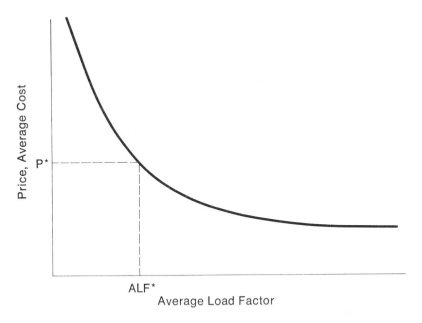

In the regression results shown in Table 1 we see that the realized average load factor (which is an excellent proxy for profits or the operating ratio) is strongly (inversely) related to the number of firms per market. The average load factor is also related to distance, since the fare-distance relationship understates slightly the cost-distance relationship, causing the break-even average load factor to decline with distance. (Since airline markets are interdependent, we would not expect each and every market to be characterized by actual load factors which are equal to the estimated break-even levels; the pattern is, however, discernible statistically.)

A further point of interest is the futility of cross-subsidy schemes, except through binding exit and service-level restraints. Among the markets served by trunk carriers, it would appear that in practice little cross-subsidy occurs, and what there is (in terms of relative contribution to "fixed" costs) probably has the opposite effect to that intended. Since the small-to-medium-size markets have fewer firms in competition, their average load factors and profits tend to be somewhat higher than those of the large markets.

The implication of this equilibrium for regulatory control is straightforward. The regulator, by setting the fare in a market, indirectly determines the equilibrium average load factor (and the level of slack capacity), assuming the aircraft size is given. If the fare is increased, causing the break-even load factor to decrease, frequency competition will soon cause the average load factor to fall. Conversely,

Table 1

CROSS-SECTION ANALYSIS OF MARKET AVERAGE LOAD FACTORS

(1) $ALF = .588 - 2.11 \times 10^{-5} D + 7.62 \times 10^{-7} N - 7.06 \times 10^{-2} C$
       (1.4)   (9.1)   (6.5)

$R^2 = .213$
$Df = 347$

(2) $ALF = .257 - .019 \ln D + .073 \ln N - 1.46 \ln C$
       (1.8)   (7.1)   (5.5)

$R^2 = .144$
$Df = 347$

ALF = market average load factor (that is, total passengers/total seats).
  D = market distance (in miles).
  N = average number of daily passengers in market.
  C = number of carriers in market.
  ( ) = coefficient T-statistics.
Data Source: Civil Aeronautics Board, Bureau of Economics, CAB Docket 21866-6, Exhibit BE-1216 (July 6, 1970).

if one determines that the average load factor is excessively low, the regulator should lower the fare. It is a classic case of cost being price-determined, rather than price-determining. Moreover, the regulator's control on entry (number of firms per market) is obviously the crucial tool for controlling profits.

While the "competitive" regulated equilibrium does result in average cost approaching the regulated price, it does not directly suggest the appropriate price; that is, any price within a bounded set satisfies the naive constraint that the "fair price" yield a "fair profit." Consider the depiction of the average cost curve in Figure 1. If the market is small, there may be no price which would generate a volume of passengers sufficient to reach "break-even," in which case scheduled service is not viable. However, past some minimum-demand density, the set of feasible prices grows, and with it the range of feasible equilibria. We might characterize the state of market equilibrium under CAB regulation as having prices closer to the top than to the bottom of the feasible range. (Some notable exceptions to this, however, are the low-price, high-load factor equilibria in the CAB-regulated East Coast-Puerto Rico and West Coast-Hawaii markets.) Set against this are the few price-competitive intrastate markets with lower-price, higher-load factor equilibria than occur in similar CAB-regulated markets.[8]

The high-price, low-load factor equilibrium provides a lead-in to the issue of "excess capacity." While, as noted above, frequency competition expands slack

---

[8] There also remains the question of the purely technical efficiency of production in the regulated industry. Since the participants have enjoyed a sheltered existence, some degree of excess costs might be anticipated. An unbiased comparison of the costs of the regulated with the unregulated California carriers (see Jordan, *Airline Regulation*) or with a hypothetical efficient carrier (see Keeler, "Airline Regulation and Market Performance") is fraught with problems of holding all dimensions of service and quality comparable. The technically efficient tradeoff curve could, of course, be inside the one derived from the cost experience of the regulated firms.

capacity, this additional slack capacity is not without its benefits. Indeed, some level of slack capacity is desirable in an efficient scheduled transport system. Since the level of frequency and slack capacity affect the convenience of the service, it follows that in order to determine the existence of "excess" capacity, one must be able to determine the optimal level of slack capacity. It is not necessarily the case that the lowest feasible price will produce the "optimal" average load factor.

Another study has shown the relationship between the level of slack capacity of a scheduled transport system and a generalized measure of the convenience of the service—the expected schedule delay per passenger.[9] This variable measures the average difference between a traveler's preferred departure time and the time he can obtain a flight with an available seat. One can demonstrate that for a given market the expected schedule delay per passenger decreases as the number of flights increases and as the average load factor decreases. Figure 1 can then be recast according to a tradeoff between average cost and service quality (expected schedule delay) since both are related to the average load factor.

Figure 2 shows a hypothetical case. For a given market there exists a range of "fair prices" which are consonant with a "fair return" on investment. Related to each price, however, is an implicit level-of-service quality. The range of feasible combinations of price and quality may be regarded as the opportunity locus of the regulator.[10] The "optimal" price, and by extension the "optimal" level of slack capacity, depend on the value travelers attach to this dimension of quality, avoiding schedule delays.

Under reasonable assumptions concerning the value travelers might place on avoiding schedule delays, a pattern of optimal load factors and prices may be calculated. While the average load factors arising from the regulated markets have ranged recently from 45 percent to 55 percent, the range of optimal average load factors would appear to be significantly higher, from 50 to 55 percent in small markets of short length to 70 to 75 percent in larger or longer-distance markets. It appears that fares range from being approximately efficient in small or short-distance markets to being 35 to 45 percent too high in large or long-distance markets.[11]

How Does This Happen?

While the level and structure of fares and service quality in the airline market are demonstrably inefficient, it is interesting to consider whether the results are the

---

[9] Douglas and Miller, "Quality Competition."

[10] Note again that a technically efficient market would be characterized by the production of a given level of output at a given level of quality (expected schedule delay) at a minimum cost. This requires not simply the avoidance of "waste," but the optimal selection of aircraft sizes, routing and schedules, a condition that may or may not obtain even in an unregulated competitive market.

[11] See Douglas and Miller, *Economic Regulation,* pp. 87-94.

77

Figure 2

AVERAGE COST PER PASSENGER VERSUS EXPECTED
SCHEDULE DELAY PER PASSENGER

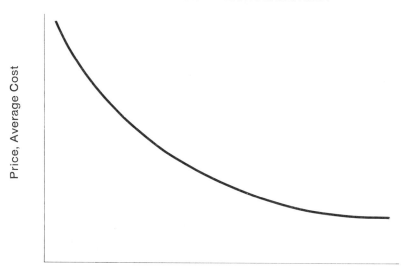

Expected Schedule Delay

consequence of a guided, explicit maximizing process, or whether they can more generally be attributed to the dynamics of the industry and a regulatory process whose results were not anticipated by any of the participants.

In the former, "maximizing" vein, we might consider a number of possible goals or variables that might be maximized. The first candidate, the maximization of joint profits, can be easily rejected. Although, as noted above, many of the restraints imposed by regulation are consistent with cartel behavior, many are not—for example, the diminution of monopoly markets by entry and the restraints against active collusion on capacity (scheduling) competition.[12] Moreover, the profit record speaks for itself.

Second, one might suggest that the implicit goals which produced the current situation were those of constrained maximization. That is, some measure such as net profits, capital investment or overall output was maximized subject to the constraint that profit rates not exceed (over time) those which might be justifiable as "fair." Clearly, if the constraint on the return to capital is an accurate measure of the cost of capital, economic profits thus constrained would not exist. If fair return exceeds the cost of capital, then maximization of net profits becomes equivalent to maximizing capital investment. And, if output is measured by available capacity produced, since capital investment is largely composed of flight equipment

---

[12] I will discuss below the implications of the "temporary" authority to negotiate capacity agreements recently granted the carriers.

and facilities, the maximization of this variable is roughly equivalent to the maximization of either net profits or capital investment.

While I would not argue here that the fair return defined by the CAB accurately measures market cost, it does not appear to have been a frequent binding constraint. Nevertheless, either of these variants (replacing "fair" cost of capital with the market cost of capital) appears to be consistent with the observed equilibrium, both in the fares chosen in the viable range and in other characteristics of pricing. For example, third-degree price discrimination expands the level of output and capital use possible while satisfying the profit constraint. The one variant of maximizing behavior which is the closest approximation to a revenue-constrained optimum—maximization of revenue passenger-miles—is not consistent with the observed pattern of regulation and the structure of prices. Specifically, maximization of revenue passenger-miles would require one to choose the level of price and service quality that minimizes the total perceived costs of air travel to the traveler. But this would be a condition of an efficient equilibrium and price structure.[13]

While the regulated equilibrium appears to be consistent with the constrained maximization of capital (or equivalently, capacity), there are no persuasive reasons why this outcome should have been chosen as a direct goal of regulation. Rather, I would suggest that it is an outcome of a process going on between the regulator and the industry whose character was neither anticipated nor sought by either party. Moreover, many of the regulatory policies of competitive restraint are understandable in terms of the longer history of airline regulation and its explicit statutory coupling of industry promotion with the public interest.

Before 1950, in fact, one might view the promotion activities of the CAB as paramount. Rightly or wrongly, Congress expressed a demand for development of an extensive scheduled air system, and willingly appropriated funds for subsidy of nonviable services. The Civil Aeronautics Board, of course, was the instrument responsible for the organization and supervision of this program. Under such a mandate, the pattern of competitive restraints is altogether understandable: in order to establish a given level of output (in the aggregate) with a minimum amount of subsidy, cartel-type restraints are called for. In other words, the minimization of subsidy in a loss equilibrium is equivalent to the maximization of joint profits. Hence, practices such as entry barriers, market division, price discrimination and monopoly-level price setting were established. Furthermore, since some markets were viable, it is understandable that efforts toward explicit cross-subsidy were attempted. While cross-subsidy does not represent a strictly efficient

---

[13] The conditions for technical and allocative efficiency and the equivalence under certain assumptions of traffic maximization and constrained welfare maximization are described formally in George W. Douglas, "Equilibrium in a Deregulated Air Transport Market," paper presented at Seminar on Problems of Regulation and Public Utilities, Dartmouth College, August 21, 1971.

way of funding deficit services, its deficiency in a world of second-best is probably not overwhelming.[14]

In assessing regulatory policy itself, I have not addressed the wisdom of the promotion goal or the development of air services in nonviable markets, assuming instead that this was required by Congress. But it might be advisable at this point to consider why in principle some subsidy service in some nonviable markets may be justified on grounds of economic efficiency. The justification follows from the usual declining costs (scale economy) argument, that the marginal social cost at some low level of output is less than the average social cost. Conceptually, scale economies of scheduled transport service in a specific market arise from capacity economies related to vehicle size and from the time inputs of the traveler himself. One can show, for example, that in a market that is efficient in aircraft size and frequency, both the average cost to the firm and the average cost to the passenger (including his time and convenience) decline as the number of passengers increases.[15] But as George Eads has pointed out, the subsidy mechanism actually employed has generated many inefficiencies of production, thereby vitiating most (or all) net gains from the existence of the subsidized services.[16]

The underlying nature of the regulatory/promotional requirements of the CAB changed substantially in the decade following World War II. In this period, a new class of carriers—local-service or "feeder" airlines—was introduced, and these carriers eventually absorbed most of the nonviable markets. With the growth in traffic and productivity, the "trunk" airlines rapidly became self-sufficient, and virtually all their remaining markets were (or became) viable. Hence, the CAB now presided over a viable, self-sufficient trunk airline industry which quickly became dominant in intercity common-carrier passenger transport. The form of the regulatory process, however, was largely unchanged, and the competitive restraints were eased only slightly and slowly. On the other hand, the joint maximization (subsidy minimization) policy was abandoned; the CAB's policy instead might be characterized as a monitoring of profits and an ordering of reductions or increases of fares (generally in some across-the-board formula) to restrain or enhance profits.

We may now consider what may be characterized as the principal behavioral rule in price regulation (that prices are viewed as the instrument by which profits are restrained or increased) and how this behavior affects equilibrium. Consider again the tradeoff between average load factors and average cost. In Figure 3 I

---

[14] Cross-subsidy might be defended on equity grounds as well: the air travelers in both markets are most likely drawn from the same subset of the general population.

[15] This follows even in the absence of scale economies to the firm in the production of available capacity, since the optimal average load factor (and, with it, average cost) declines as the market size increases. See Douglas and Miller, "Quality Competition."

[16] See George C. Eads, *The Local Service Airline Experiment* (Washington, D.C.: The Brookings Institution, 1972).

80

have portrayed a hypothetical relationship of this sort, including as a cost the regulatory-determined fair rate of return. If this rate of return accurately represents the cost of capital as perceived by the firms, a price level of P* should elicit an equilibrium average load factor of ALF* (or close to it). Suppose, however, that productivity increases outpace factor-price increases, causing the average cost curve to shift down, or to the left. The break-even load factor commensurate with price level P* would be reduced, as would the actual average load factor, in a new equilibrium. Regulatory lag in an era of rapid increases in productivity could be expected to create declining equilibrium average load factors.

A second variant of this outcome might be shown in a divergence between the regulated "fair" return and the carriers' perceived cost of capital. If the fair return exceeds the cost of capital, we could construct an industry reaction curve lying to the left of that constructed for the "fair" return on invesment (see Figure 4). In this case, a price P* leads to equilibrium at ALF**. If the regulatory response were to attempt to restore "fair" profits with a price increase (raising P* to P**), the equilibrium would instead move to a yet lower level of average load factor (ALF***). This "ratchet effect" would lead to increasing prices, approaching the point at which capital and capacity would be maximized.[17]

A variant of the ratchet effect would posit different cost functions among the competing firms. A fare increase designed to increase average profits to the fair rate (even if this equaled the market rate) would only cause the more efficient firms to expand capacity further and thereby would cause the market average load factor to decline.

Another trigger for the ratchet effect would be the chronic overoptimism of the carriers concerning their own traffic growth. (Thus, each carrier may anticipate a 20 percent increase in its own traffic, even though aggregate traffic may in fact increase only 12 percent.) This optimism implies that either the rivals are exceedingly slow to learn of their interdependence, or, perhaps more realistically, that they are pursuing a long-run strategy of predatory scheduling. Such a strategy, of course, should not be validated by the pricing response of the regulator and could be easily quashed by freeing entry.[18]

One should take note here of the currently fashionable view espoused by the airlines, the present CAB chairman, and some academic observers. This is the view that equilibrium under scheduling competition yields a loss equilibrium in the

---

[17] See Douglas and Miller, *Economic Regulation,* chapter 9. Output maximization (measured by capacity) may be seen to occur in the context of the ascending price ratchet when the demand elasticity approaches unity, which removes the incentive to continue marginal additions to schedules. At this point, the first order conditions for frequency maximization are reached.
[18] The CAB was finally persuaded in principle of the regulator's role in the ratchet dynamic in the domestic passenger fare investigation in 1971. The board also broke with tradition in the same proceeding, establishing for rate-making purposes "target" average load factors of 54 percent for trunk carriers (a figure that is yet too low in my opinion). See CAB Order 71-4-54, April 9, 1971, p. 23.

Figure 3

DECREASE OF AVERAGE LOAD FACTOR OVER TIME
DUE TO REGULATORY LAG

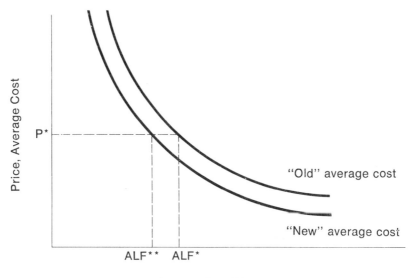

Average Load Factor

Figure 4

RATCHET EFFECT WHEN FARES ARE INCREASED TO
RAISE RETURN ON INVESTMENT (ROI)

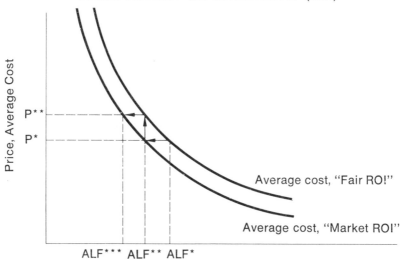

Average Load Factor

context of the familiar "prisoner's dilemma." [19] In essence, this view holds that in a market where scheduling has already reached (or approached) break-even, each carrier would perceive that a unilateral increase of one flight would still be profitable (by diverting traffic from competitors). If several carriers share the market, and each adds one flight, relative market shares are not affected, but each one's average load factor declines below break-even, and they all suffer losses. (Perhaps one of the greatest ironies is the zeal with which this hypothesis is forwarded by representatives of the carriers, since it rests on the most naive and myopic assumptions about carrier behavior.)

It is difficult, perhaps impossible, to sort out the reasons why carriers tend to schedule flights beyond the level which would achieve the (CAB-defined) break-even load factor. The point is that it is almost irrelevant which hypothesis of firm behavior is "correct." The appropriate regulatory response to each should be a studied indifference to the current level of profits, so long as the prices chosen lie in the viable range. The prices should be chosen instead so as to elicit a desirable level of slack capacity and service. While profits should be monitored, the regulatory response should principally lie in restraining excess-profit levels by allowing or encouraging entry and price competition.

Of paramount concern at present is the possible unfortunate resolution of the excess-capacity problem through regulator-sponsored-and-approved capacity agreements. Foreclosing competition through capacity would come close to perfecting the "imperfect cartel" at the expense of travelers and economic efficiency. While the CAB has seized upon the current petroleum "crisis" to enlarge the practice of capacity agreements adopted reluctantly (as a temporary expedient) in 1972, the institutionalization of this practice is not yet certain, and it is opposed by the Departments of Transportation and Justice. While it is clear that excess capacity has developed, the development is attributable to the management practices of the carriers which would undoubtedly cease if not validated by the CAB. The European experience with cartel organization under the guise of efficiency should be a forewarning of the counterproductive nature of these "solutions." There, although capacity collusion via "pooling" is institutionalized, the system provides services of poorer quality than those of the U.S. airline system at considerably higher prices.

In summary, the inefficient production and marketing of scheduled air travel services have their antecedents in the regulatory policies of the Civil Aeronautics Board. Most of the inefficiencies may be attributed to a misperception by the CAB of the dynamics of the industry they regulate, a misperception of the altered circumstances of regulation in a nonsubsidized viable industry, and the usual misidentification of fair price with fair profits of the regulated firms.

---

[19] This view has been put forward by Fruhan and has recently gained currency in the industry and at the CAB. See William E. Fruhan, Jr., *The Fight for Competitive Advantage: A Study of the United States Domestic Trunk Air Carriers* (Boston, Mass.: Harvard University Press, 1972).

IS EFFICIENT REGULATION
OF AIR TRANSPORTATION POSSIBLE?

Arthur S. De Vany

The basic purpose of this paper is to see if it is possible for regulation of air transportation to achieve the basic objectives it is supposed to achieve and to see how close current regulatory policy is to attaining those objectives that are possible. I shall begin by briefly reviewing the bases for the regulation of air transportation given by economic theory or by proponents of regulation, and shall then look to see if current research shows that air transportation satisfies any of the conditions necessary for regulation to improve efficiency, and I shall assess the efficiency of current regulation in light of this research. Following that, I shall attempt to show which regulatory goals are mutually attainable and which ones are not, so as to reveal the nature of the tradeoffs that must be made in regulatory choices and the pitfalls or unintended consequences of some of the choices. I shall conclude by suggesting steps that might be taken by the regulator to improve the efficiency of the air transportation system.

Efficiency, Views of Market Failure, and the Role of Regulation

It is somewhat more difficult to characterize efficiency in air transportation than it is to characterize efficiency in other areas. The reason for this is that efficiency requires a correct level of output, and that the output be of the correct quality as well. The consideration of quality is missing or ignored in other markets. Output of the industry is defined as passenger trips over some system of routes. Quality is taken to be the time required to make trips, which in turn depends upon the speed of the aircraft and the availability of seats on departing flights. The air transportation system will be efficient when two conditions are fulfilled: (1) the marginal value of capacity (that is, the reduction in travel time attributable to an additional flight) must equal the marginal cost of capacity, and (2) the price or fare must equal the marginal cost of output at the efficient level of capacity (that is, the fare the last passenger is willing to pay for a trip should just cover the additional cost incurred in carrying him, when capacity is adjusted so as not to impose additional delays on other passengers).

The fundamental justification for regulation is that an unregulated market would fail to provide the efficient level of output and capacity. Some of the reasons offered why unregulated air transportation would not achieve economic efficiency are as follows:

Decreasing costs. Open competition (free entry and no limitations on price) would result in losses if price were equal to marginal cost since marginal cost is less than average cost. A monopoly would be able to produce at lower cost than many small firms, and regulation limiting the number of airlines serving a route would be justified. In addition, price regulation would prevent monopoly abuses.

Oligopoly. It may be that, given cost conditions and the extent of passenger demand, a given route would support only two or three airlines. Together, they might collude and restrict output and flights, and raise prices above the efficient level. (This situation might justify price regulation, but not limitations on entry.)

Monopolistic competition. It may be that a sufficiently large number of airlines would emerge so that they would engage in rivalry in scheduling in an effort to differentiate their product from that of competitors and gain some small measure of monopoly power. In the view of Chamberlin, this process would result in excess capacity, too high a price, and a chronic entry and exit of airlines in the market.[1] This view would justify limiting entry and also regulating price if the limited firms retained some monopoly power.

Ruinous competition. One opposing view of the effects of competition is that it results in too little rather than too much capacity. The argument is that marginal operators will skim off the cream of the principal firms and cause them to curtail their flights. By a number of processes it is claimed this leads to an overall reduction in the level of service offered. This view justifies some limitations on entry and possibly on prices if the efficient number of firms is small.

Externalities. The existence of positive externalities may justify subsidies to airlines, though it does not follow that regulation is therefore also necessary. Congestion or noise externalities could justify regulation limiting capacity if the proper congestion tolls or noise charges are not levied.

This listing is not exhaustive, and the discussion is incomplete, but it serves to identify some of the views held on the nature of competition in air transportation markets and some of the issues that need to be examined in any assessment of the efficiency of regulation. Each separate view of the competitive process tends to identify a separate set of issues and regulatory problems and suggest a different regulatory policy. I will now review some of the evidence bearing on these views or models of the industry.

---

[1] Edward H. Chamberlin, *The Theory of Monopolistic Competition* (Cambridge, Mass.: Harvard University Press, 1933).

Behavior of the Industry under Current Regulation

We must take the industry as currently regulated as given, model it, and use the evidence gained to shed light on the hypotheses given above.[2]

The model assumes that the airlines regard fares as exogenously determined by the CAB. Competition takes the form of superior equipment, ticketing, baggage handling, and flight frequencies. The first question is this: Given a set fare, what effect will scheduling competition have when there are one, two, three or more airlines on a route? The answer is that when there are just one or two airlines, the monopoly solution tends to prevail. Monopoly provides too few flights, reduced convenience and too little output—that is, price will be in excess of marginal cost in one- or two-airline markets.

When there are three or more airlines, the competitive solution holds. In these markets, flights are added until the actual load factor is driven down to equal the break-even load factor at the regulated fare. At any given fare, in any market, more flights will be scheduled and more output will be produced when there are three or more airlines than when there are only one or two. Once there are three airlines, though, it does not seem to matter much if a fourth, fifth, or sixth airline is added.

Monopoly routes tend to earn a higher profit than competitive routes, not because prices are higher or route structures more favorable, but because profits are competed away in the competitive markets. Thus, one of the important policy instruments employed by the CAB is determination of the number of airlines permitted to serve a given route. Given any market and any fare, the more airlines certificated, the greater will be the number of flights scheduled, the lower will be the load factor, the more passengers will be carried, and the more closely will earnings approach a competitively determined normal rate of return on investment.

Price is the other important variable by which the CAB influences airline behavior. The effect of price on airline flights and output is shown in Figure 1. The outermost curve labeled Q^c is the competitively determined supply of output (passenger trips), and the competitive supply of flights is labeled F^c. Q^m and F^m are the respective supply curves if the route were served by a monopoly. All supply curves are upward-sloping and then turn back. This reflects the fact that as the CAB permits price to rise from the minimum level at which any service would be

---

[2] The analysis of the industry given here is based on George W. Douglas and James C. Miller III, "Quality Competition, Industry Equilibrium, and Efficiency in the Price-Constrained Airline Market," *American Economic Review*, September 1974; and on Arthur S. De Vany, "A Forecast of Air Travel and Airport and Airway Use in 1980," *Transportation Research*, vol. 6 (1972), pp. 1-18, "The Revealed Value of Time in Air Travel," *Review of Economics and Statistics*, vol. 56 (February 1974), pp. 77-82, and "Effects of Price and Entry Regulation on Airline Output, Capacity and Efficiency," *Bell Journal of Economics and Management Science*, forthcoming, Spring 1975. I have made no attempt to cite other literature. This paper is a rather personal account of my research and the reasons for the opinions expressed herein.

Figure 1

EFFECT OF REGULATED PRICE ON FLIGHTS AND OUTPUT

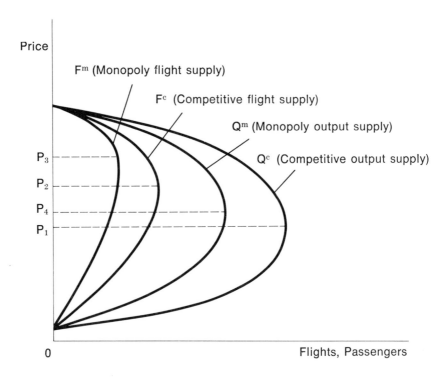

offered, both flights and output increase up to a point. The price at which output is maximized for the competitive group of airlines (P_1) is the efficient price. This price is below the price that maximizes the number of flights this group would offer (P_2). Monopoly flights and output are maximized at higher prices than competitive flights and output (P_3 and P_4 respectively), but are at less than the competitive levels at every price. This analysis indicates that efficiency cannot be obtained in monopoly (one- or two-carrier) markets, and can only be obtained in competitive markets if the efficient price is established by the CAB.

I have made the claim that routes served by three or more airlines would be served efficiently if the correct price were set. This requires justification. The evidence indicates that in these markets airlines do not schedule flights in such a way as to maintain market share. (If they did, this would give the inefficient monopoly solution.) With three or more airlines, each airline finds that additional flights tend to realize a load factor equal to the load factor experienced on the airline's other flights. This means that the average and marginal revenues of flights are equal, so that when the profit-maximizing airline adds flights until marginal cost equals marginal revenue, a zero-profit equilibrium is reached. In other words, each airline takes load factor to be a constant and schedules the number of flights that maximizes profits, but the equilibrium load factor in the market will be the one that just reduces profit to zero—that is, to a normal rate of return on investment. If the efficient price is set by the CAB, then the marginal revenue realized by the airline on its flights will equal the marginal value placed on the flights by the traveling public. Then, since the airline equates its marginal cost with marginal revenue, the marginal cost of the flights will equal their marginal value, and the result will be efficiency.

Recent estimates of the marginal cost and marginal value of flights indicate that the CAB has approved fares in the competitive markets that are higher than the efficient level. Prices appear to be close to the level that would maximize the number of flights in the markets. This would correspond to P_2 in Figure 1. Notice that, at this price, output is less than it would be at the efficient price (P_1). The reason is that the higher price discourages travel more than the extra flights encourage it—which is another way of saying that the public places less value on these flights than it costs to provide them. They are therefore wasteful. In the ten competitive markets I have studied, the estimated waste caused by the excessively high price averages $2.3 million a year per market.

In the monopoly markets the CAB appears to have done a better job of setting fares, given the restriction on entry. That is, the fare in each of these markets is close to the output-maximizing level. However, the result is still inefficient, in that fewer than the efficient number of flights are provided and output is less than the efficient level. The monopoly restrictions on output result in an average loss of value per market of $272,000 per year for the ten markets I have studied.

On the basis of this summary of evidence, we can assess the validity of some of the views of the air transport industry presented earlier.

Decreasing costs. The evidence is that cost per flight is constant or increasing in all markets, and tends more to be increasing in monopoly markets than in competitive ones. In addition, average cost of output is rising in all markets, reflecting the fact that load factors must be falling in the neighborhood of equilibrium if the equilibrium is stable. Thus, regulation of air transportation is not justified on the basis of decreasing cost.

Oligopoly. There is some evidence that two airlines are more likely to collude than three or more. If there are three or more airlines in a given market, the likelihood of collusion is very small, unless it is enforced by legal sanctions. Thus, entry restrictions are not justified, and price control may be only weakly justified in cases where fewer than three airlines would offer service.

Monopolistic competition. The evidence is that product differentiation through flight scheduling produces an effect analogous to perfect competition, with each firm believing that it can sell all the flights it wishes to supply at the going load factor. The result is that each firm, while earning zero profits, produces at minimum average cost for the equilibrium load factor. The equilibrium load factor is a function of the regulated price, and, as shown in Figure 1, this price may be set too low or too high, inducing either too little or too much capacity. Given that the price set in competitive markets is above the efficient level, the resulting excess capacity appears to support the monopolistic competition thesis. However, if price were freed of any regulatory restraints, it would fall to the efficient level under competition and the resulting level of capacity would be efficient.

Ruinous competition. There is an element of truth in this argument, but its implications are opposite to those usually drawn. A group of competitive firms operating on the fringe of a market may skim the cream from flights of established firms. This is only possible, however, where there are some excess profits to be gained. But the availability of these profits indicates a monopoly restriction of flights and output. On balance, therefore, the fringe operators serve to increase flights and output to the competitive level. If the regulated price in these markets is at the efficient level, the fringe operators will bring about efficiency. If, however, the price is higher than the efficient level (as the evidence suggests), then the extra flights provided by fringe firms would be wasteful. But this would be a problem resulting from current regulation, and the problem cannot therefore be used to justify closing entry.

In summary, the evidence does not suggest that the traditional basis for regulation given by economic theory applies with any real force to air transportation. The question still remains whether regulation is capable of achieving any gain in efficiency even in those cases where there might be a strong basis for it within the traditional analysis.

The Feasibility of Efficient Regulation

It has been recognized that convenience is an important aspect of air travel, and that the most important determinant of convenience—reliable schedule frequency —depends upon the regulatory policies adopted. The traditional analysis of regulation ignores the role that the regulatory agency may play when it sets prices and establishes entry policies, thereby determining the overall level of convenience or quality of the product.

Suppose, for example, that the CAB is faced with a traditional regulatory problem of dealing with a monopolist. According to the traditional view, the price should be reduced below the monopoly level until it equals marginal cost. This will increase monopoly output to the efficient level. But this does not work in the case of air transportation. First, monopoly marginal cost of output is greater than social marginal cost, and so a price equal to marginal cost would still be too high (price should equal average cost, which is the social marginal cost). Second, if price is adjusted downward from the monopoly level, the number of flights offered will be reduced and waiting time will be increased. This will move the monopolist closer to efficiency. But it will not be possible to eliminate the monopoly restriction of flights and output to secure an efficient outcome. Thus, there is no strong assurance that regulation will be able to eliminate monopoly inefficiencies in the case of the airlines, and it is entirely possible for output and flights to be reduced to a point even below their monopoly levels if the attempt is made to reduce price to a level that would eliminate excess profits.

The regulatory dilemma facing the CAB has its origins in the fact that the quality of the product, as well as the level of output, are functions of the control variables available to the board. The control variables may be taken to be price, number of airlines certificated to provide service, and limitation of schedule frequencies (though the CAB, until very recently, has not exercised control of schedules). Suppose that the CAB considered output, flights, fare levels, and earnings to be the variables it wished to influence through use of the control variables. Given the nature of the industry, the tradeoffs between these variables are as shown in Figure 2. The outermost locus of points indicates the levels of flights and output that would be produced if three or more airlines were authorized to serve the market. Alteration of fares from low to high levels moves equilibrium in the direction indicated by the arrows on the curve. When one starts at a low level, an increase in fares increases both output and flights. The efficient fare level is where Q is at a maximum, and fare increases beyond this point increase flights but decrease output. Thus, the region from Q_{max} to F_{max} is a region of negative tradeoffs between output and flights. Every point on this outer curve is a point of zero profits, so price variations do not influence earnings when there are at least three airlines. If the number of airlines is reduced to one or two, the feasible region of choices is contracted to the inner curve in Figure 2, and earnings are increased. Another negative tradeoff occurs between earnings and output or flights, when the number of airlines is the control variable.

Still another way to influence earnings is to limit flights (which has been done in the capacity limitations approved by the CAB). Suppose, as the evidence indicates, that the CAB has set price in competitive markets at the level that maximizes flights rather than output (point F_{max} in Figure 2). Now, the effect of reducing flights by, say, 15 percent is to reduce output by 10 to 15 percent. (This represents a move along the curve originating at F_{max} connecting the competitive locus with the monopoly locus.) Earnings will rise when flights are reduced so long as the elasticity of demand with respect to flights is less than unity (which my estimates indicate to be the case). In the process of increasing earnings by reducing flights at the already inefficiently high price, output is reduced but efficiency is improved. The reason is that the price induces an inefficiently large number of flights, so that reducing flights may save resources. Cutting flights enough would move the otherwise competitive market to the monopoly solution. Unfortunately,

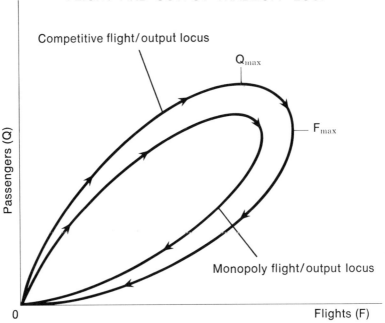

Figure 2

FLIGHT AND OUTPUT TRADEOFF LOCI

Competitive flight/output locus

Q_{max}

F_{max}

Passengers (Q)

Monopoly flight/output locus

0   Flights (F)

there is a great deal of confusion on this point. It is thought by some that competitively supplied flights will be inefficiently high in numbers, and that mono-
polization would, therefore, improve efficiency. But this is possible only when the
price is set inefficiently high in the first place.

The evidence indicates that the CAB is not pursuing a policy that would
promote efficiency. Its policy is in fact difficult to understand and is somewhat
contradictory. By certificating at least three airlines in many markets, the CAB
has made the achievement of efficiency in these markets possible, but has ensured
zero profits. But, by selecting a fare higher than the efficient one, the CAB has
encouraged an excessive number of flights and on balance has discouraged travel.
The capacity agreements will increase earnings, but will also afford the airlines a
greater opportunity to collude to achieve the (inefficient) monopoly solution.

It is not clear why the CAB would certificate four to six carriers on a route,
thus ensuring zero profits, and then attempt to assist these carriers in restraining
flights in order to achieve excess profits. Such a policy would seem to indicate that
what I have called zero profits are viewed as constituting losses by the CAB. Yet
in the absence of a market-determined competitive rate of return, there is little to
guide the CAB in deciding what the rate of return ought to be. The rate of return
currently earned by airlines in the price-regulated competitive markets cannot be

used as a guide, inasmuch as the CAB has followed policies that have introduced substantial variation in airline earnings. Because of this variation, resources in the industry will require a supernormal rate of return.

One thing that has contributed to the variation in earnings is the supply response of airlines to changes in the regulated fare. Suppose fare is raised on a competitive route. Each airline is induced to increase flights in response to the higher price, as any competitive firm would do. However, suppose demand is price-elastic. The overall number of flights in the market will then decline. With each airline expanding flights in a situation requiring fewer total flights, losses will be incurred. The return to equilibrium, where these losses are brought back to zero, would be accomplished by flight cutbacks by all firms, or by exit from the market by the weakest airline. Now, if the CAB attempts to bolster this weak airline, the process whereby equilibrium would be attained will be blocked. There really is no way of saving the marginal carrier that does not do violence to efficiency or further violence to the already weak airline. Further fine-tuning of fares in an effort to find one level at which the weak carrier can survive simply adds more variation to earnings. And an overall restriction of flights would reduce efficiency unless the fares are above the warranted level. In this situation the weak airline would hang on only if the route contributed a marginal profit to its whole system of routes (even though taken by itself it might be loss-producing) or if (because of the "use it or lose it" form of right issued by the CAB), the airline was willing to bear present losses in the hope of future profits.

Fare adjustments are an improperly used instrument for stabilizing airline earnings. It can be shown that the across-the-board variety of fare increase often approved by the CAB is capable of dealing with inflation only. Because elasticity of demand differs by trip length, across-the-board fare increases will raise revenue in short-haul markets and lower it in long-haul markets. In the long run, total cost will be adjusted to equal total revenue and fares will not affect earnings. The policy of raising fares during business downturns is especially odd. When a slump occurs, the value of time to travelers falls even more than income falls, raising the price elasticity of demand during the slump, and thus warranting a reduction in fares. Increasing fares in the slump worsens the impact of the recession on airline earnings.

There are other pitfalls in regulation, other areas where an action may have unintended and even perverse consequences. Our knowledge of the structure of the relationship between the policy instruments available to the CAB and the results desired is incomplete, but I think what we do know suggests that the board has only limited opportunity for success in improving the efficiency of air transportation. With few exceptions, the research carried out by the CAB staff has been undistinguished and incapable of shedding light on the board's problems, which require a knowledge of structural relationships in the industry.

If economic efficiency is the public-interest objective (and I am not sure it is), then I have a few suggestions to help the board achieve it:

(1) Allow three or more airlines on each route.

(2) Allow certificates to go unused without loss.

(3) In setting fare do not consider airline earnings, as this will lead to perverse fare changes except when adjustment is being made for inflation.

(4) Seek that fare which maximizes passenger trips over the route under consideration. If both flights and output expand when the fare is raised, the fare is too low. If flights expand but output contracts (or if both contract), the fare is too high.

(5) Do not make unsophisticated across-the-board fare adjustments. At least recognize the differential impact such adjustments will have on long- and short-haul routes and on carriers whose route mix is predominately long or short.

This list could be expanded considerably to take into account the complexities of dealing with a network of interconnecting routes and a host of other factors. I have tried to make some simple suggestions based on the rather limited model of the industry that I have summarized here. I would say in conclusion that the opportunities for regulation to improve on the efficiency that would exist in open competitive markets for air transportation are limited, and the regulatory pitfalls are many.

SUMMARY OF DISCUSSION

The major discussion following these papers centered around the economic philosophy implied in Professor Jordan's paper. Briefly stated, the objection made was that economists, by explaining how things happen, are frequently accused of endorsing the status quo, and that Professor Jordan's attempt to delineate the objectives of CAB regulation and to suggest policies that would achieve them more efficiently might be interpreted as endorsing CAB policy. By its very nature, economic policy analysis is caught up in an adversary process, and what economists usually write in communicating with each other is likely to be taken out of context and misrepresented unless the economist makes a very strong disclaimer at the very beginning of his analysis. The problem, of course, centers around the role of an economist—is he "positive" or is he "normative"?

The point was made that there may exist considerable economic ignorance on the part of policy makers and their constituents. If this is the case, then to impute desired policy objectives from actual policy-maker behavior may result in error. Also, one economist in the group suggested that an appropriate role for an economist is that of being an "economic doctor"—that is, pointing out ways to increase efficiency and thus "improving the patient's health."

Professor Jordan responded that the economist must remain strictly positive if he (or she) expects to have any impact on policy. That is, once an economist adopts any public-interest criterion such as economic efficiency, he quickly loses credibility. Jordan urged economists to shy away from rote adherence to an economic efficiency norm if this adherence involves the neglect of other objectives equally or even more relevant. As an example, he related an incident where a graduate student asked his assistance in establishing the best way of cartelizing the Canadian rutabaga industry for sales to the U.S. An economist, says Jordan, should be as open to granting this kind of advice as he (or she) would be in providing analyses of the efficiency costs of CAB regulation. When economists do in fact show this objectivity, then they will achieve credibility.

There were several comments on the papers by Professors Douglas and De Vany. First, it was remarked that the non-price competing cartel models described by the authors would apply to other "competitive" industries under government regulation. Examples include interstate trucking, intercoastal shipping, and fixed-fee brokerage commissions. Second, it was pointed out that one must not lose sight of the fact that CAB regulation has protected the existing carriers, even if their profits have been "normal." Some inefficiency has been insulated from market forces through limitations on entry and measures to prop up losing carriers and thus prevent exit. Third, one participant said he found it difficult to reconcile the existence of some monopoly markets, some competitive markets, and normal returns overall. Quite likely, the effect is one of slightly higher-than-normal returns, or else some chronic losses in certain competitive markets.

One government official noted that his analysis showed a significant division between one and multi-carrier markets rather than De Vany's significant division between one or two versus three or more. Also, there was more discussion of Douglas's point that increasing market density gives rise to "economies of scale" in a particular dimension. Although technically capacity is produced at constant costs, the cost of a service of given quality declines because when output expands waiting time falls because of more frequent departures (at given load factors). Consequently, *ceteris paribus,* as market density increases, optimal load factors rise and optimal fares fall.

PART THREE

PROBLEMS OF PUBLIC POLICY REFORM

INTRODUCTION

As was mentioned in the introduction to this volume, one underlying theme of this conference was the interface between the academic community and transportation policy makers. Generally, the question here had to do with an observed variance between the recommendations of professional economists and other academic experts and the actions of policy makers. Are academicians failing to communicate? Are their analyses open to suspicion and misgiving? Are they looking at the "wrong" problems? Or are there simply limits on how far a policy maker will go in doing what is "right" as opposed to doing what is politically expedient?

In this provocative paper, Professor Eads notes the almost universal academic criticism of the institution of transportation regulation. He notes also the almost universal apathy about the situation in other quarters. Not only does he see no prospect for deregulation, he is even pessimistic about the prospect of "holding the line" against regulatory entrenchment.

Professor Eads attributes the variance between the results of academic research and the actions of policy makers to several failings in the advocacy and decision-making processes. First, he argues that economists have failed to devote sufficient analytical resources to considering the overall costs of regulation. Second, and even more important, he argues that the way economists look at the problem is not very efficient from the standpoint of its impact on public policy. That is, positive arguments about allocative efficiency losses seldom carry the day. Instead, what is needed is more research into the equity aspects of regulation—who is helped by regulation and at whose expense does the help come? Who would be hurt by deregulation and who would benefit?

Professor Eads explains the lack of a ground swell for deregulation on the part of the potential beneficiaries of deregulation in the following way. First, those who would be hurt by deregulation are small in number, know full well the losses they would incur, are highly organized, have effective communications, and bring their views to bear on policy makers (especially congressmen) in an efficient manner. On the other hand, those who would benefit by deregulation (especially the ultimate consumers of transported products) are large in number (making the benefit per person small), are to a large degree either ignorant of their stake in regulatory change or are confused about it, are unorganized, have little communication, and bring practically no force to bear on these public decisions.

Against this background, Professor Eads concludes that the battle for deregulation will be long and difficult, with little chance for success. If it is won, it will require more work by academicians, better packaging of the proposal, and "statesmanship" on the part of political decision makers.

ECONOMISTS VERSUS REGULATORS

George Eads

Introduction

For the last decade, a growing band of economists has been assaulting those modern-day citadels, the independent regulatory commissions. Study after study has been produced, often with great fanfare, demonstrating that regulation is ineffective in protecting the consumer against monopolistic exploitation,[1] that regulation often has been instituted at the behest of the regulated,[2] that regulation produces serious distortions in the incentive structure facing the regulated firms,[3] or that regulation results in massive net welfare losses to society.[4] Indeed, the weight of economic evidence has become so great that any economist venturing to support regulation today is apt to find himself in a very lonely position. What only a short time ago was considered heresy now has assumed the status of conventional wisdom.

In no single area has the evidence against regulation been either as consistent or as voluminous as in transportation.[5] Indeed, the evidence has become so clear that federal agencies such as the President's Council of Economic Advisers,[6] the

---

[1] The classic study here is George J. Stigler and Claire Friedland, "What Can Regulators Regulate?: The Case of Electricity," *Journal of Law and Economics* (October 1962), pp. 1-16.

[2] See, for example, George J. Stigler, "The Theory of Economic Regulation," *Bell Journal of Economics and Management Science,* Spring 1971, pp. 3-21.

[3] See, for example, William Capron, ed., *Technological Change in Regulated Industries* (Washington, D.C.: The Brookings Institution, 1971).

[4] See, for example, Thomas Gale Moore, *Freight Transportation Regulation* (Washington, D.C.: American Enterprise Institute, 1972).

[5] In addition to Moore (ibid.), see John R. Meyer et al., *The Economics of Competition in the Transportation Industries* (Cambridge, Mass.: Harvard University Press, 1959); Ann F. Friedlaender, *The Dilemma of Freight Transportation Regulation* (Washington, D.C.: The Brookings Institution, 1969); *Improving Railroad Productivity,* Final Report of the Task Force on Railroad Productivity to the National Commission on Productivity and the Council of Economic Advisers (Washington, D.C.: U.S. Government Printing Office, 1973); Robert W. Harbison, "Toward Better Resource Allocation in Transport," *Journal of Law and Economics,* October 1969, pp. 321-38; Almarin Phillips, ed., *Competition and Regulation* (Washington, D.C.: The Brookings Institution, forthcoming, 1975); William A. Jordan, *Airline Regulation in America: Effects and Imperfections* (Baltimore, Md.: The Johns Hopkins University Press, 1970); and Theodore E. Keeler, "Airline Regulation and Market Performance," *Bell Journal of Economics and Management Science,* Autumn 1972, among others.

[6] *Economic Report of the President,* February 1970, pp. 108-9; February 1971, pp. 122-30; and January 1972, pp. 130-34.

Antitrust Division of the Department of Justice,[7] and the Department of Transportation [8] have all gone on record favoring reduced regulation. In the fall of 1971, the Nixon administration even sponsored a bill that had as its aim a limited relaxation of regulation in the field of surface freight transportation.[9] Surely, one might conclude that the walls at least of the ICC are about to come tumbling down.

Those who are preparing for the burial of this agency would do well to check the health of the patient. If one were to look at results, not rhetoric, one might almost be convinced that regulation even in surface freight transportation is on the rise, not on the verge of collapse. The proposed regulatory modernization act of 1971 got nowhere. Instead, what was almost produced was a bill that would have put the federal government in the railroad boxcar supply business. And when the Northeast railroad "crisis" became acute, the solution turned to was not relaxed regulation, but quasi nationalization with the inevitable increase in regulation it will (or would) require.

In arriving at the solution it did, Congress was not going against the wishes of the public. To the extent that it had an opinion, the public's view was that the government was not doing enough to "help" the bankrupt Northeast railroads. For example, when the Department of Transportation presented proposals to rely to a degree on market forces to determine which of the trackage of the Northeast roads should be retained, cries of anguish arose from shippers, state legislators and governors.

This response is not atypical. To put it bluntly, there just is no discernible public demand at present for deregulation. Regardless of what economists' studies demonstrate about regulation-induced waste and inefficiency, the public remains convinced (or at least not hostile to the proposition) that certain industries are best run by an appointed committee of men, odd in number, no more than half of whom are members of any one political party.

This apathy on the part of the public toward deregulation is crucial, for it is quite clear that any moves to relax regulation will not come from either the regulatory agencies or, except in the rarest of cases, from industries currently being regulated. No regulatory agency is about to propose legislation that will reduce its powers and hence its budget. According to the agencies, if there is a

---

[7] See, for example, "Antitrust, Regulation and the Monopoly Mentality—Competition as a Spur to Progress," remarks by Donald I. Baker, deputy assistant attorney general, Antitrust Division (Prepared for delivery at the Practicing Law Institute, Mayflower Hotel, Washington, D.C., December 7, 1973).

[8] See, for example, statement of John A. Volpe, secretary of transportation, before the Subcommittee on Transportation and Aeronautics, Committee on Interstate and Foreign Commerce, House of Representatives, 92d Congress, 2d session (March 27, 1972), on H.R. 11824, H.R. 71826, and H.R. 11207.

[9] The Transportation and Regulatory Modernization Act of 1971 (H.R. 11826, S. 2842).

problem, its solution lies not in constricting, but in expanding its powers. If unregulated motor carriers win traffic away from regulated common carriers by means of lower rates and better service, this indicates that the unregulated carriers must be brought under the regulatory umbrella. If the California intrastate air carriers demonstrate consistent profitability, high load factors, and fares half the level of their regulated counterparts, or if the charter air carriers threaten to win traffic away from the scheduled carriers by offering services more in line with the demand of the public, this "unfair and ruinous" competition must be halted.

Similarly, both management and labor in regulated industries sense their continuing self-interest in maintaining regulation. The gainers from deregulation might be able to compensate the losers and still have something left over, but the Teamsters, the Air Line Pilots Association, and the rail unions are smart enough to discount the probability that any such compensation ever would be carried out, and to recognize just who the biggest losers are likely to be.

Therefore, if reduced regulation is ever to become more than a gleam in economists' eyes, it must have the strong support of both shippers and the traveling public. These groups must be convinced that deregulation is enough in their interest to induce them to devote the substantial resources that will be required to secure its enactment. And if these two groups cannot be convinced, economists might as well quit writing about "regulatory wastes" for all the good it will do.

Mobilizing these groups to support relaxed regulation is likely to prove difficult for two reasons. First, while economists tend to believe that inefficiency is bad per se, the bulk of the population seems willing to tolerate inefficiencies resulting from regulation because they believe that in return they are obtaining "fair treatment" or "equity." It does economists little good to observe that in many cases whatever "equity" is produced by regulation may be purchased at a high cost in efficiency, or that what may appear to the public to be "equity" indeed may be highly inequitable. Economists have not, in general, been willing to perform the studies that would allow us to back up such claims. Most of us have contented ourselves with analyses that measure such esoteric concepts (esoteric to the general public, at least) as "deadweight loss." By doing so, we have failed absolutely to undermine the strongest support for regulation among the general public.

Second, even if all the costs and benefits of relaxed regulation could be quantified, gains are likely to accrue to a large segment of the population some time in the future. Any losses from deregulation are likely to be borne by a much more compact portion of the population and are likely to be more immediate. The diffuse and uncertain nature of the gains tends to undermine any incentive the beneficiaries may have for devoting financial resources and time to the support of deregulation while the concentrated and relatively certain nature of the losses tends to encourage the opponents to fight any moves toward that end.

The "Efficiency versus Equity" Dilemma

There is little evidence to support the proposition that regulation has ever been enacted for the purpose of promoting or restoring economic efficiency. But there is no problem in uncovering cases in which regulation has been promoted on the grounds that it will produce "fair" or "equitable" treatment. The recent clamor for the institution of gasoline rationing was typical. Rationing was favored over use of the price mechanism to equilibrate supply and demand not because it is more efficient, but because it is "fair." During the latter half of the nineteenth century the railroad pricing policies that led to a public demand for Congress to "do something about the railroads" generated this outcry not because the pricing policies were inefficient but because they were "unfair" or "unjust." Recent support for federal action to rescue the Northeast railroads stems largely from concern by the public that reliance on the market to restructure this system would result in certain cities "unfairly" losing rail service.

In certain cases this idea of "fairness" can be enough to make an economist wince. The highly discriminatory structure of air fares is extremely popular with the general public (except for businessmen, who have been the class discriminated against). The recent decision of the CAB to bring discount fares more in line with costs brought forth cries of anguish from certain segments of the public and resulted in the introduction of legislation to require the reestablishment of the fares, even though the CAB decision was based on sound economic principles.

The public also considers as "unfair" attempts to correct through use of the price mechanism situations that are both inefficient and highly discriminatory (at least as an economist understands the word "discriminatory"). In its annual report for 1972, American Telephone and Telegraph (AT&T) estimates that, on the average, about fifty cents of each residential customer's basic monthly charge goes to pay for directory assistance.[10] Since there are approximately 60 million residence main telephones in the United States,[11] this implies a total attributable cost of approximately $360 million per year for this one service. The annual report also reveals that the company's studies show that a sizable majority of directory-assistance calls are made by relatively few customers. Thus, failure to levy an explicit charge for directory assistance not only results in overuse of the service and the devotion of too many resources to its provision but also produces a highly discriminatory cross-subsidization of one group of subscribers by another. However, AT&T reports that its efforts to institute a charge for directory assistance, which it strenuously asserts is not for the purpose of increasing revenues "but simply and only to remove the burden of cost from the general body of customers

---

[10] American Telephone and Telegraph Company, *1972 Annual Report,* p. 13.
[11] I would like to thank Ed Lowry of AT&T for locating this figure for me.

and assign it to those who benefit from a disproportionate use of this service," have resulted in strong public protests.[12]

What is to be done? Merely to reply that the public needs to be educated is to underestimate the depth of the problem. As Richard Posner has observed, cross-subsidization is deeply embedded in the regulatory framework.[13] At times it is explicit, as when the CAB attempts to "strengthen" the local-service air carriers by granting them access to denser routes.[14] More often it is implicit, as when the chairman of the board of AT&T makes reference to the possibility that his company can no longer carry out its "unusual obligation" to provide telephone service wherever and whenever demanded if companies are allowed to compete with AT&T for more lucrative portions of the telecommunications business.[15] The economists' standard response to cross-subsidization—that if certain "public interest" services must be provided, it is more efficient to support them by means of a direct subsidy—does not strike a responsive chord either with the public or with the regulatory agencies. Both seem to find this proposal's primary virtue—that it would allow the true cost of the subsidized service to be revealed, facilitating thereby a comparison of these costs and benefits—to be a distinct liability. The regulatory agencies are reluctant to have to fight a budget request through the Office of Management and Budget and Congress each year. The public seemingly would prefer to remain ignorant of the true cost of the service, believing it to be "free" or, even better, to be paid for out of the profits of those greedy monopolists, the regulated firms, in partial expiation for their protected status.

If this attitude of the public is to be changed, economists must begin a long, slow campaign of revealing the true cost of any "equity" achieved by regulation. An excellent example of a situation where this was at least begun is contained in a staff report entitled "Service to Small Communities" prepared by the CAB's Bureau of Operating Rights. This report clearly showed that the cost to the federal government of supporting short-haul, low-density air service using large aircraft was not the two or three dollars per passenger that some had claimed but instead amounted to more than $20 per passenger on average, and in one extreme case amounted to over $200 per passenger.[16] The report also calculated the savings that could be

12 AT&T, *1972 Annual Report*, p. 13.

13 Richard A. Posner, "Taxation by Regulation," *Bell Journal of Economics and Management Science,* Spring 1971, pp. 22–50.

14 George C. Eads, *The Local Service Airline Experiment* (Washington, D.C.: The Brookings Institution, 1972).

15 "An Unusual Obligation," Remarks by John D. deButts, chairman, American Telephone and Telegraph Company, delivered at the annual convention of the National Association of Regulatory Utility Commissioners, September 29, 1973.

16 "Service to Small Communities," A Staff Report of the Bureau of Operating Rights, Civil Aeronautics Board, March 1972, part 1, pp. 8, 20, 25, 32, and Appendix P-4, p. 3. The point where the subsidy cost was $206.13 per passenger was Martinsburg, West Virginia. Allegheny was suspended at Martinsburg on December 1, 1970, and the point was transferred to a scheduled air taxi.

achieved if the current support program (which includes a combination of direct and indirect subsidy) were transformed entirely to a direct subsidy program relying on competitive bids.[17]

Yet even this excellent study did not produce an improvement in the system of support for these "public interest" air services. A bill to experiment with the proposed bidding scheme was introduced in Congress but attracted little notice or public support.[18] Recently, the proposal was declared "dead" by the newly appointed director of the Bureau of Operating Rights.[19] He announced that the CAB was considering adopting instead a "flow through" subsidy scheme under which subsidy would be paid to local service carriers and "passed through" to commuter carriers operating routes under contract from the former carriers. This plan would combine many of the disincentive features contained in t'ie old method of subsidy payment with a set of new ones and, if adopted, would indicate that even after more than twenty-five years and excellent staff work, the CAB has not learned much about how to provide efficient short-haul, low-density air service.

Economists must not underestimate the importance of countering the allegation that if society opts for deregulation it will be giving up equity in exchange for efficiency. In those cases where deregulation would produce gains in both equity and efficiency or would produce efficiency gains with no loss of equity, economists must be able to demonstrate conclusively the fallaciousness of the claimed tradeoff. Where the tradeoff does exist, economists must be prepared to supply quantitative estimates of the efficiency losses (both their total magnitude and their distribution) that must be endured in order to gain "equity." In such cases, economists must be prepared for the likelihood that society may put less value on avoiding these losses than the economists do.

The Harvest Is Plentiful, but the Laborers Are Few

Theodore Keeler's estimates of the likely airline fare that would obtain in a deregulated air transport system demonstrate that the savings to air travelers from deregulation would be enormous in the aggregate.[20] Frequent air travelers would benefit particularly. Yet, there exists no organized air traveler lobby fighting for airline deregulation. Why is this?

---

17 Ibid., part 2 and part 3.

18 S. 3460, 92d Congress, 2d session, introduced April 7, 1972.

19 Remarks by William B. Caldwell, Jr., director, Bureau of Operating Rights, before the annual meeting of the Western Conference of Public Service Commissions, Portland, Oregon, June 6, 1973.

20 Theodore Keeler, "Airline Regulation and Market Performance," *Bell Journal of Economics and Management Science,* Autumn 1972, p. 417, Table 6. See also, William A. Jordan, *Airline Regulation.*

The answer may be found in the work of Mancur Olson, who has identified the problem as one of market failure.[21] Regardless of the size of the aggregate savings, the important thing is that they are so broadly spread throughout the entire population that no single individual or clearly identifiable group would gain sufficiently from deregulation to justify the investment of the funds and the time required to accomplish it. Furthermore, no mechanism exists that would allow an organization, if created for the purpose of securing airline deregulation, to impose a tax on the potential beneficiaries to finance a lobbying campaign. Each individual would have an incentive either to deny that he would benefit or to understate the extent to which he would benefit, knowing full well that it would be impossible to exclude him from the benefits of deregulation should deregulation somehow be achieved.

The opponents of deregulation generally do not face a similar problem. Regulated industries and unions already possess organizations capable of mobilizing the resources needed for effective opposition. Indeed, to the extent that Stigler is correct,[22] the fact that regulation was secured by such interests in the first place is proof that an effective organization exists. Furthermore, the strict control over entry that generally accompanies regulation assures that the number of potential "losers" is neither large nor increasing in number.

If the class of potential gainers from deregulation constitutes a large segment of the population and if the gain from deregulation can be shown clearly to exceed the loss, one might expect the government to be the proper instrument for correcting this "market failure." However, as I have just noted, any move toward deregulation is likely to evoke a response from a well-financed and politically effective opponent. This does not produce an atmosphere conducive to a dispassionate governmental weighing of costs and benefits. Furthermore, the branches of government most familiar with the industries in question—the regulatory agencies—are also likely to oppose deregulation, both because of pressures from the industries with which they are continuously associated and because of their natural inclination to avoid committing the bureaucratic equivalent of suicide. Support for deregulation may come from agencies without identifiable industry or labor constituencies—agencies such as the Council of Economic Advisers and the Antitrust Division of the Department of Justice. However, what makes them possible supporters of deregulation also limits the effectiveness of their support. Lacking clearly identifiable constituencies, they also lack lines of influence to the relevant congressional committees.

The last few years have seen the rise of certain "public interest" lobbies such as Common Cause. Might not such groups prove effective in mobilizing support for deregulation? They might, but it is not likely, for such groups are generally unwill-

21 Mancur Olson, Jr., *The Logic of Collective Action* (New York: Schocken Paperbook edition, 1968), chapter 1.
22 Stigler, "Theory of Economic Regulation."

ing to devote their relative meager resources to battles which are likely to require years, not months, and which do not evoke strong feelings from their potential funding sources. Deregulation is never likely to evoke the sort of emotions raised by the SST, even though its burden on the public may be much larger. Only if, through years of effort, economists manage to undermine the general support for regulation that the public now shows and develop a latent opposition to regulation are groups such as Common Cause likely to consider active support for deregulation to be in their best interest.

Another possible source of support would be from the "public interest" law firms such as the ones associated with Ralph Nader. However, such groups should not be counted on for much either. Although these groups complain loudly of the inefficiencies of the regulatory agencies and bemoan the frequency with which they get into bed with those they are supposed to regulate, they nevertheless have an inherent bias in favor of more, not less, regulation. They believe that regulatory agencies, if sufficiently "public spirited" and supplied with adequate budgets and qualified staffs, will protect the consumer. They also tend to support "equity" at the expense of efficiency, even when the "equity" they advocate is in fact highly inequitable. Furthermore, even if they can be convinced to support reduced regulation, they cannot be counted on to win more than skirmishes. They simply do not have the resources to fight the large battles required if significant deregulation is to be achieved.

Where Do We Go from Here?

In the last decade, economists have finally begun to understand how regulation works and what its effects on the economy are. My conclusion that the faults of regulation outweigh its virtues does not rest on any belief that the free market is likely to work perfectly, but upon my conviction, based on observation, that the market, though imperfect, works better than the sort of regulation society is likely to get, barring commissions composed of omnipotent, omniscient, benevolent dictators.

Having made this belated discovery, and in the light of the pessimistic picture painted in the sections above, how should we proceed from here? It is quite clear that we are not likely to see a repeat of Joshua's remarkable victory at Jericho—the mere publication of our results will not bring down the walls of the ICC, CAB, FMC, and so on, with a great crash. The "battle" for deregulation more likely will resemble a classical medieval siege with much logistical preparation, slow and dirty slogging in the trenches, small assaults that will often be repulsed, and victory through attrition and exhaustion.

In a limited number of cases, it may be possible to make unexpectedly rapid progress if groups having a financial interest in deregulation far out of proportion to their numbers can be identified and induced to lend their support. In the case of surface freight transportation, for example, a small group of important shippers were shown the benefits in lower rates and improved service that deregulation would bring. They were willing to finance a modest lobbying effort. This as much as anything else has accounted for the progress that has been made in moving toward relaxed regulation in this area, limited though this progress has been.

In general, however, what is required is a slow but systematic attempt to undermine the notion that regulation in some way protects the consumer from Big Business. The public has to be shown over and over again that regulation primarily serves the interests of the regulated and that whatever "equity" it produces usually is purchased at a high cost to the consumer. In addition, a concerted effort has to be made to convince the public that the "equity" of internal subsidy is indeed highly inequitable. To paraphrase Caves, the little old grandmother flying between New York and Los Angeles must be made to see that "fairness" does not require her to subsidize the air travel of well-to-do businessmen between smaller towns.[23]

Particular attention must be given to blocking attempts to extend regulation wherever they are proposed. We may not be able to do much about the way that the airlines are regulated, but we can build a powerful case that these mistakes should not be repeated in the case of the now unregulated commuter carriers. Likewise, the nonregulated status of the California intrastate air carriers, the truckers carrying agricultural commodities, and the inland bulk water carriers must be preserved. Blocking "the tendency of regulation to spread" [24] may be easier than securing positive action on deregulation since the losers from expanded regulation may be sufficiently aware of their potential losses to be willing to fight. Nevertheless, the general tendency of the public to believe that intelligent and well-meaning men can protect the public interest better than the workings of the "invisible hand" means that even here the job will be far from trivial, and even here a number of defeats should be anticipated.[25]

---

[23] Richard E. Caves, *Air Transport and Its Regulators* (Cambridge, Mass.: Harvard University Press, 1962), p. 436.

[24] This has been noted by Kahn. See Alfred E. Kahn, *The Economics of Regulation* (New York: John Wiley, 1971), vol. 2, pp. 28-32.

[25] My pessimism seems to be shared by others who are not economists. According to a survey conducted by the magazine, *Transportation and Distribution Management,* about 70 percent of the transportation and traffic managers who responded indicated their belief that the present system of regulating common carriers discourages the efficiency of freight transportation systems within the United States. Some 87 percent stated that they would prefer less regulation. Yet 57 percent stated that they expected more, not less, regulation of transportation during the next ten years. *Transportation Distribution and Management,* vol. 14, no. 2 (March/April 1974), pp. 38-40.

SUMMARY OF DISCUSSION

This paper generated a lively discussion over several facets of economics advocacy. First, what is the proper role of an economist? Is he (or she) strictly "positive"? Should he even care whether his analysis affects public policy? To the degree analysis does affect policy, can the economist remain totally "objective" in communicating his results? Can an economist advocate without losing credibility as a researcher? As might be expected, views varied.

A second issue was the degree to which economists have in fact influenced policy. Several members of the audience cited examples of changes in regulation which were prompted by academic research; they also cited proposed changes which were not promulgated for the same reason. There appeared to be general agreement that economists can have an impact when the results of their research have intuitive appeal to policy makers and when proposed programs, in turn, can be readily justified to constituents.

Others at the conference suggested that economists may affect policy through educating the populace to think analytically, specifically to consider opportunity costs. Economists are a very small minority and even persons in society who have more than a passing acquaintance with economic logic constitute a small fraction of the voting public. If economics education were broadened and started earlier, then there might arise a public "demand" for regulatory reform. Examples were cited where informed public opinion has had an effect on regulation (for example, West Coast-Hawaii and East Coast-Puerto Rico air fares are lower than comparable fares within the "lower forty-eight" because representatives from Hawaii and Puerto Rico have lobbied effectively before the Civil Aeronautics Board).

Among the non-economists at the conference there was general agreement that economists seldom package proposals in a way that is useful to a policy maker. Moreover, few economists are willing (or able) to market their proposals in a political advocacy environment. Finally, on a related note, it was pointed out that economists tend to ignore the political effects arising out of the income redistribution implicit in their proposals. If ways could be found to "buy off" losers from regulatory change, then reform would be much more likely. In technical terms, a "Pareto move" with compensation is much more likely than one without.

PART FOUR

EVALUATIONS OF FEDERAL
TRANSPORTATION PROGRAMS

INTRODUCTION

Yale Brozen

The same moral emerges in each of the analyses of the allocation of scarce capital among competing uses undertaken in the four papers in this section. Political processes—and the rules they produce for determining the uses to which capital is to be put—result in a staggering waste of resources. The waste is great whether measured (1) in terms of capital used where the value of its services is very much less than the value it could produce in alternative uses or (2) in terms of the objectives avowed in the debate leading to the provision of funds for the program in question.

Perhaps the moral is that project evaluation to determine the appropriate use of capital in politically governed activities is a fool's errand. Politicians are little concerned with economic waste. They are even less concerned (if that is possible) with the avowed objectives of programs once those programs are enacted. They are most interested in providing funds that can be used to reward their friends and precinct captains and to garner votes in their districts by showing how they can milk the rest of the country for the benefit of their constituents—particularly for their unionized constituents and the constituents who are members of their local contractors' associations.

With the cynicism inculcated by reading the four papers, perhaps one might be willing to argue that project evaluations might be useful for educating the taxpaying public in how their money is being wasted and suggesting that they should not hold still for the rape they are undergoing. But even this purpose seems to be poorly served. Such analyses as these seem to be disregarded or ignored. Perhaps their only use is to fill the professional journals and proceedings and to obtain promotions for their authors.

To illustrate the waste in terms of the avowed purpose of the appropriating legislation, let me cite one thing I learned from the first paper, written by Professor Ross Eckert. The primary avowed purpose of the Airport Development Aid Program (ADAP) was to provide a system which would eliminate the congestion existing in 1969, when the program was enacted, at such major airports as Chicago's O'Hare, New York's La Guardia, and Washington's National. Further, it was intended that the airport system be expanded sufficiently to keep future congestion to acceptable levels despite the expected growth of traffic. Despite this purpose, the rules incorporated in the program divert most of the funds to those airports where no congestion existed or was likely to develop. Perhaps it is not unreasonable to suspect that congestion was simply a smokescreen for enabling congressmen to raid the pockets of airline passengers for the benefit of hometown contractors and construction workers.

The Urban Mass Transit Assistance Program (UMTA) was sold partly on the contention that infusions of capital would upgrade transit services. This upgrading would presumably attract riders. More riders were needed, it was argued, to keep mass transit alive to serve the poor. But, according to Professor George Hilton, the infusion of capital has taken such forms as subsidizing the construction of the rapid transit line in the median strip of the Dan Ryan Expressway in Chicago. This has diverted passengers from the Illinois Central rail facility, which now faces an early death because of the deficit induced by the Dan Ryan line. The net result will be the replacement of a previously built private facility with a newly built public facility. The only gainers will be the contractors and construction workers who built the line and those who would have been competing with them for the available construction work if they had not been kept busy with the subsidized work. In other areas, some of the subsidy apparently serves to provide larger wage increases for unionized transit workers. The operating costs saved by the use of subsidized capital are used to pay transit workers more than what would be the going rate. Again, the smokescreen of preserving mass transit has hidden the real effect—the enrichment of members of construction and transit unions.

These days we talk about how nice it was that Amtrak kept the trains going so that they could save our supplies of gasoline and jet fuel. But Professor James Miller reports that Amtrak uses twice as much fuel per passenger mile as buses, and there is not even the redeeming social virtue of providing a more convenient service. Moreover, the frequency of service Amtrak provides is much less than that provided by buses. When the full costs of the various modes of transportation are considered, Amtrak shows a distinct disadvantage.

When it comes to the federal highway program—the subject of Professor Herbert Mohring's paper—it may be noted that this, too, like airport development, had the avowed purpose of eliminating congestion and providing for future growth of traffic. But this, too, like ADAP, has rules built into it diverting funds to the construction of roads in areas where there is no congestion problem. Four-lane limited-access roads in Nevada serving light traffic do little to relieve congestion in Chicago, New York, or Hoboken. And building a $5 million interchange a few miles beyond an existing interchange outside Las Vegas to serve the forty cars a day driving to a recreational facility must have produced the world's most expensive entrance to such facilities and does remarkably little to relieve congestion.

116

AN EVALUATION OF THE AIRPORT DEVELOPMENT AID PROGRAM

Ross D. Eckert

The United States has subsidized the construction of state and local civil airports since the close of World War II. Between 1946 and 1969, $1.2 billion in grants were provided.[1] In 1970 annual subsidies rose by nearly 300 percent with the creation of the Airport Development Aid Program (ADAP)—a ten-year, $2.8 billion expansion in facilities financed by taxes on airline tickets and noncommercial fuel.[2] In 1973 Congress raised the annual ADAP subsidies from $280 to $310 million. These funds are available only for such airfield investments as runways, taxiways, and aprons. Terminals, parking, access roads, and concession-related facilities are ineligible. Grants must be matched by local airport authorities on a fifty-fifty basis for large airports, but on a seventy-five to twenty-five basis for medium and small airports. By June 30, 1974, nearly $1 billion of ADAP funds will have been spent.

The purpose of the program is to capitalize the nation's airport system sufficiently so that expected growth in traffic can be accommodated without having congestion rise to unmanageable levels. The program is unlikely to accomplish this goal for two reasons. First, most of the investments already bought will have little effect in reducing congestion. Second, by expanding facilities without imposing peak-hour landing fees, demand and congestion are encouraged. The program has not only perpetuated the problem it was designed to solve but has probably made the problem worse. These discouraging outcomes make an evaluation of the airport subsidy program timely, especially in view of the energy "crisis."

Rationing Demand without Prices

Landing fees, where they exist at all, are low and based on aircraft weight rather than the time of flight. As Professor Michael Levine has shown, fees are low because airport authorities use the income from terminal concessions to subsidize airfield use,[3] where operations are rationed on a first-come-first-served basis. Fees

---

[1] U.S. Congress, Senate, Subcommittee on Aviation of the Committee on Commerce, *Hearings on Airport/Airways Development,* 91st Congress, 1st session (June 1969), part 1, pp. 36, 64.
[2] For a short history of this legislation, see Ross D. Eckert, *Airports and Congestion: A Problem of Misplaced Subsidies* (Washington, D.C.: American Enterprise Institute, 1972), pp. 3-7.
[3] Michael E. Levine, "Landing Fees and the Airport Congestion Problem," *Journal of Law and Economics,* vol. 12 (April 1969), p. 79.

for landing a fully loaded Boeing 707 at major airports are often less than $100, and those for general (noncommercial) aviation rarely exceed $10. As of 1967, the majority (61 percent) of the nation's 12,000 airports levied no landing fees.[4]

Landing fees do not vary during the course of the day, but demand of course does. Because of passenger preferences, flights at many airports tend to bunch in early-morning and late-afternoon hours. Without fee discounts during off-peak hours or premiums during on-peak hours, more runway use is demanded at preferred travel times and the result is congestion. Serious congestion leads some airlines and passengers to adjust their schedules to avoid spending time in a stack awaiting landing or queuing on taxiways awaiting takeoff. Although delays alone shift some use to off-peak times, these incentives could be accentuated by peak-time landing fees.

Time-uniform fees in the presence of peaked demands lead to inefficiencies of several kinds.[5] First, scarce runway space is allocated by willingness to incur delay rather than by willingness to pay. The policy of FAA control towers usually is to give priority to flights on the basis of early arrival in the queue. This enables such lower-valued flights as recreational, instructional, or short-haul-carrier trips to be given preference over higher-valued movements such as transcontinental airline trips simply by an earlier arrival in line. Not all long-haul-carrier flights are of higher value to society than all short-haul-carrier or general-aviation trips; smaller planes used for corporate or professional purposes are occasional exceptions. But most carrier flights will be of higher value, and thus willing to pay more for landing space, than most general-aviation flights. Failure to permit users to bid for landing rights will inevitably lead to some inefficiency in runway use. This conclusion is buttressed by the experience at New York's three major jetports when, in 1968, a minimum peak-hour fee of $25 was applied to general-aviation and air-taxi traffic. The fact that this traffic abruptly dropped by 30 percent at peak hours suggests that much of it was of marginal value.[6]

---

[4] U.S. Congress, Senate, *National Airport and Airways System,* Senate Report No. 1355, 90th Congress, 2d session (1968), p. 74; and Eckert, *Airports and Congestion,* pp. 20-22.

[5] Generally, see Alan Carlin and Rolla E. Park, *The Efficient Use of Airport Runway Capacity in a Time of Scarcity,* Memorandum RM-5817-PA (Santa Monica, Calif.: The RAND Corporation, 1969), pp. 3-12; Eckert, *Airports and Congestion,* pp. 13-32; Paul Feldman, "On the Optimal Use of Airports in Washington, D.C.," *Socio-Economic Planning Science,* vol. 1 (1967), p. 1; Michael E. Levine, "Landing Fees"; James D. Likens, "The Welfare Costs of Non-Optimal Utilization of the Washington-Baltimore Airports," paper presented at the annual meeting of the Western Economic Association, Davis, California, August 28, 1970; James C. Miller III, "Short-Run Solutions to Airport Congestion," *Atlanta Economic Review,* October 1969, pp. 28-29; Jora R. Minasian and Ross D. Eckert, "The Economics of Airport Congestion, Use and Safety," *California Management Review,* vol. 11 (Spring 1969), p. 11; Joseph Yance, "Pricing to Reduce Airport Congestion," *Highway Research Record,* 1969, p. 296; and "Movement Time As a Cost in Airport Operations," *Journal of Transport Economics and Policy,* vol. 3 (January 1969), p. 28.

[6] Eckert, *Airports and Congestion,* p. 28.

Second, as Professor Arthur De Vany suggests,[7] some air-carrier traffic is redundant because of incentives to compete in flight scheduling—incentives provided by the fixed and noncompetitive structure of airline fares. Flight-scheduling competition is viable because landing and takeoff fees are so cheap. Higher fees at peak times would raise operating costs and make some low-load-factor flights unprofitable.

Third, passengers and airlines lose time by waiting, and safety is reduced. Two Rand Corporation economists, Alan Carlin and R. E. Park, estimated that the costs of congestion for the three New York-area jetports during 1967-68 amounted to $48.7 million.[8] The costs of congestion for the whole nation would be many times larger.

Fourth, without prices the airport authority cannot be certain when an expansion of capacity is economically warranted. Such indices as the number of landings or minutes of delay are misleading since they do not measure the value of avoiding some amount of congestion. Only prices can indicate whether an increase in capacity will generate benefits (in reduced delays) greater than the costs it generates.

Fifth, the absence of prices is almost certain to result in an airport that is overcapitalized. Imposition of peak-hour landing charges permits a given number of flights to be accommodated by a smaller airport than could accommodate those flights in the absence of a peak-hour charge since the demand at peak times would be reduced. If 800 operations were distributed over a twelve-hour period rather than a six-hour period, a smaller airport would be "needed." A 1970 study of runway capacity at New York's John F. Kennedy International Airport by the National Academies of Science and Engineering suggested the magnitude of possible economies. If minimum peak-hour charges had been raised to $100 for all flights—an amount larger than was then paid by most carrier flights and four times the maximum fee paid by general aviation—the reduction in general-aviation flights and consolidation of competing flights among carriers would roughly equal the entire projected growth in traffic at Kennedy by 1980. This was the same growth that a $200 million investment in runways was thought necessary to accommodate.[9] This conclusion underscores the desirability of making more efficient use of existing facilities before embarking on elaborate plans for increasing capacity.

The FAA's preferred short-run method of reducing severe congestion is to limit hourly operations at particular airports by administrative fiat rather than to encourage airport authorities to impose peak-hour landing fees. Hourly quotas are

---

[7] Arthur S. De Vany, *The Value of Time in Air Travel: Theory and Evidence,* Research Contribution No. 161 (Arlington, Va.: Center for Naval Analyses, 1971).

[8] Carlin and Park, *Efficient Use of Runway Capacity,* pp. 56-57.

[9] National Academy of Sciences and National Academy of Engineering, Environmental Studies Board, *Jamaica Bay and Kennedy Airport* (Washington, D.C., 1971), pp. 23-44.

now in effect at three eastern airports and Chicago's O'Hare.[10] At Washington National, for example, the quotas are forty operations per hour for air carriers, eight for air taxis, and twelve for general aviation. The overall quota and its division among categories of users is based on the FAA's judgment as to what the local facilities will tolerate safely. The number of flights per hour per airline is determined by a "scheduling committee" among the air carriers. A general-aviation user, however, must make detailed advanced reservations for each arrival or departure. The purpose of the regulations is to limit the amount of general-aviation traffic by preventing a large number of general-aviation flights from showing up unannounced during peak times. The policy has withstood opposition from general-aviation interests, and general-aviation use of the four airports has dropped sharply.

Although administrative quotas are a simple means of decreasing traffic by a given amount, they do not accomplish the goal as efficiently as peak-hour prices would. Without information on the value of flights at different times, the FAA cannot know what the optimal number of hourly operations at a given airport is. How can the FAA know if decreasing flights from fifty to forty per hour will generate travel costs (from fewer movements at popular times) exceeding the benefits from lower congestion? Moreover, the FAA cannot know the most efficient division of flights between carriers and general aviation unless prices are charged. Although it is unlikely that many general-aviation flights would outbid fully loaded Boeing 727s for landing rights, it is conceivable that a few would do so and that many might outbid air taxis and short-haul-carrier operations. While such bidding could occur under a pricing regime, it is prohibited under the system of administrative quotas. Dividing quotas among individual airlines through bargaining processes is probably a better means of allocating flights than having the FAA decide alone. But it is still a more cumbersome (less efficient) method than pricing, especially if the number of airports subject to quotas were to be increased. Quotas are simple to impose, but they substitute administrative guesswork for what prices routinely provide—determining how scarce runway space should be allocated among competing claimants and determining when the expansion of facilities is justified economically.

Aside from time-variable landing fees, a second mechanism for shifting airport use to slack times might be time-variable airline ticket prices. However, such fares have not been common. "Night-coach" reductions of 20 to 35 percent have been regularly used by only two trunk carriers, primarily for flights to Atlanta and Miami from Chicago, New York, and Los Angeles. During the fall of 1973, three other carriers instituted experimental night-coach fares in markets of 2,000 miles or more in distance. Discounts ranged from 14 to 20 percent with travel limited to certain hours and days of the week, excluding holiday periods. These discounts were scheduled to terminate in February 1974. Generally, the Air Transport Asso-

---

[10] For a general description of quotas and how they work, see Eckert, *Airports and Congestion,* pp. 34-38.

ciation of America, usually a reliable policy voice for the major carriers, has opposed extensive use of peak/off-peak fares,[11] and where these fares have been instituted the purpose appears to be to produce new demand for off-peak travel rather than to lessen peak-hour congestion.

Whether night-coach fares have had a marked impact on congestion would have to be investigated on an airport-by-airport basis. In any case, they should not be considered as a substitute for peaked landing charges. First, they apply only to selected flights and airports. For example, West Coast travelers are precluded by FAA regulations from landing at Washington National Airport unless they stop first at Chicago. Night-coach discounts on flights to Dulles which are not substitutes for landings at National do not reduce National's congestion. Second, higher ticket prices do not shift general-aviation demand to off-peak periods and might increase it during peak periods if changes in airline schedules open up additional landing "slots" at peak hours. Third, airline fares are regulated by the CAB. The FAA could have little effect on the structure of ticket prices through withholding ADAP funds from airports, but such action might exert a powerful effect on landing fees. Fourth, several economic models of air-carrier behavior suggest that increases in airline fares could worsen congestion by encouraging carriers to intensify flight-scheduling competition through added seat capacity. If so, congestion would be improved by reductions in fares. Whereas increased landing charges would have unambigous anticongestion effects on general-aviation and air-carrier use alike, the effects of changes in ticket prices are far less certain.[12]

Experience under ADAP

By June 30, 1973, the United States had obligated $656 million in ADAP funds, and $300 million had been appropriated for the fiscal year 1974. But constraints imposed by law and by the political processes of making grants have prevented these funds from being used to decrease congestion. Instead, resources are misallocated by airport location, size, and type of project.

Funds are misallocated by airport location because Public Law 91-258, the Airport and Airway Development and Revenue Act of 1970,[13] requires that subsidies for air-carrier and reliever airports be distributed according to a strict formula: one-third according to each state's land area and population as a percentage of the national totals; one-third according to the number of passenger enplanements at air-carrier airports in each state as a percentage of total enplane-

---

[11] U.S. Congress, Senate, Subcommittee on Aviation of the Committee on Commerce, *Hearings on Airport/Airways Development,* part 1, pp. 132, 155; and part 2, p. 647.

[12] See De Vany, *Value of Time;* and Arthur S. De Vany, "The Economics of Quality Competition: Theory and Evidence on Airline Flight Scheduling," unpublished, 1969; and James C. Miller III, "Market Solutions to Airport Pollution," unpublished, 1972.

[13] 49 U.S.C., section 1102 et seq. (1964).

ments at such airports nationally; and one-third at the discretion of the FAA. Although congestion has been confined to several "large hub" airports in a few states, the act compels division of the available monies among all states, most of which have airports that will never face congestion. For example, the nation's thirty-three large hub airports generated 73 percent of all passenger enplanements in 1973, but received only 42 percent of total ADAP funding during 1971-1973; non-hub and small-hub airports, which numbered 313 in 1973, generated 13 percent of enplanements but received 31 percent of the program's funding. Part of this aid to small airports may have come from the one-third of ADAP funds which can be allocated at the FAA's discretion to airports having low demand but political clout.

Funds are misallocated by airport size because one-third of the program is distributed according to past enplanements. Instead of channeling ADAP funds into "reliever" airports, designed to drain traffic from nearby congested facilities, the distribution formula of Public Law 91-258 forces more money to be spent at the older, larger airports located in areas that are less desirable. Of all ADAP funds obligated by June 30, 1973, less than 5 percent went to reliever airports.

Funds are misallocated by type of project because environmental constraints written into the law preclude some investments which are likely to have a major impact on congestion. One of the main talking points in the debate over Public Law 91-258 was the FAA's contention that ADAP was needed to finance new airports. But the law's environmental clause, section 16(c), prevents the FAA from funding projects having adverse environmental effect until public hearings and studies indicate that no feasible or prudent alternative exists. These requirements have stymied the reinforcement of existing runways at Los Angeles International Airport, thwarted the extension of runways at Kennedy in New York, and made it necessary for a new runway at Chicago's O'Hare to be financed entirely without ADAP support. During ADAP's first three years only 8 percent of its funds was spent on completely new runways, and not a single new air-carrier airport was started under the program. Instead, more than one-half the funds were rushed through during the last quarter of each fiscal year and went for such projects as overlaying existing runways, repaving and extending taxiways and aprons, constructing airfield roads and drainage, and reimbursing local authorities for purchases of land. Most of these projects will probably have less impact on congestion than would new runways or new reliever airports.[14]

The 93rd Congress had an opportunity last year to take a second look at ADAP, to recognize its failures, and to cut it back. Instead, Congress expanded it by $30 million per year through enacting the Airport Development Accelera-

---

14 Generally, see Eckert, *Airports and Congestion*, pp. 8-9. But there are doubtless exceptions. One might be the purchase of land at Los Angeles International Airport to permit clear approach zones for existing runways and to lessen noise damage to nearby homeowners. See *Department of Transportation News*, June 15, 1973.

tion Act of 1973. The federal share of the airport subsidy was raised from 50 to 75 percent for all but the thirty-three "large hub" airports—each of which generates at least 1 percent of total air-carrier enplanements. Congress justified this on the ground that many investments at smaller facilities had been postponed because local authorities and airlines could not afford to match the federal share on a fifty-fifty basis.[15] But these postponements may have reflected instead the fact that the direct local beneficiaries of these investments placed a lower value on putting more of their own resources into airports than they did on putting them to other uses. An increased federal share could have been justified economically only if it were confined to reliever airports rather than made available to all airports of small or medium size. Thus, the Airport Development Acceleration Act raises the likelihood that still more resources will be misallocated by airport size, subsidizing facilities that are unlikely to experience significant congestion.

The act also prohibited local airport authorities from imposing head taxes on departing passengers. As of January 30, 1973, thirty-one authorities had levies varying between $.50 and $3.00.[16] Head taxes are poor meters of runway use, which is more a function of the number of operations per hour than of the number of passengers, but they are ideal for local financing of terminal facilities since terminal size is more a function of the number of passengers than of the number of operations. For this reason, head taxes should not have been federalized.

The act would have further increased subsidies and misallocated airport resources had two of its provisions in earlier drafts not been deleted. First, the annual funding of $310 million was $110 million less than the $420 million in the Senate's version of the act,[17] and was $40 million less than a similar bill that President Nixon vetoed in 1972.[18] Many aviation groups still deem $310 million insufficient, and attempts will probably be made in coming years to raise annual ADAP funding.

The legislation did not extend subsidies to airport terminal construction, which the Senate and most aviation groups had favored but which the House of Representatives has traditionally opposed.[19] Terminals are lucrative investments for local authorities because of the income from concessions and are well suited to airline and nonfederal governmental financing. Moreover, terminal projects are almost

---

[15] Perhaps in anticipation of the passage of this act, with its higher federal share, some local authorities held back their grant applications during 1973. Congress appropriated $280 million in ADAP funds for fiscal year 1973, but only $206.6 million were obligated. During the first four months of fiscal year 1974, the FAA's rate of project obligation was twice that of the similar period for 1973.

[16] U.S. Congress, Senate, Committee on Commerce, *Airport Development Acceleration Act of 1973: Report on S. 38,* Senate Report No. 93-12, 93rd Congress, 1st session (1973), p. 21.

[17] Ibid., p. 2.

[18] U.S. Congress, Senate, Committee on Commerce, *Report on S. 3755,* Senate Report No. 92-1005, 92d Congress, 2d session (1972), p. 2; and "Nixon Vetoes Added Assistance for Airports," *1972 Congressional Quarterly Almanac,* pp. 945-48.

[19] U.S. Congress, Senate, Committee on Commerce, *Report on S. 38,* p. 14.

endless in number, vary greatly in cost, and are subject to more "gold-plating" than runways—all of which would increase pressures to expand ADAP even more.

Pricing and Experiments

It is ironical that past airport subsidies have, for the most part, bought investments that will be ineffective in reducing congestion and will indeed be likely to promote it. Below-cost landing fees have produced more airport users—air carrier and general aviation alike—than if there had been no subsidies to begin with. Once given, the subsidies are painful to withdraw because the user groups are lobbying for still more subsidies. Congestion will continue as long as subsidies continue, unless additional rationing schemes are superimposed. I have argued that pricing systems are superior to administrative quotas for achieving efficient use of existing facilities before new investments are made. These pricing systems could be of two kinds—peaked landing fees and exchangeable landing rights.

With peaked landing fees, airport authorities would raise peak-hour fees until delays were reduced to safe and manageable levels. Since no one has accurate a priori information as to what these congestion levels and their related fees would be at any particular airport, some experimentation and adjustment would be necessary. An initial price could be set for a period of, say, three weeks during which the reactions in demand would be monitored carefully. If congestion fell off only slightly then the price could be raised for a second three-week period. Queues would ultimately decline though several price changes might be required. One advantage of pricing over administrative rationing is that the fees can be changed easily when circumstances warrant, and local airport authorities already have experience in setting other fees which vary with time (automobile parking, for example). Fees would have to vary over two or three periods of the day at most, much like telephone tariffs; fees that changed every hour or so would probably be too complex.

An alternative to variable landing fees would be to create transferable landing rights or "slots" for peak-hour use.[20] The airport authority would first determine the desired rate of operations per hour and then create lease rights for each slot. Holders would be free to exchange these lease rights. For example, a landing right could be issued for a flight at any time between 9:00 and 9:30 A.M. daily. If a given airport experienced peaking by day as well as by hour, the right could differentiate between weekdays, Fridays, and weekends. Initially the rights could either be sold to the highest bidders at public auction or be vested in current users in proportion to their use as of a designated date, after which they could be

---

[20] The best discussion of this proposal is found in Carlin and Park, *Efficient Use of Runway Capacity,* pp. 150-55. See also Levine, "Landing Fees," p. 105; and Eckert, *Airports and Congestion,* pp. 50-56.

exchanged so that rights would ultimately be acquired by highest-valued users through ordinary market transactions. Thus, even if general-aviation users, flying clubs, and trade associations representing them were entirely displaced at some airports—which is not very likely—it would be through voluntary transactions in which both parties gained. The principal drawback of exchangeable landing rights is the difficulty in choosing the optimal rate of operations per hour. Airport authorities may initially select a rate that is too high or too low, since setting the optimal rate requires information which only prices can provide accurately. However, the rate could later be changed by the issuance of new rights or cancellation of old rights in the same proportion as they were initially distributed so that each user would gain or lose in proportion to his initial slot holdings.

Since there has been little experience with peak-hour landing fees and no experience with exchangeable landing rights, airport administrators are likely to be unsure of the results of using these mechanisms. Some uncertainties could be eliminated by experimentation at two or three airports. The experiments could determine whether prices can improve the economic efficiency with which airport resources are used and could reveal any unforeseen problems in implementing pricing systems. They could be sponsored by the FAA under its authority to make planning grants for airports under section 13 of Public Law 91-258. Three possible experiments are outlined briefly here.

The first would impose a system of peak-hour fees at a large already congested airport. (While it would be easier to experiment with pricing at a smaller uncongested facility, the prices of flights would be relatively low and the information generated about the responsiveness of demand would be less valuable.) To ensure the cooperation of local authorities, the grant contract would stipulate that the airport would not lose any ADAP funds to which it would have been entitled on the basis of the previous calendar year of operation. The airport would also be protected against any loss in landing-fee revenue (although airport income is more likely to rise than to fall as landing fees are raised). The grant could extend over a two- or three-year period. Prices should be set by the local authority, but the FAA would provide the authority with available information about the nature of the airport's demand for flights and would collect data on the results of the experiment.

A second experiment would involve exchangeable landing rights. As before, the local authority would be protected against a decline in landing-fee income and ADAP funding. Permits for "slots" could be granted for, say, a three-year period, renewable for another three years at the end of the first eighteen months. This should give users the advance information and degree of certainty that they need to plan their operations sensibly, and the possibility of having these valuable rights renewed would give them a stake in the experiment's success. The main problem in this experiment—setting the initial hourly operations rate—could be eliminated by selecting the experimental airport from the three now subject to FAA quotas. Neither the hourly FAA quota nor its division among different cate-gories of users may be economically optimal now, but the quota system has the advantage of having been in operation for some time and airport users are already accustomed to it. To convert from a quota system to a system of exchangeable landing rights would require only that the quota slots be made fully transferable and that dates for their expiration and renewal be stipulated. The slots that air carriers already have could be vested in each airline, or they could be auctioned off. General-aviation slots could be treated in a similar manner. Although auction-ing slots would have certain advantages, vesting rights according to current use would increase the acceptability of the experiment among users and would permit its implementation quickly and easily at any airport subject to FAA quotas.

A third experiment would be to establish either of these pricing systems at the two federally operated airports near Washington, D.C. The delays involved in making planning grants under Public Law 91-258 would be avoided, and it may be noted that a system of FAA quotas already exists at Washington National. Moreover, the rivalry between the two airports (National being preferred to Dulles by most travelers because of its proximity to downtown Washington) would yield information on the effects of pricing on the use of a competitive outlying airport.

Actual experimentation with pricing should clarify the advantages of prices over administrative rules as solutions to congestion. Although the experiments might last several years, there would be enough information available within six or eight months to permit answers to several important questions: Is pricing admin-istratively feasible? Can airport authorities set fees that reduce congestion at peak times? Do they raise fees in response to rising demand and lower fees when demand falls? Can local authorities set an hourly movement rate that enables landing rights to be exchanged? Do higher landing fees or higher prices of slots lead users to shift flights to off-peak hours? Do general-aviation users obtain some (although perhaps fewer) landing slots either by paying higher fees or by having brokers or trade associations purchase the slots and then rent them to individual users?

If the FAA cannot induce local authorities to adopt rational pricing systems even on an experimental basis through planning grants, it might withhold ADAP funding for new facilities until each congested airport had demonstrated through pricing that it was making efficient use of existing facilities. Peak-hour fees are not prohibited by any federal law or regulation and have been upheld in court.[21] Moreover, the FAA's action could be supported by section 18(8) of Public Law 91-258, which requires "as a condition precedent to . . . approval of an airport development project" that the FAA should determine that the local airport opera-

---

[21] Aircraft Owners and Pilots Association v. Port Authority of New York, 305 F. Supp. 93 (1969).

126

tor has maintained a structure of fees and rentals "which will make the airport as self-sustaining as possible."

The FAA has opposed the introduction of pricing or landing-rights systems on a variety of grounds.[22] First, the FAA is unwilling to abandon a "proven" quota policy, which has safely reduced delays to historically low levels, for a pricing experiment that might have uncertain results. But the FAA cannot know, absent prices, whether its quotas have reduced congestion by too much or too little. Moreover, only after experimentation with pricing will it be clear whether quotas are superior to prices for the allocation of airport resources.

Second, the FAA has emphasized that the setting of airport landing fees is beyond its control since fees are determined by contracts made between airlines and local airport authorities. But the FAA, through ADAP and other aviation programs, might convince local authorities not to make new contracts of this kind, and might encourage the modification of some existing contracts. The FAA influences nonpricing aspects of local airport operations and could also push for pricing systems if it so desired.

Third, the FAA argues that the use of exchangeable landing rights would raise the possibility of one airline monopolizing a given city-pair route through the purchase of the fixed number of slots. But an airline so inclined would have to purchase an enormous number of slots to accomplish its goal—most of the slots at all airports in both cities—since slot rights are tied only to the time of flight and not to flight origin and destination. Thus, monopolizing behavior of this kind is extremely unlikely.[23]

Fourth, it has been suggested that the increased income airports would obtain from peaked landing fees would amount to an "embarrassment of riches" which would put the airport under pressure to spend the increased income quickly. Moreover, the money might be siphoned off to nonaviation purposes where environmental considerations restricted expansions in airport capacity.[24] But the increased income is not likely to be an embarrassment for long. It could be used to purchase new facilities where environmental restrictions permitted, general-aviation facilities in suburban areas, permission for noise and air polluton from adjacent homeowners, or the assorted projects which are now federally funded but have only marginal impact on congestion. Aside from the manner in which the money is spent, the raising of peak-hour fees will itself have the benefit of reducing congestion by rationing existing airport facilities more efficiently. Individual travelers

---

[22] Letter from John H. Shaffer, administrator, Federal Aviation Administration, to William J. Baroody, president, American Enterprise Institute for Public Policy Research, November 13, 1972, with accompanying memorandum, "Comments on *Airports and Congestion: A Problem of Misplaced Subsidies.*"

[23] If it were thought necessary, a system of exchangeable landing rights could include a rule to limit the number of slots that one airline could hold at a given airport or hour.

[24] Carlin and Park, *Efficient Use of Runway Capacity,* pp. 115-16; and Ronald W. Pulling, letter to the editor, *Wall Street Journal,* October 15, 1973.

have relatively little interest in the manner in which increased landing-fee income is used so long as what they pay buys them a trip with fewer delays.

Fifth, the FAA is opposed to experimentation with pricing until there is at hand most of the information that would guarantee an experiment's success. The FAA asserts that "detailed [econometric] specification of the demand function is required because of the known weekly and seasonable variations in travel patterns throughout a year" and that "the operational feasibility of peak-load pricing . . . is strongly dependent upon these two factors." [25] But estimates of demand elasticities, although useful, are not prerequisites for an experiment. Higher prices at peak times will shift use, and the experiments will indicate the likely magnitudes of shifts at a given airport. Information on these magnitudes could be used to design a structure of fees for the entire airport system. However desirable it might be to have econometric estimates ex ante, they would serve as a guide to setting initial prices only. Changes in demands, capacities, and other factors would eventually lead to changes in prices. Again, the relative advantages of variable landing fees over nonvariable prices (or quotas) can be understood and compared only after experimentation with variable pricing.

Sixth, the FAA argues that experimenting with landing fees at only one airport ignores the whole network of airports: the structure of fees that lowers the peak at one facility, such as Washington National, may disrupt traffic patterns at the eighty-odd airports with which National connects. But every airport must contend with some of the consequences of decisions made at other airports. Any independent action that affects one airport's capacity (action such as the construction of new runways) is bound to have some system-wide repercussions to which other airports must adjust. The fact that the nation's airport system routinely adjusts to changes in capacity, revised airline fares and schedules, slowdowns by FAA controllers, and imposition of FAA quotas suggests that the system could also adjust to the selective imposition of peak-hour landing fees. It would be inefficient to require one airport to take into account all the system-wide effects of its action before it could modify the demand for its facilities. Such a policy would freeze airports into current capacities and patterns of demand, and would prevent the introduction of landing fees (time-uniform or time-variable) or anything else that would alter the pattern of runway use. Put simply, the FAA's contention that congestion at one airport cannot be analyzed sensibly without considering congestion at each and every other airport with which it forms a pair cannot be taken seriously. Whatever action one major airport takes to resolve its congestion will eventually lead to adjustments by airports that connect with it—adjustments leading to an eventual equilibrium situation. And pricing is likely to simplify these adjustments rather than complicate them since it would provide direct information on the value of peak-hour movements and thus on increments to airport capacity.

---

[25] "Comments on *Airports and Congestion: A Problem of Misplaced Subsidies.*"

The central theme of the FAA's objections to system-wide or experimental use of peaked landing fees appears to be that it might create costs or dislocations in the aviation and airport systems. However, the FAA just as consistently fails to acknowledge the costs and dislocations caused by the existing structure of non-variable landing fees. The economic value of preventing a lower-valued flight from displacing a higher-valued flight is not easily "seen" but it exists nonetheless. From the perspective of the nation's economy, a judgment in favor of time-uniform over time-variable landing fees can be made only after a weighing of the gains and losses from both options. The FAA has failed to raise any telling objection either to the system-wide implementation of time-variable fees or the experimentation with them at selected airports over a limited period of time.

Energy and Airports

Congestion wastes fuel, whether the aircraft is queuing on the ground awaiting takeoff or in a "stack" in the air. As a result of rising fuel prices and a national policy to conserve energy, airlines and other users have cut back on flights.[26] But a reduction in flights is only a minimal response to the energy "crisis." The nation's energy problems strengthen rather than weaken the case for adopting economically rational airport pricing policies, and reducing or postponing ADAP subsidies.

First, peaked landing charges would provide an efficient mechanism for determining which flights should be dropped. Without higher fees, airlines could conserve fuel by eliminating off-peak rather than on-peak flights. With higher fees only the most valuable flights could bid successfully for both landing rights and aviation fuel. Peak-hour, low-load-factor, and short-haul flights—usually among the least efficient users of aviation fuel on a seat-mile basis—would be the most likely to be cut if landing and takeoff fees were raised.

Second, and completely aside from the question of airport pricing, reductions in general-aviation and air-carrier flights would eliminate the argument for many contemplated ADAP investments in new airport capacity. Why should the government continue to spend $310 million per year on airport expansions designed to accommodate increased flights when the number of flights is actually declining because of higher fuel prices? Some projected airport subsidies could be eliminated and others could be postponed. The monies saved could be reallocated to energy research and exploitation or to other pressing national demands.

The most desirable policy, looking from the standpoint of the nation's scarce resources, would be to reduce peak-hour flights by increasing landing fees in addition to other existing schemes for curtailing flights. And fewer peak-hour operations would weaken whatever rationale may remain for perpetuating a national program of unnecessary subsidies which have contributed both to airport congestion and to the rising scarcity of fuel.

---

[26] "Austerity in the Air," *Time Magazine*, December 24, 1973, p. 25.

THE URBAN MASS TRANSPORTATION ASSISTANCE PROGRAM

George W. Hilton

As Cervantes definitively demonstrated, there are two interpretations of anything. Inevitably, observers have developed differing hypotheses to explain the decline of the urban transit industry. Society in the course of the twentieth century has gone from a 90 percent dependence on the streetcar for urban trips to today's almost equally high dependence on the automobile. The urban transit industry, which had produced 23 billion rides as recently as 1946, had declined to producing 8 billion by 1963, and the industry's financial performance was such that its survival was questionable.

The first interpretation of the decline of the transit industry is found in *The Urban Transportation Problem* by John R. Meyer, John F. Kain, and Martin Wohl,[1] along with some additional writings by the same authors. Meyer, Kain and Wohl argue that the decline is the result of changes in geographical and demographic patterns of cities, almost all of which have tended to produce more diffused urban areas. Substitution of television for theaters and cinemas, trucks for railroads, computers for unskilled clerical labor, airports for railroad stations, Negroes for immigrants as slum dwellers, and similar conversions have all tended toward decline of central business districts. Meyer, Kain and Wohl particularly stress that the automobile is used in complementarity with single-family housing, so that the trend toward suburbanization gave the automobile a strongly positive income elasticity of demand: as consumers' incomes increased, demand for services of automobiles increased more than proportionately. By contrast, transit proved to have either negative or insignificantly positive income elasticity of demand. The automobile proved to be the least costly method of moving people on the light-density routes which suburbanization created. Urban motorists were found to pay their way overall, but rush-hour drivers probably receive a subsidy because of the governmental use of average-cost rather than marginal-cost pricing of roads. The result is a congestion of traffic into and out of central business districts analogous to the queuing created by nonprice rationing elsewhere in the economy. In addition, the nature of road pricing gives no incentive for the use of transit in accordance with its comparative advantage for home-to-work trips.

---

[1] John R. Meyer, John F. Kain, and Martin Wohl, *The Urban Transportation Problem* (Cambridge, Mass.: Harvard University Press, 1965).

131

Though the point is not particularly stressed in the Meyer, Kain and Wohl volume, the same authors and some other writers have argued that the organization of urban transit systems into monopolies causes their labor costs to be excessive (by producing strong unions), and causes them to be unresponsive to demand changes, as compared to a "jitney" system of owner operation of buses.[2] In such a system, transit would be provided by a continuum of vehicles—from private automobiles registered to handle passengers incidental to trips to and from work to buses run by full-time owner-operators.

A rival to this interpretation is another presented in *Urban Transportation and Public Policy,* by Lyle C. Fitch and Associates,[3] to the effect that urban transit has declined because it has been undercapitalized. Fitch and his collaborators have argued that channeling public funds into roads through the highway trust fund and similar fiscal devices created an imbalance in transportation policy which resulted in the inability of transit systems to compete with the automobile on equal terms. Rush-hour travelers, who had proved themselves relatively unresponsive to price changes, were presumed to be highly responsive to improvements in the quality of service. Such improvements might take the form of replacement of existing buses with newer and more commodious buses, or substitution of rail lines for bus lines, or the bringing forth through experimentation of new systems of public transit.

The interpretations of the decline of urban transit in Meyer, Kain and Wohl and in Fitch are not entirely irreconcilable: the treatment of the consequences of user charges on roads undifferentiated by hour, for example, is essentially the same in both books. The two interpretations, however, lead to diametrically opposite policy conclusions: the interpretation in Meyer, Kain and Wohl leads to a prescription that transit should move to more demand-responsive labor-intensive systems, and the interpretation in Fitch leads to a recommendation that transit be made more capital-intensive through infusions of federal funds into the industry. Fitch explicitly recommended that federal intervention be restricted to capital grants on the ground that it was the quality of service which urgently required upgrading, and that operating subsidies might result in waste or dissipation of funds in gains for the unions.

The Urban Mass Transportation Assistance Program provides a partial test of the relative validity of the two hypotheses, inasmuch as it was based entirely on the latter; in fact, the Fitch volume had its origin in a public document that led to the Urban Mass Transportation Act of 1964. The Urban Mass Transportation Act funded the program and provides its basic statutory authority. The program

---

[2] John F. Kain and John R. Meyer, "Transportation and Poverty," *Public Interest,* no. 18 (1970), pp. 75-87; and Ross D. Eckert and George W. Hilton, "The Jitneys," *Journal of Law and Economics,* vol. 15 (1972), pp. 293-325.

[3] Lyle C. Fitch and Associates, *Transportation and Public Policy* (San Francisco, Calif.: Chandler Publishing Co., 1964). See also Thomas E. Lisco, "Mass Transportation, Cinderella in Our Cities," *Public Interest,* no. 18 (1970), pp. 52-74.

has two major categories of expenditure—demonstration grants and capital grants —along with a variety of minor categories for higher education, executive training, and planning of projects. These minor categories will not be treated here because of space limitations. Both the demonstration grants and capital grants are allocations of federal funds to public bodies, though the act provides that the funds may be spent for equipment operated under contract by privately owned carriers. Funds have been expended at a ratio of $2 of federal money to $1 of local. Demonstration grants are intended for experimentation with new uses of existing technology (such as buses on a monthly subscription basis and demand-responsive scheduling of buses) or for development of new technology (such as tracked air-cushioned vehicles, personal rapid transit, and hovercraft). Capital grants are made for conversion of transit systems from private to public ownership, replacement of buses with new ones, purchase of ferryboats (to a limited extent) and building or re-equipment of rail transit systems. About two-thirds of the funds of the Urban Mass Transportation Administration (UMTA) go into rail systems, and many of the proponents of the program, and apparently some of its former administrators, have looked upon the program as mainly designed to build rail systems parallel to freeways built by highway departments.

The program was explicitly intended to produce certain external benefits: reduction in traffic congestion and atmospheric pollution; increased mobility for the poor, the young and the elderly; and incentives for the creation of compact transit-oriented urban patterns of the New York-San Francisco type in contradistinction to cities of the low-density, automobile-oriented sort, such as Los Angeles and Houston.[4] Profitability and even ridership were subordinate to the production of the desired externalities. Evaluation of the externalities was mainly subjective, inasmuch as UMTA does not require benefit-cost analysis of its applicants. The externalities were sought through the arrest and reversal of the decline of transit without a change in the industry's economic organization into local monopolies of linear routes with an organized labor force. In fact, section 13(c) of UMTA's statutory authority provided a powerful strengthening for the present economic organization by requiring that any grant be approved by the unions involved. In order to secure an agreement of the union under section 13(c), the transit enterprise had to provide protection of job rights, thus making sure that capital would be used in complementarity to the employees, not as a substitute. Among other things, this made it impossible for UMTA to establish owner-operated "jitney" systems. It also ensured that any demand-responsive systems that UMTA might establish would be staffed at union pay scales. UMTA was, however, without power to subsidize the variable expenses of transit systems, and without power over fares, except insofar as a change in fares might be part of an experimental program under a demonstration grant.

---

[4] For example, see Urban Mass Transportation Administration, *Capital Grants for Urban Transportation: Information for Applicants*, 1972.

The Demonstration Grant Program

The Demonstration Grant Program has carried on well over one hundred projects almost all of which can be classified under three headings: the bus programs, the rail programs, and projects concerned with new or experimental systems.

The bus program contained one set of projects which was markedly successful and several others which were uniformly unsuccessful. The successful class of projects involved granting bus priority on freeways. In Seattle, beginning in 1970, UMTA sponsored a set of reversible lanes and exclusive on-off ramps for buses, allowing them quick access to and egress from the central business district, and also allowed the buses nonstop running for distances up to eight miles along Interstate 5. An integral part of the project was the establishment of a park-and-ride lot for 550 automobiles at the north end of the reversible lanes. Ridership on the buses ran between 10,700 and 12,100 per day.[5]

A more permanent project of the same character was undertaken on a reversible lane in the median strip of the Shirley Highway, the principal freeway running south from Washington, D.C. Reserved lanes for buses to downtown Washington were also established. By March 1973 ridership in the morning rush hours was reported to have reached 12,855 and daily diversion of automobiles from the Shirley Highway was estimated at more than 3,000.[6] Also in this category of projects, the Texas Transportation Institute at Texas A&M University developed a technique whereby the admission of automobiles to the Gulf Freeway in Houston was limited by traffic lights at on-ramps. Automobiles were admitted at a rate consistent with free-running speeds on the freeway. The elapsed time for buses in a six-mile section of the freeway was shortened from twenty minutes to twelve minutes and freeway capacity was increased about 12 percent. The technique, which entails admission of buses to the freeway by separate entrances to keep them out of the queues of automobiles, is considered highly successful and is being installed on I-35 running south from Minneapolis.[7]

UMTA began express bus services on freeways in Baltimore, Buffalo and Providence, and this service also proved viable at the expiration of the UMTA demonstration period. Unfortunately, UMTA's other bus programs have been uniformly unsuccessful. Subscription bus services designed to pick up workers at their doors and deliver them to factories in the morning and to provide the reverse trip in the afternoon were tried in Flint and Peoria but neither proved viable.[8] The Flint project had to be abandoned before its scheduled completion. A pair of bus lines was established at Hempstead, Long Island, to connect a lightly populated

---

[5] Project WASH-MTD-2. For experience under this and other projects, see George W. Hilton, *Federal Transit Subsidies: The Urban Mass Transportation Assistance Program* (Washington, D.C.: American Enterprise Institute, 1974).

[6] Project TRD-82.

[7] Project TRD-14.

[8] Projects MICH-MTD-2 and ILL-MTD-3-4.

suburban area with the Long Island Rail Road Station. It was hoped the home-to-station trip could be provided for less than 10 percent of the cost of owning a second automobile, but this experiment also proved unsuccessful.[9]

UMTA established eighty-three routes in fifteen cities intended to provide outward mobility for ghetto residents to factories or other places of suburban employment. These projects, which were intended to offer a service that the existing routes of transit companies generally provide imperfectly or not at all, proved highly unsuccessful—one of the least productive set of projects in UMTA's entire experience. All routes reported losses ranging from $.39 per passenger trip in Chicago to $7.40 per passenger trip in St. Louis. The sponsor of the project in St. Louis reported that many had used the bus to find jobs, then had bought automobiles and quickly forsaken the bus. The performance of this program was so unsatisfactory that the General Accounting Office undertook a review of the projects and in a memorandum to the administrator of UMTA suggested that the program was such a demonstrable failure that continuance was not warranted and would in fact constitute a subsidy of operations rather than an experiment, thereby rendering the expenditures in violation of UMTA's statutory authority.[10]

UMTA has undertaken a demand-responsive project in Haddonfield, New Jersey, an established suburban community of Philadelphia. The project is unprofitable, is attracting something more than a third of the anticipated ridership and is apparently providing at bus fares a service that represents latent demand for taxicab service not manifested at local taxi rates.[11]

Under the demonstration program UMTA established only one rail line but that line provided a good indication of what could be expected from the inauguration of rail lines under the capital grant program. The line was the Skokie Swift of the Chicago Transit Authority, making use of five miles of track between the village of Skokie and the north terminus of the north-south rapid transit line in Chicago to provide an express service over the route of a recently abandoned interurban line. The service was inaugurated on April 20, 1964, and by 1967 reached a peak of 7,500 riders per day. The Chicago Area Transportation Study surveyed the ridership of the Skokie Swift in 1966 in an effort to estimate its impact on travel patterns and demand for rival or complementary facilities. Of its southbound passengers 12.3 percent had formerly driven to the Chicago Loop, 11.2 percent had formerly driven to elevated stations, 2 percent had been passengers in the automobile to the Loop, 3 percent had been automobile passengers to the elevated; about 20.8 percent had formerly taken the bus to the elevated and 7.7 percent had taken the bus to the Loop, about 9.4 percent had taken suburban

[9] Project NY-MTD-11.

[10] U.S. Congress, House of Representatives, Subcommittee of the Committee on Appropriations, *Hearings on Department of Transportation and Related Agencies Appropriations for 1973*, 92d Congress, 2d session (1972), pp. 656-59.

[11] Project NJ-DMG-2.

railroad trains to the Loop, 27.7 percent had not made the trip, and the remainder used other methods or left their former modes of travel unknown. The Chicago Area Transportation Study concluded that institution of the rail line had diverted from the principal highway facility, the Edens-Kennedy Expressway, about 900 automobiles per day. This diversion was imperceptible when compared to the growth or variance of vehicle counts on the facility which had utilization well in excess of 100,000 vehicles per day.[12] Since 1967 the Skokie Swift has shared the decline in passenger volume of the Chicago Transit Authority system as a whole. The peak two-hour load southbound on winter weekdays has fallen from 2,350 in 1967 to 1,750 in 1972.

The other projects in the rail portion of the demonstration grant program were mainly efforts at improvement of electric railway technology: tunneling methods, ventilation systems, control mechanisms, fare collection devices, and the like. By far the largest of these projects was a joint effort with the management of the Bay Area Rapid Transit (BART) district to develop an automatic train control mechanism for the BART system.[13] Upon BART's initiation of service, the mechanism proved to malfunction, giving erroneous indications to the trains and not having fail-safe properties. In the course of testing, pre-revenue operation, and revenue operation of the Hayward line in the fall of 1972, BART suffered six accidents, all of which involved system malfunctions. Until 1974 this problem prevented the BART system from beginning full operation between downtown San Francisco and the East Bay area. The problem can presumably be rectified but at a cost which has not yet been estimated.

UMTA's program in new technology has allocated the largest part of its funds to technologies for automatic unmanned vehicles operating on guideways. These are known generically as personal rapid transit. UMTA has made an experimental installation of such a system to connect two campuses of West Virginia University with downtown Morgantown, a small linear route of 2¼ miles with three stations. It was hoped at the outset that the system might be installed for $13.5 million. By 1971 the estimate had been raised by $37.5 million and by 1973 it had reached $64.3 million. To date the system has not been made operable though UMTA hopes that the installation can be put in service in 1974.[14] Other pilot installations of new technologies have fared a little better. A line of tracked air-cushion vehicles was proposed for Los Angeles in 1970 but was subsequently dropped, possibly as a consequence of the earthquake in the area in 1971. A hovercraft put in service between the San Francisco and Oakland airports proved to have operating costs of 23 cents per seat-mile and to have poor riding qualities.[15] It was quickly aban-

---

[12] Project ILL-MTD-1. See Chicago Area Transportation Study, *The Skokie Swift: A Study in Urban Rapid Transit,* 1968, p. 23.
[13] Projects CAL-MTD-2 and CAL-MTD-7.
[14] Project WVA-MTD-3.
[15] Project CAL-MTD-3.

doned. A grant was made for study of a gravity vacuum-tube vehicle but the project was abandoned before any installation was attempted.[16]

Many of the demonstration grants of all types were trivial in character—as, for example, larger destination signs on buses, improved design of shelters, and so on—so that no important consequences could have been expected from them.

The Capital Grant Program

The low level of success in the demonstration program inevitably caused more and more of UMTA's funds to be channeled into the capital grant program. Currently more than 85 percent of UMTA's expenditures go for capital grants. These capital grants are used mainly for three purposes: conversion of privately owned systems to public ownership, replacement of buses and building rail systems or re-equipping existing rail lines.

Because UMTA requires that an application for funds for conversion to public ownership be accompanied by a plan for re-equipment of the transit system, funds used for these conversions are not separated from the funds used for purchase of new buses. Conversion to public ownership has produced a consistent pattern of increases in operating costs and decreases in the rate of decline of ridership, or possibly reversal for a short period of time. The increase in cost comes partly from the strengthening of the union's position through the section 13(c) agreement —partly because the conversion replaces a private entity with a public body which is customarily not required to maximize net receipts or minimize losses. The diminution in decline in ridership comes partly from an increase in the quality of service which the new buses produce, partly from the fact that public bodies frequently pursue policies of lowering fares. For example, with a grant of $9 million from UMTA the Golden Gate Transit District was formed to assume the suburban services of Greyhound Lines between San Francisco and Marin County, California, in the expectation that the deficit from the service would be borne from the tolls on the Golden Gate Bridge. Greyhound had lost about $800,000 per year on the service and had not been eager to continue its franchise. The district assumed the franchise without buying Greyhound's assets on January 1, 1972. In its first year the district increased ridership about 57 percent above Greyhound's level, mainly by providing more commodious equipment and rerouting buses closer to the financial district of San Francisco. Only minor changes were made in routes and fares. The deficits rose from $800,000 under Greyhound's operation to $2.7 million in a single year mainly because of increased drivers' wages.[17] In Providence, Rhode

---

16 Project TRD-85.
17 Interview with H. Donald White, general manager, and Jerome Kuykendall, assistant general manager, Golden Gate Transit District, January 5, 1973.

Island, the conversion temporarily reversed the secular decline of ridership on the transit system, making up for approximately two years' decline.[18]

The majority of projects but the minority of funds in the capital grant program have been devoted to bus replacement. By January 31, 1973, UMTA had bought 12,725 buses for the American transit industry, mainly through two-to-one matching grants. About 80 percent of American transit buses were being purchased in this fashion. This program has proved extremely popular with the transit industry. Frank Hassler of the Transportation System Center of the Department of Transportation informally estimates that the bus replacement program has yielded a benefit-cost ratio of 1.7 to the recipients, which he considers markedly higher than the benefit-cost ratio of any other UMTA program.[19] The bus replacement program yields a stream of benefits to transit enterprises in the form of reduced maintenance expenditures, simply because new vehicles require less maintenance than old. The consequences of this have been studied in detail by Captain William B. Tye III, assistant professor of economics and management at the United States Air Force Academy, who wrote his dissertation on the subject. Tye studied the effect of UMTA grants on the practices of the Chicago Transit Authority and the Cleveland Transit System, both of which pursued the normal practice in the industry of using the newest buses in their fleets in base service or all-day operation, and downgrading buses to "tripper" service in rush hours only as they became older and their operating costs increased.

In Cleveland Tye found that operating, maintenance and unreliability costs of representative buses in 1960 were 11.23 cents per mile and that these costs grew at the rate of 4 percent per year as the vehicle aged. Taking the cost of capital as 5.3 percent, he computed the optimal times for replacement of buses at various rates of use, notably at rates of 50,000 miles per year and 22,000 miles per year (corresponding roughly to base service and tripper use). He found that, in the absence of capital grants, the increase in operating costs caused optimal replacement of a bus after fifteen years at 50,000 miles per year and after twenty-four years at 22,000 miles per year. Tye then computed the actual rate of use of buses of a given age in the Cleveland Transit System with the rate of use which his calculations had led him to anticipate. He found the system underutilized its buses of a given age by about 24.5 percent or in other words replaced buses too early, or was overcapitalized. This he believed was inconsistent with the argument implicit in the UMTA program that the transit industry is undercapitalized. He found that the Chicago Transit Authority underutilized equipment to only about a tenth of the extent that Cleveland did, and thus replaced buses at approximately an optimal rate.

Tye then compared the replacement practices of the two systems under the presumption that two-thirds of the replacement cost of buses was provided by a

---

[18] Rhode Island Public Transit Authority, *Annual Reports,* 1969, 1970 and 1971.
[19] Interview with Frank Hassler, August 2, 1973.

138

UMTA grant. The vehicle being operated in Cleveland at 50,000 miles per year, which previously had an optimal life expectancy of fifteen years, would now optimally be replaced after about six. The bus operating for 22,000 miles per year, which previously had a life expectancy of twenty-four years, would now be replaced after thirteen years. In general, at rates of utilization under 40,000 miles per year the optimal life of a bus was cut approximately in half. Calculations for Chicago were similar.

Tye then computed the cost of producing 50,000 miles without grants and with two-to-one matching grants. The federal contribution lowered the cost to the Cleveland Transit System by about one-fourth. Including the federal contribution, the total cost, however, rose by about 8 percent. Tye concluded that approximately 23.8 percent of the federal contribution in Cleveland and 22.5 percent in Chicago amounted to waste from the substitution of depreciation for variable expenses. Tye stressed that the waste came exclusively from incentives to premature replacement of buses. He assumed no changes in maintenance methods but, as he pointed out, the program also gives operators an incentive to neglect maintenance, to accelerate depreciation, and to put capital into trivial peripheral items.[20]

The bus program, however, ought properly to be looked upon as a political offering to lightly populated areas incidental to a program which is mainly engaged in the building of rail systems. Some 64 percent of UMTA funds of all sorts currently go into rail projects. To date UMTA has financed four rail lines in Chicago (including the Skokie Swift financed under the demonstration program), one in Cleveland and one in Boston. The experience of all these lines is consistent with that of the Skokie Swift.

The largest of the projects is the rapid transit line in the median strip of the Dan Ryan Expressway running south from the Chicago Loop for 9.5 miles, opened late in 1969. By 1972 the line was handling an average of 108,600 passengers per day. In mid-1970, when the ridership was approximately 90,000 passengers per day, the Chicago Transit Authority (CTA) surveyed passengers using the terminal station at 95th Street to determine their former mode of travel. The CTA found that 37.7 percent had previously used buses for the entire trip to the Loop, 34.8 percent had previously made combination bus-rail trips mainly by transfer from bus to the existing CTA north-south rapid transit line, 8 percent were diverted from suburban trains of parallel mainline railroads, 8 percent were ex-drivers, and 6 percent had not made the trip before at all. Because the south terminus has a parking lot and the intermediate stations are simply interfaces with bus lines, the 8 percent figure presumably overstates the total diversion of drivers.[21]

20 William B. Tye III, "The Capital Grant as a Subsidy Device: The Case Study of Urban Mass Transportation," *The Economics of Federal Subsidy Programs* (A compendium of papers submitted to the Committee on Priorities and Economy in Government of the Joint Economic Committee, U.S. Congress, 1973), part 6, "Transportation Subsidies," pp. 796-826.
21 "In Chicago Buses Help Fill the Trains," *Railway Age,* July 13, 1970, p. 44.

Table 1
AVERAGE DAILY VEHICLE COUNTS AT PEAK POINTS,
DAN RYAN AND KENNEDY EXPRESSWAYS

Year	Dan Ryan	Kennedy
1968	122,300	103,000
1969	126,100	108,200
1970	121,500	104,300
1971	144,100	109,200
1972	159,000	117,000

Source: Chicago Area Transportation Study, letters of August 7, 1972, and February 13, 1973; Chicago Transit Authority, "Mass Transportation Riding Habits," March 12, 1973.

The fact remains that the vehicle counts on the Dan Ryan Expressway in Table 1 show a decline in 1970 (the line's first full year of operation) approximately equal to one year's secular growth of traffic on the expressway. Vehicle counts on the Kennedy Expressway, on which the CTA opened a rapid transit line early in 1970, also show continuing secular growth in vehicle counts after a year's decline. Table 2 shows the effect of the opening of two lines on the ridership of the Chicago Transit Authority system. The annual ridership of CTA buses declined monotonically. The number of rail passengers on the CTA declined monotonically except for 1970, when (as a result of the opening of the two new lines) the decline was reversed to the extent of approximately a year's decline. The decline then continued as before. The total ridership of the CTA declined monotonically throughout the period from 1967 to 1972.

Experience in Boston and Cleveland has been similar. The new Quincy line of the existing Harvard-Ashmont subway took somewhat less than a thousand vehicles a day off the Southeast Expressway, a freeway which regularly handles between 80,000 and 120,000 passenger cars per day.[22] The extension of the Cleveland Transit System's rapid transit line to Hopkins Airport is estimated by the Cuyahoga County engineer to have taken approximately the equivalent of six months' growth in traffic off I-71, the parallel freeway.[23]

These appear to make up a consistent set of demonstrations that the institution of rail systems is not a cost-effective way of securing the external benefits sought from such systems. Professor Kain has recently argued that Atlanta, with a system of express buses allowed to operate at free-running speeds on existing freeways (through admitting automobiles with traffic lights on entrance ramps

---

[22] Department of Public Works, Boston, "South Shore Transit Extension—Effect on Southeast Corridor Travel Patterns," *Annual Report,* 1972, supplemented by an interview with the author, Max Kaplovitz, August 25, 1972.

[23] Letter of Albert S. Porter, Cuyahoga County engineer, March 8, 1973. See Martin Wohl, "An Analysis and Evaluation of the Rapid Transit Extension to Cleveland's Airport," Working Paper 708-43 (Washington, D.C.: The Urban Institute, 1972).

Table 2

REVENUE PASSENGERS OF THE CHICAGO TRANSIT AUTHORITY

Year	Bus	Rail	Total
1967	389,770,830	120,737,566	510,508,396
1968	346,976,958	110,792,832	457,769,790
1969	317,024,210	103,071,290	420,095,500
1970	296,176,300	105,598,382	401,874,682
1971	282,659,196	103,499,016	386,158,185
1972	277,152,147	100,468,879	377,621,026

Source: Chicago Area Transportation Study, letters of August 7, 1972, and February 13, 1973; Chicago Transit Authority, "Mass Transportation Riding Habits," March 12, 1973.

with the techniques developed at Texas A&M), could generate more external benefits than are anticipated from the rail system planned for the city, with less than 2 percent of the investment required for the rail system.[24] Rail systems are extremely capital intensive, with construction requiring between $5 million and $20 million per mile. Beyond that, however, section 13(c) of UMTA's statutory authority makes them relatively expensive to operate.

The BART system was begun with a local bond issue but subsequently BART has secured UMTA grants so that now federal funds have provided some 17.7 percent of the investment in the $1.6 billion system. Injection of UMTA funds into BART has made it subject to section 13(c). Former employees of Greyhound Lines who were hired after the section 13(c) agreement was made were engaged at wage rates as much as $2 per hour higher than BART's own original employees. This dual wage structure caused a strike of BART's operating and clerical employees. The unions won the strike. They not only ended the dual wage structure but secured a variety of pension, medical and other fringe benefits, all of which added more than $8 million to BART's operating expenses and thus to its anticipated deficit. Instead of failing to cover its variable expenses by something on the order of $10 million, BART is now estimated (by its finance director) to incur an operating deficit of about $20 million per year. [25]

Evaluation of the UMTA Program

To date the Urban Mass Transportation Assistance program has not been successful. The failure can be demonstrated either by an examination of the experience of the transit industries since establishment of the program or by an examination

[24] John F. Kain, "The Unexplored Potential of Freeway Rapid Transit in Regional Transportation Planning: An Atlanta Case Study," in Andrew Hamer, ed., *Unorthodox Approaches to Urban Transportation: The Emerging Challenge to Conventional Planning* (Proceedings of a conference held at Georgia State University, November 16-17, 1972), pp. 38-53.
[25] *San Francisco Chronicle,* September 19, 1973, pp. 1, 16.

141

of externalities which the program was supposed to provide. Ridership on American transit enterprises has continued to decline since the inauguration of the program. Ridership in 1963 (near the inauguration of the program) was about 8 billion rides per year. By 1972 the figure had sunk to 5.3 billion. The decline was distributed over the entire nation. Edmond L. Kanwit found that the decline in ridership was uniform in pattern between metropolitan areas and little related to UMTA's expenditures: "These losses have been both relative and absolute and at most only slightly slowed by federal, state and local efforts to shore up transit." [26] Inevitably the industry's financial performance worsened steadily throughout the decade. The industry first reported a net deficit in 1963 and by 1972 the deficit was $513 million. Frequently the deficit doubled annually in the 1963-1972 period.

Given the continued transit decline, the UMTA program has been unable to generate the externalities sought of it. Generally, cities of the concentrated transit-oriented type which UMTA is intended to preserve and to generate continued to decline throughout the 1960s. All of the American cities of the transit-oriented type—New York, Chicago, Philadelphia, Cleveland, San Francisco, Boston, New Orleans, Pittsburgh and Newark—had absolute population declines between 1960 and 1970. Cities of the Los Angeles-Houston type which UMTA is intended to keep from developing rose steadily in population relative to traditional cities. Los Angeles gained 300,000 population, while Houston went from 938,000 to 1,213,000 and became the sixth largest American city. Of the major automobile-oriented cities, only Detroit lost population. The fastest-growing American city was San Jose, which more than doubled its population in the course of the decade in spite of an incidence of automobile ownership and dependence on the automobile for trips greater than that of any other major city. In the older major cities, growth of population and economic activity was almost entirely in suburban locations of the character of Los Angeles, Houston and San Jose, rather than in the transit-oriented inner portions.

Such other external benefits as have been sought from the UMTA program cannot have been realized under the circumstances. The immobility of the elderly, the young and other groups that cannot drive has persisted. The immobility of the urban poor has been dealt with by an increase in automobile ownership rather than by anything which UMTA has done. Insofar as atmospheric pollution from motor vehicles has been reduced, it has been reduced by emissions controls rather than by stimulation of transit. Moreover, the demonstration program under UMTA has failed to develop viable alternatives to existing modes of transportation. The public remains served by the same mix of automobiles, buses, rail vehicles and ferryboats as it was before.

---

[26] Edmond L. Kanwit, "The Urban Mass Transportation Administration: Its Problems and Promises," in David R. Miller, ed., *Urban Transportation Policy: New Perspectives* (Lexington, Mass.: Heath Lexington Books, 1972), pp. 77-123.

The failure of the UMTA program justifies a conclusion that the interpretation on which it was based—the belief that the industry was undercapitalized as argued in Fitch and similar sources—was and is incorrect. The failure of the UMTA system appears consistent with the interpretation of the decline of transit in Meyer, Kain and Wohl and other works that make the same general argument.

As was stated at the outset, Meyer, Kain and Wohl's volume and similar later writings demonstrate that transit is characterized either by a negative or insignificantly positive income elasticity of demand and a relatively low price elasticity of demand. Automobile transportation is characterized by a strongly positive income elasticity demand and also, apparently, by a relatively low price elasticity of demand. Under these circumstances the cross elasticity of demand as between the two must be relatively low. Consequently, making transit more capital-intensive is unlikely to change the behavior of many drivers. Drivers are likely to be changed in their behavior significantly only by measures which make driving more costly to them.[27] In general, there is nothing in UMTA's statutory authority which would enable UMTA to do this. UMTA has no powers over the user charges levied on roads. The one set of UMTA projects that can be considered a success is that which involves operating buses on reserve lanes of freeways or allowing buses to operate at free-moving speed on the freeways by regulating the admission of automobiles to the freeway. Either of these places higher queuing costs on drivers than on transit passengers. These measures do, in fact, make driving more costly to drivers and thus they affect drivers in a way that instituting a rail-transit system or substituting new buses for old do not.

Similarly, there is nothing in UMTA's statutory authority to change the economic organization of the transit industry—quite the contrary. Through section 13(c) UMTA strengthens unions in the field and thus tends to solidify the present noncompetitive organization of the industry. Moreover, UMTA strengthens unions in the industry by making the industry more capital-intensive in a fashion complementary to the union and so lowering the elasticity of demand for transit employees. Thus UMTA not only fails to change the economic organization of the industry but in fact makes its operation more costly. As a result, the UMTA program does nothing to relieve the characteristic problem that only radial routes from a central business district generate enough traffic to warrant transit routes, but that demand for such trips is typically declining absolutely. Indeed, by increasing operating costs, the UMTA program aggravates the problem.

Furthermore, the UMTA program makes more capital-intensive an industry whose economic organization tends to make it overly capital-intensive even in the absence of the program. The high level of wages for unionized drivers makes transit systems opt for a relatively large vehicle, a diesel bus of fifty-passenger

---

27 See Leon Moses and Harold F. Williamson, Jr., "Value of Time, Choice of Mode and the Subsidy Issue in Urban Transportation," *Journal of Political Economy,* vol. 71 (1963), pp. 247-64.

capacity. A recent federal study, "Evaluation of Rail Rapid Transit and Express Bus Service in the Urban Commuter Market," demonstrates that such buses, running on linear routes and stopping at most street corners, provide a standard of service appropriate only for densely traveled lines running through neighborhoods of people with low time valuation.[28] Urban transit service generally, the report shows, could be provided with a higher standard of speed and convenience in vans of about eight-passenger capacity, such as jitney operators typically select. The report demonstrates that diesel buses of the present sort are appropriate for a line-haul function. In a line-haul on reserved rights-of-way they can provide a standard of service comparable to rail systems, but at considerably lower cost. Thus, both on the urban-transit function and the line-haul function, the industry was already overly capital-intensive before the UMTA program began.

Explaining the decline of an industry is an activity which is particularly characteristic of economic historians, but it is the sort of thing which economists of all sorts usually do well.[29] Indeed, economists devote much of their time to predicting the future when what they do best is interpret the past. Interpretations of secular declines are frequently thought to be only of academic interest. In this case, however, the federal government through accepting an erroneous interpretation of the decline of a major industry has undertaken a program which, given its statutory authority, could not have been successful, which has wasted several billion dollars of capital, and which has on the whole aggravated the problem with which it was intended to deal.

---

[28] J. Hayden Boyd, Norman J. Asher and Elliot S. Wetzler, *Evaluation of Rail Rapid Transit and Express Bus Service in the Urban Commuter Market* (Arlington, Va.: Institute for Defense Analyses for Department of Transportation, October 1973).

[29] Inevitably, in UMTA's education programs research funds found their way into the hands of an economist who held a position consistent with the Meyer, Kain and Wohl interpretation. In April 1972 a grant of $142,884 was made to the University of Missouri, St. Louis, to be administered by Professor Joseph B. McKenna, who proposed to develop a mathematical model of demand for transportation in St. Louis from which engineers could develop plans for a system suitable to the demand conditions. Professor McKenna considered the reverse of sensible procedures the customary method of designing a linear system and then planning land use in an attempt to generate the desired level of traffic. He had identified himself with opposition to a plan for an eighty-six-mile rail system for St. Louis. The East-West Gateway Coordinating Council and the Bi-State Development Agency objected to the grant, apparently out of fear that the research would strengthen Professor McKenna's case against the proposed rail system. UMTA responded by requiring that recipients of research grants clear their proposed projects with local area councils of government or other regional planning bodies. Professor McKenna shifted his research to Denver, rendering the issue moot locally. See "St. Louis Disturbed by Grant to Study Subway Alternative," *New York Times,* April 16, 1972, p. 59.

AN ECONOMIC POLICY ANALYSIS OF THE AMTRAK PROGRAM

James C. Miller III

By enacting the Rail Passenger Service Act of 1970 (P.L. 91-518), Congress and the executive branch sought to "salvage" U.S. rail passenger transportation. To accomplish this end, the act provided for the establishment of a nongovernmental profit-making corporation which would take over from the railroads (at their option) and thereafter operate a national system of rail passenger service, with improved operating standards and competitive fares. With the capital acquired from participating railroads ($197 million), and from the federal government in the form of direct grants ($40 million) and loan guarantees ($100 million), the corporation presumably would become self-sustaining within a two-year "experimental" period.

The Amtrak "experiment" has failed, inasmuch as the objective of a self-sustaining enterprise has not been achieved. While there has been a turnaround in rail passenger service and traffic on Amtrak's routes, the total effect has been one of replacing the passenger subsidy from railroad stockholders and nonpassenger users with an ongoing subsidy out of the public purse. In addition to describing the Amtrak program and explaining why the experiment failed, this paper will attempt to draw lessons from the failure which should be of value to policy makers engaged in running the program as well as those contemplating or administering similar programs in other sectors of the economy (as, for example, the United States Railway Association).[1]

Brief History of Amtrak

Enabling Legislation. By the late 1960s intercity rail passenger service appeared on the verge of extinction. From a level of 39.9 billion revenue passenger-miles

---

The author wishes to acknowledge helpful comments and other assistance from George Douglas, Robert Gallamore, George Hilton, Bol Kuanyin, Robert D. Tollison, and the Texas A&M University Organized Research Program. Responsibility for all errors, omissions, and opinions remains, of course, with the author.

[1] Under provisions of the Regional Rail Reorganization Act of 1973 (signed into law on January 2, 1974), a newly formed United States Railway Association will reorganize the seven bankrupt Northeast railroads and will turn them over to a semipublic, nonprofit Consolidated Railroad Corporation. In many respects this reorganized provision of rail freight service parallels Amtrak's provision of rail passenger service.

in 1947, intercity train travel fell to just over 6 billion revenue passenger-miles in 1970.[2] Also, at the end of the decade, fully one-half of the remaining intercity trains were in discontinuance proceedings at the Interstate Commerce Commission (ICC).[3] In April 1970, the Senate Commerce Committee reported favorably on a bill which would (1) have granted federal operating subsidies for a "basic national system" of passenger trains, (2) have provided financial support to the railroads for the rehabilitation of old equipment and the purchase of new equipment, and (3) have provided for federal supervision over service standards.[4] The bill failed to reach a vote before Congress adjourned for the summer.

Meanwhile, the Department of Transporation (DOT) and its Federal Railroad Administration (FRA) began to develop an alternative program, with two major emphases differing from the emphases of the congressional approach. First, they wished to minimize the extent of needed federal support, and second, they planned to attack one of the alleged root causes of the rail service dilemma—"disinterested" railroad management.[5] To minimize federal support, DOT proposed that the railroads be asked to "buy out" of their passenger losses by purchasing common stock in a new enterprise venture. To solve the problem of "disinterested" carrier management, DOT proposed setting up a separate corporation whose sole task would be to provide rail passenger service.

On October 30, 1970, President Nixon signed into law the Rail Passenger Service Act of 1970,[6] essentially the DOT bill. The purpose and approach of the act is summed up in section 101:

> The Congress finds that modern, efficient, intercity railroad passenger service is a necessary part of a balanced transportation system; that the public convenience and necessity require the continuance and improvement of such service to provide fast and comfortable transportation between crowded urban areas and in other areas of the country; that rail passenger service can help to end the congestion on our highways and the overcrowding of airways and airports; that the traveler in America should to the maximum extent feasible have freedom to choose the mode of travel most convenient to his needs; that to achieve these goals requires the designation of a basic national rail passenger system and the establishment of a rail passenger corporation for the purpose of providing modern, efficient, intercity rail passenger service; that Federal financial assistance as well as investment capital from the private sector of the economy is needed for this purpose; and that interim emergency Federal

---

[2] *Yearbook of Railroad Facts,* 1973 edition (Washington, D.C.: Association of American Railroads, 1973), p. 32.

[3] *The Role of Intercity Rail Passenger Service: A Study of Amtrak's Mission* (Boston, Mass.: Harbridge House, 1973), p. III-5.

[4] U.S. Congress, Senate, Committee on Commerce, *Rail Passenger Service Act of 1970,* Report No. 91-765, 91st Congress, 2d session (April 9, 1970).

[5] A preliminary version of the DOT approach is contained in Senator Winston Prouty's minority view, ibid., pp. 76-88.

[6] Public Law 91-518.

financial assistance to certain railroads may be necessary to permit the orderly transfer of railroad passenger service to a railroad passenger corporation.

Title II of the act required the secretary of transportation to recommend a "basic system" of essential rail passenger services which would form the corporation's initial route network. The secretary had thirty days to come up with and publicize the proposed system. Then, within ninety days of enactment in which to take into consideration comments by interested parties, the secretary's revised basic system would become final and would not be reviewable by the courts.

Title III of the act created a National Railroad Passenger Corporation, first known as "Railpax" (or "Railpox" by its critics) and later known as "Amtrak." Eight of the corporation's fifteen-member board of directors would be appointed by the President with the advice and consent of the Senate. One of the eight would be the secretary of transportation, and one would be a "consumer advocate." Three additional members would be elected by stockholders, and the remaining four would be elected by preferred stockholders (if any). Common stock would be sold initially to participating railroads only, with preferred stock (if any) being sold to nonrailroad interests. An annual report to Congress, including legislative recommendations, would be required of the new corporation.

Under title IV of the act, the corporation was required to take over intercity rail passenger service and begin operations by May 1, 1971. The rail passenger service taken over would include the secretary's "basic system" as well as any additional service the corporation wished to include and any service which would not otherwise have been included but for which a state, regional, or local agency agreed to defray two-thirds of the corporation's losses. Actual operations would continue to be provided by the railroads and by railroad employees, under the corporation's direction. Also, and quite importantly, the corporation would be exempt from ICC regulation of rates, fares, and charges, and from ICC control over passenger-service route entry and train discontinuances.[7] Payments to the railroads for their services would be made through contracts based on costs actually incurred with a 5 percent increment to cover some common costs and other nonidentifiable but passenger-related expenses.[8]

The act established the corporation's capitalization. The corporation would be paid for common stock. Participating railroads would have to pay the lesser of: (1) one-half of their "fully distributed passenger deficit" for the calendar year 1969, (2) their "avoidable loss" on intercity passenger service for 1969, or (3)

---

[7] The exemption from ICC control over abandonment applied to setting up the basic system. Routes in this initial system would have to be maintained until July 1, 1973, and then discontinuance of any portions would have to receive ICC approval.

[8] In the event the corporation and the railroads were unable to reach a mutually satisfactory contractual arrangement, the ICC was given the power to prescribe terms and conditions.

twice the "avoidable loss" incurred during 1969 over the routes the carrier had included in the secretary's revised basic system.

There was also direct federal assistance. Title VII of the act authorized the secretary of transportation to make (or insure) loans to railroads for the purpose of purchasing the corporation's common stock, so long as the aggregate amount did not exceed $200 million. Title VI authorized the transportation secretary to pay the corporation $40 million to assist in getting the organization underway. It also provided that the secretary could guarantee loans made to the corporation in an amount not to exceed $100 million.

Amtrak's Experience to Date. Transportation Secretary John Volpe issued his preliminary report on the "basic system" on November 30, 1970, and included in it a network linking seventeen cities. Secretary Volpe's revised "basic system" was issued on January 28, 1971, and included four additional cities, with a concomitant expansion in the network.[9] The new corporation expanded this network slightly and put it into operation on May 1, 1971.[10] In addition to the financial backing conferred on the corporation by the $40 million federal grant and the $100 million in loan guarantees, the corporation agreed to receive $197 million over a three-year period as the participating railroads' "entrance fee" into the program (that is, the railroads would pay $197 million for the purchase of common stock). Four railroads took the option of not joining in exchange for continuing passenger service on their own until January 1, 1975: Southern Railway, Denver and Rio Grande Western, Chicago and Rock Island, and Georgia Railroad.[11]

The new corporation, now renamed Amtrak, quickly ran into financial difficulty. After exhausting its $40 million grant, it began relying on railroad (common-stock) entrance-fee payments to defray its operating losses. By the fall of 1971 (after only six months of operation), Amtrak had begun to use the $100 million in federal loan guarantees to cover operating losses.

Facing an anticipated loss of $152.3 million during fiscal year 1972, Amtrak petitioned Congress for additional funding of $170 million. Congress responded with amendments to the original legislation, authorizing an additional $225 million capital grant (of which $170 million was later appropriated), plus an addi-

---

[9] U.S. Department of Transportation, Secretary of Transportation, *Final Report on the Basic National Rail Passenger System,* January 28, 1971.

[10] National Rail Passenger Corporation, *Annual Report,* October 29, 1971.

[11] In 1972, these four carriers accounted for approximately 17 percent of intercity rail passenger service. See U.S. Congress, House of Representatives, Committee on Appropriations, *Department of Transportation and Related Agencies Appropriations Hearings for Fiscal Year 1974,* 93rd Congress, 1st session, part 2, p. 1053. Under provisions of the act, railroads not joining the venture had their passenger service "frozen" until January 1, 1975. After that, they could petition the ICC for approval of discontinuances, with the presumption that the corporation would then pick up any essential routes. In any event, nonparticipating railroads were required to cooperate with the corporation in providing interconnecting service.

tional $100 million in loan guarantees.[12] This legislation also limited the salaries of Amtrak officials to $60,000 per year and required additional reporting to Congress on the problem of the recurring deficit. Finally, the legislation admonished Amtrak to get on with the business of adding new and experimental routes, and also to take more control of the passenger service operations away from the railroads.

Table 1 shows Amtrak's sources and application of funds for fiscal years 1972, 1973, and 1974, together with totals for all three years. Note that offsetting the $1,217.0 million in fund applications are only $542.9 million in operating revenues. Note also that government support ($278.4 million in direct grants and $200 million in loan guarantees) accounts for over 39 percent of total funds. (The railroad's contribution—entry-fee payments for common stock—accounts for just over 15 percent.) Moreover, Amtrak's operating deficit remains sizable, although it would appear to show some signs of diminishing. For fiscal year 1972 the operating deficit was $152.3 million; for fiscal year 1973, it is expected to be $124.0 million; and for fiscal year 1974, $95.6 million. Since the narrowing of the deficit is only predicted, not actual, we must not place a great deal of faith in such claims. Even making a linear extrapolation from the estimated changes in shortfall (approximately $28 million per year), it would be 1980 before the operating deficit would be eliminated (not counting capital expenditures or depreciation).

While admittedly Amtrak is losing money, may it not be doing better than the operation it took over? First, we note that Amtrak appears to have reversed (temporarily, I would say) the secular decline in rail travel on the routes it took over. Yearly total figures are not readily available, but on the basis of monthly samples, Amtrak has reported total ridership increases on the order of 10 percent per annum.[13] How has Amtrak accomplished this turnaround? Several factors are obvious. First, it has benefited from extensive advertising, both commercial and (more important) "free" in the form of extensive media coverage. Second, Amtrak has lowered rates on many of its price-sensitive routes (New York-Boston, for example). Third, Amtrak has refurbished many of its cars, making them cleaner and more comfortable. Fourth, Amtrak has trained railroad personnel to be more courteous and helpful to customers. Finally, Amtrak has instituted a number of marketing advances, including a nationwide system of schedules, computerized reservations and ticketing, improved food service, package tours, and modernized terminals.[14]

But before we judge performance, there are other comparisons to make. For the eight months of operations during calendar year 1971 (the latest period for which I have the requisite data), Amtrak's operating loss was $77.7 million, or 3.3 cents per revenue passenger-mile. With an average fare of $8.14, this meant a

[12] P. L. 92-316, *Amendments to the Rail Passenger Service Act of 1970,* June 22, 1972.
[13] National Rail Passenger Corporation, *Annual Report,* February 1, 1973, pp. 19-20.
[14] National Railroad Passenger Corporation, *Amtrak at Two: A Progress Report,* 1973.

Table 1
AMTRAK SOURCE AND APPLICATION OF FUNDS
($ in millions)

	FY 1972 (actual)	FY 1973 (plan)	FY 1974 (plan)	Three-Year
Cash at Beginning of Period	$ 12.2	$ 3.2	$ 3.9	$ 12.2
Source of Funds				
Operating revenues	152.7	179.4	210.8	542.9
Federal grants	77.6	107.8	93.0	278.4
Federal guaranteed loans	17.0	83.0	100.0	200.0
Railroad capital payments	65.0	65.1	54.7	184.8
TOTAL	312.3	435.3	458.5	1,206.1
Application of Funds				
Operating expenses (not including depreciation)	305.0	303.4	306.4	914.8
Capital expenditures:				
Equipment and facilities	21.4	126.1	100.0	247.5
ROW and corridor improvements	—	—	50.0	50.0
Subtotal, capital expenditures	21.4	126.1	150.0	297.5
Accrued liabilities	(5.1)	5.1	—	0
Repayment — prior loan	—	—	4.7	4.7
TOTAL	321.3	434.6	461.1	1,217.0
Cash at End of Period	$ 3.2	$ 3.9	$ 1.3	$ 1.3

Source: Secretary of Transportation, *Report to Congress on the Rail Passenger Service Act* (Washington, D.C.: U.S. Department of Transportation, March 15, 1973), p. 102.

150

per-passenger operating deficit of $6.26.[15] By comparison, in 1970 (before Amtrak), the railroads' deficit solely related to passenger service was $252 million, or only 2.3 cents per passenger-mile. On an average fare of $1.46, this meant a per-passenger deficit of $1.32.[16] If the entire 1970 service deficit were attributed to intercity passengers, the result would be a passenger-mile deficit of 4.1 cents, or $7.78 on a $8.14 fare as compared with Amtrak's per-passenger loss of $6.26.[17] Also, by comparison, during 1970 the direct federal subsidy to local service air carriers amounted to $45.9 million, or less than one cent per local-service passenger-mile. On an average local-service fare of $23.71, this amounted to a per-passenger subsidy of only $1.73.[18]

It must therefore be concluded that, measured by individual performance figures, Amtrak is not succeeding very well. This is all the more difficult to comprehend when it is realized how much rail passenger service shrank when Amtrak took over. As is shown in Table 2, between April 30, 1971 (before Amtrak) and October 31, 1971 (after Amtrak), total train-miles per day fell by 57 percent. Presumably, it would be the "marginal" or chronic money-losing routes that Amtrak (and the secretary) would have chosen to discontinue. Yet, while operating 57 percent fewer train-miles and 34 percent fewer trains, Amtrak has incurred per-passenger-mile deficits at least comparable with those obtained by the railroads.

Reasons for Amtrak's Failure

This section attempts to identify reasons for the apparent failure of the Amtrak experiment.

The Secular Decline in Rail Travel. Economists have long cited population, income, price, and travel time (as well as other "quality" characteristics) as being the major determinants of the demand for travel. The demand for travel is especially related to income and is usually estimated to be income elastic (that is, a given percentage increase in income will usually lead to a greater percentage

---

[15] Association of American Railroads, *Statistics of Railroads of Class I in the United States, Years 1961 to 1971,* 1972, p. 16.

[16] *Yearbook of Railroad Facts,* pp. 21, 32, 34 and 35.

[17] Reported figures do not break down the deficit by commuter versus intercity travel. In 1970, before Amtrak, intercity travel accounted for approximately 27 percent of railroad passengers carried and 58 percent of revenue passenger-miles. Association of American Railroads, *Statistics of Railroads,* p. 7.

[18] See U.S. Civil Aeronautics Board, *Handbook of Airline Statistics,* 1971 edition, pp. 111, 209 and 215. It should be noted that this estimate is based on all local service carrier traffic, not just that for which subsidy is provided. Eads, for example, reports that for traffic that would not be accommodated by local service or commuter airlines on a subsidy-free basis, the per-passenger subsidy for 1969 is on the order of forty dollars. See Eads, *The Local Service Airline Experiment* (Washington, D.C.: The Brookings Institution, 1972), p. 186.

Table 2

INDICES OF THE LEVEL OF INTERCITY RAIL PASSENGER SERVICE

Indices	April 30, 1971	October 31, 1971	Percent Change
Train Miles/Day			
Northeast corridor (NEC)	16,231	16,453	+01
Other than NEC	147,548	57,481	−63
Total	163,779	73,934	−57
Number of Trains/Day	290	192	−34
Route Miles	49,533	24,379	−51

Source: U.S. Department of Transportation, *Status of Intercity Railroad Passenger Service* (Washington, D.C.: U.S. Department of Transportation, November 1971), p. 20.

increase in travel). Of course, the greater the population, the greater the demand for travel; the relationship here is considered to be approximately proportional, or perhaps slightly greater than proportional. The relationship between price and the demand for travel is generally considered to be price inelastic (that is, while a given price change will have an inverse effect on quantity demanded, this effect is less than proportional). The same is true of travel time, another component of the "full cost" of travel.[19] Thus, between 1950 and 1970 total travel in the United States rose from 506 billion passenger-miles to 1,181 billion passenger-miles.[20] During the same period, the U.S. population rose from 154 million to 208 million, and per capita income rose from $1,877 to $4,756.[21] Costs of travel fell for some modes (especially air), and there were marked increases in transit speeds. (See Table 3.)

But while total travel has grown significantly, its growth has not been shared by the railroads. As shown in Table 3, most of the growth has been in auto travel. In percentages, air travel has grown even more. Bus travel has remained approximately constant. Rail travel has fallen from 32 billion revenue passenger-miles in 1950 to just 11 billion revenue passenger-miles in 1970.

The reasons for the secular decline in rail travel are fairly straightforward. First, and most importantly, the wider availability of automobiles, their increased comfort, higher speeds, lower (real) costs of operation, and the substantial completion of a network of high-speed, limited-access interstate highways have made the personal automobile the dominant form of intercity travel. While bus transportation has lost in market share, it has held its own absolutely through increased speeds and more comfortable equipment. Air travel, of course, has increased its share of travel markedly through increased comfort, higher speeds, relatively con-

---

[19] In other words, a traveler has an opportunity cost on his time, usually fairly accurately measured by his wage rate. This is one reason why the demand for travel is so sensitive to the level of income.

[20] U.S. Department of Commerce, *Statistical Abstract of the United States, 1972*, p. 536.

[21] Ibid, pp. 7 and 315.

Table 3

TIME SERIES CHARACTERISTICS OF AUTO, BUS, RAIL, AND AIR TRAVEL, 1950-1970

Characteristic and Year	Auto	Bus	Rail	Air
Total Travel (billions of passenger-miles) [a]				
1950	438	26	32	10
1955	637	25	29	23
1960	706	19	22	34
1965	818	24	18	58
1970	1,026	25	11	119
Average Price (revenue per passenger-mile in current cents) [b]				
1950	N.A.	1.89	2.74	5.56
1955	N.A.	2.05	2.70	5.36
1960	9.76	2.71	3.03	6.09
1965	11.02	2.88	3.14	6.06
1970	11.89	3.60	4.02	5.96
Average Speed (miles per hour) [c]				
1950	48.7	49.8	37.4	180
1955	52.0	52.3	39.8	208
1960	53.8	55.5	40.7	235
1965	57.8	57.4	41.3	314
1970	60.6	58.8	40.3	350

[a] Data from U.S. Department of Commerce, *Statistical Abstract of the United States, 1972*, p. 536. Air travel includes "general aviation" as well as commercial.

[b] Data from *Statistical Abstract, 1972*, p. 548, and U.S. Department of Transportation, *1972 National Transportation Report* (Washington, D.C.: Government Printing Office, July 1972), p. 75. Auto entries are not in current (1972) cents; also, the "1965" auto entry is based on a report for 1968.

[c] Data from *Statistical Abstract, 1972*, pp. 549, 557 and 567. Entries for air are for domestic scheduled (commercial) service.

stant fares, and lower "full costs" of travel (because of rising incomes as well as increased speeds). Rail service, by comparison, has lost significantly. First, rail fares have risen over time. Second, rail's average speed started low and has declined relative to the speed of the other surface modes. Finally, as is well known, rail passenger service (equipment and personnel) has been decidedly inferior to other modes and has further deteriorated over time.[22]

Amtrak's Present Competitive Disadvantage. When Amtrak took over rail passenger service it sought to reverse this secular decline by making rail service "competitive." While it has made vast marketing improvements, including important recon-

---

[22] Undoubtedly this is due in part to regulatory restraints on fare changes and train discontinuances. That is, rail passenger losses forced a deterioration in service. This point should be kept in mind when attributing rail-passenger failures to "disinterested" management.

ditioning of equipment, it remains at a serious disadvantage in the cost of the service to the individual traveler. On the basis of a sample of thirty-nine city-pair markets, I estimated the direct costs faced by the passenger as a function of trip distance. The estimates are shown in Table 4, and the cost/mileage relationships are given in Figure 1.[23] For distances of less than seventy-five miles, the automobile is the cheapest mode of transport, even if only one person rides. At distances greater than ninety miles, the bus is cheaper than Amtrak (but for no distance is air cheaper). This leaves Amtrak with a cost advantage only for distances between seventy-five and ninety miles.[24]

Adjustments can be made in these figures in order to obtain a more accurate comparison of the options facing the traveler. Assuming that the traveler values his time at $5 per hour, we may use transit times to estimate the total opportunity cost on time and then add this opportunity cost to the monetary cost of the trip to obtain a measure of the trip's total cost. Results of these calculations are shown in Table 5 and Figure 2.[25] They suggest that for distances less than fifty miles auto is cheaper, whereas for distances over ninety-five miles air is cheaper, leaving, again, a fairly narrow range for Amtrak to hold a competitive cost advantage. (Bus dominates Amtrak on this basis at distances greater than 610 miles.)[26]

Finally, we might also take into consideration the time involved in waiting for a departure. There is usually a difference between a traveler's most desired time of departure and the scheduled commercial departure closest to it. (Of course, waiting time for the auto may be considered zero.) With this adjustment, valuing waiting time at $5 per hour, we come up with the passenger "full cost" relationships reported in Table 6 and Figure 3.[27] The results given in Table 6 imply that

---

[23] Equation correlation coefficients were .981, .983, and .969 for Amtrak, air, and bus, respectively.

[24] If imputations are made for fare levels which would cover Amtrak's cost, the resulting formula is passenger expense ($) = 7.637 + .07323 $\times$ distance, with a correlation coefficient of .913 (Data source: Secretary of Transportation, *Report to Congress on the Rail Passenger Service Act*, March 15, 1973, pp. 85 and 92.) If those were the fare levels actually charged, at no distance would Amtrak have a competitive advantage (for example, bus would dominate Amtrak entirely, and auto would be cheaper up to 262 miles). See Figure 1.

[25] Transit time/distance correlation coefficients were .972, .964, and .995 for Amtrak, air, and bus, respectively. (Auto transit was assumed to be the same as that of scheduled bus service.) The relevant equation for Amtrak cost-based fares was passenger expense ($) = 7.637 + .2012 $\times$ distance.

[26] Bus dominates Amtrak entirely when the passenger option is based on Amtrak cost. Also, on this basis auto dominates up to 211 miles, and air dominates Amtrak past 40 miles. See Figure 2.

[27] This "schedule delay" component of total time cost was estimated for each route using the relation, $T = 92 \cdot F^{-.456}$, where T = schedule delay (in minutes) and F = daily one-way frequency. This relation is the result of simulating departures which minimize waiting time, given a typical time distribution of demand (correlation coefficient = .497). See George W. Douglas and James C. Miller III, "Quality Competition, Industry Equilibrium, and Efficiency in the Price-Constrained Airline Market," *American Economic Review*, September 1974. Frequency delay/distance correlation coefficients were .325, .166, and .249 for Amtrak, air, and bus, respectively. The relevant equation for Amtrak cost-based fares was passenger expense ($) = 12.71 + .2052 $\times$ distance.

Table 4
DIRECT COSTS TO THE TRAVELER, AS A FUNCTION
OF TRIP DISTANCE, BY MODE, 1973

Mode	Fixed Component ($)	Variable Per Mile ($)
Amtrak	3.095	.04818
Air [a]	10.810	.06626
Bus	3.827	.03996
Auto [b]	0	.10230

[a] Coach fare, including 8 percent federal tax.

[b] Assuming one-passenger occupancy (against the national average of 1.9), standard-size auto, less a portion of depreciation, registration, and titling (such private "costs" are not relevant to choice of mode), and, finally, inflated to 1973 (as against 1972) price level.

Source: *Amtrak—All-America Train Fares, Edition 3* (Washington, D.C.: National Railroad Passenger Corporation, July 1, 1973); air—*Official Airline Guide, North American Edition* (Oak Brook, Ill.: Reuben H. Donnelley Corp., July 1, 1973); bus—ICC tariffs inspected at Greyhound bus lines terminal in Bryan, Texas during July 1973; and auto—U.S. Department of Transportation, *Cost of Operating an Automobile* (Washington, D.C.: Government Printing Office, April 1972).

Table 5
PASSENGER MONETARY COST OF TRIP, PLUS OPPORTUNITY COST
ON TIME IN TRANSIT (@ $5 PER HOUR), BY MODE, 1973

Mode	Fixed Component ($)	Variable Per Mile ($)
Amtrak	3.095	.1762
Air	12.720	.0751
Bus	3.827	.1750
Auto	0	.2373

Source: See Table 4; and Secretary of Transportation, *Report to Congress, 1973*, pp. 15 and 16.

Table 6
PASSENGER MONETARY COST, PLUS TIME IN TRANSIT AND
SCHEDULE DELAY (BOTH @ $5 PER HOUR), BY MODE, 1973

Mode	Fixed Component ($)	Variable Per Mile ($)
Amtrak	8.170	.1801
Air	14.520	.0757
Bus	6.228	.1771
Auto	0	.2373

Source: See Table 5.

Figure 1

COST-MILEAGE RELATIONSHIPS IN DIRECT PASSENGER COSTS, 1973

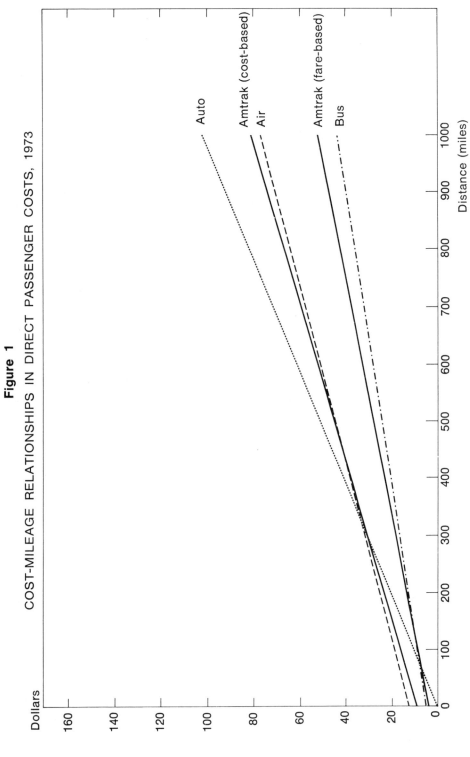

Dollars

Auto

Amtrak (cost-based)

Air

Amtrak (fare-based)

Bus

Distance (miles)

Figure 2

COST-MILEAGE RELATIONSHIPS IN DIRECT PASSENGER COSTS PLUS
OPPORTUNITY COSTS ON TIME IN TRANSIT (@ \$5 PER HOUR), 1973

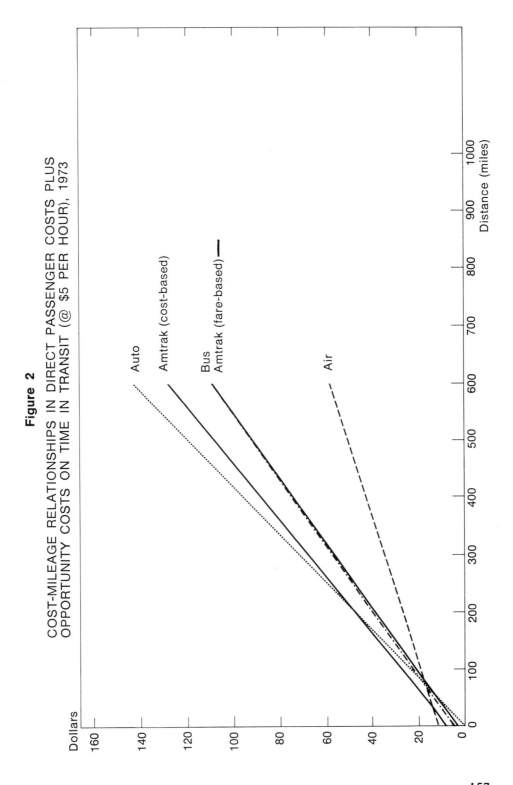

Figure 3

COST-MILEAGE RELATIONSHIPS IN DIRECT PASSENGER COSTS PLUS
OPPORTUNITY COSTS ON TIME IN TRAVEL AND OPPORTUNITY COSTS ON SCHEDULE DELAY
(BOTH @ $5 PER HOUR), 1973

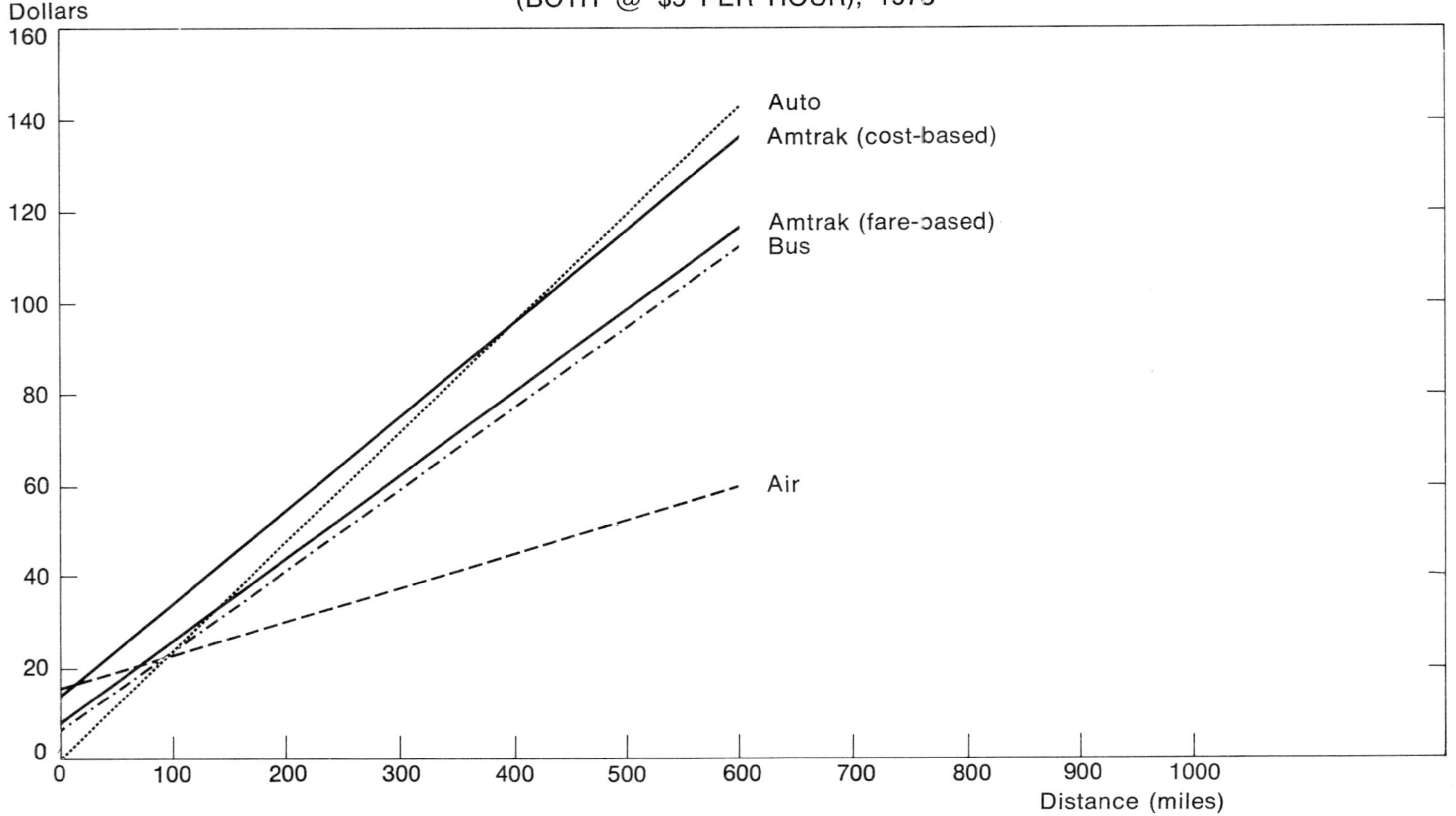

bus travel dominates Amtrak at every distance. Auto travel is cheaper up to 142 miles, and air travel is cheaper at distances over 61 miles.

These comparisons, of course, are based on broad aggregates, a representative sample of markets, and certain limiting assumptions. They do not necessarily mean that no rational person would ride Amtrak. In some markets, for example, Amtrak's speeds and frequencies are higher than they are on average and thus the service does fairly well (as, for example, in the Northeast corridor). Also, some individuals have lower opportunity costs than others, and for them Amtrak's speed and frequency disadvantage is not that important.[28] Finally, some people just prefer to ride by rail and will do so even at an apparent "full cost" differential. But the results of the comparisons should lead to a severe questioning of Amtrak's potential for making significant inroads into the markets of competitive modes of transport.

Other Reasons for Amtrak's Failure. Granted that Amtrak is at a severe disadvantage overall, could it not specialize in markets where it holds at least a *comparative* advantage? Actually, of course, specialization of this kind was an important objective of the original legislation. By "pruning" the system, it was believed a viable service could be developed and maintained. In fact, although the interstate rail passenger system shrank to something less than one-half its original size, this shrinkage was excessive and had characteristics which produced sizable losses for the corporation. For example, congressional and other pressure caused the secretary to expand the initial "basic system" from seventeen cities to twenty-one cities. Amtrak then added its own routes to this basic system, including international service and an experimental turbotrain between Washington, D.C., and Parkersburg, West Virginia. Moreover, Amtrak had to add four section 403(b) routes (New York-Chicago via Cleveland, Springfield-Boston, Chicago-Quincy, and Philadelphia-Harrisburg), where state and local governments paid only two-thirds of Amtrak's losses.[29] Moreover, Amtrak increased the number of trains it operated from 184 to 214.[30]

Another reason for Amtrak's failure has been its inability to shed chronic losing routes after they have become part of the "basic system." (Under the Rail Passenger Service Act all routes had to be continued until at least July 1, 1973, and even then discontinuances of basic-system routes would require ICC approval.) As shown in Table 7, the range of losses (both total and per passenger-mile) is quite wide. Most notably, the "West Virginian" turbotrain between Washington

28 For example, surveys show that large proportions of Amtrak riders are female and/or elderly. See Richard M. Michaels, Transportation Consultants, *Railroad Passenger Service Analysis of Train Scheduling and Operations,* February 22, 1973.

29 Secretary of Transportation, *Report to Congress,* p. 11. The New York-Chicago via Cleveland route was later discontinued when the required payments did not materialize.

30 Daniel R. Ross, "A Critical Look at Amtrak," *Proceedings of the Transportation Research Forum,* 1972, p. 15.

Table 7
AMTRAK'S PROJECTED OUT-OF-POCKET LOSSES AND PER-PASSENGER-MILE LOSSES, BY ROUTE, FISCAL YEAR 1973

Route	Out-of-Pocket Loss (in millions of dollars)	Loss Per Passenger Mile (in cents)
Short-haul		
Northeast corridor	(6.2) [a]	0.7 [b]
Chicago-St. Louis	0.9	2.7
Los Angeles-San Diego	0.7	3.9
Seattle-Portland	0.8	4.9
Chicago-Detroit	1.2	8.6
New York-Buffalo	2.6	4.6
Chicago-Carbondale	0.7	2.6
Chicago-Milwaukee	2.0	15.4
Washington-Parkersburg	1.1	33.3
Long-haul		
Chicago-Los Angeles	3.0	0.8
New York-Florida	5.1	1.1
Chicago-Seattle	4.9	2.0
Chicago-San Francisco	4.1	2.5
Seattle-San Diego	2.1	3.4
Los Angeles-New Orleans	2.0	2.4
Chicago-New Orleans	1.5	1.6
Southern Montana	2.6	3.5
New York-D.C.-Chicago	4.1	3.9
Chicago-Houston	4.5	4.0
Chicago-Florida	2.6	5.7
Chicago-D.C.-Newport News	3.0	12.0
New York-D.C.-Kansas City	4.9	14.7

[a] Out-of-pocket profit.

[b] Includes Boston-Springfield and Philadelphia-Harrisburg section 403(b) services.

Source: Secretary of Transportation, *Report to Congress, 1973*, pp. 85, 92 and 99.

and Parkersburg was projected to lose (out of pocket) over $1 million during fiscal year 1973, at an incredible 33.3 cents per passenger-mile. Not too surprisingly, the "West Virginian" was favored by U.S. Representative Harley O. Staggers (of Keyser, West Virginia), chairman of the House Commerce Committee, which presides over Amtrak legislation. Other routes also have been notorious money-losers. These include Seattle-Portland, Chicago-Detroit, New York-Buffalo, Chicago-Milwaukee, Chicago-Houston, Chicago-Florida, Chicago-D.C.-Newport News, and New York-D.C.-Kansas City. (See Table 7.) By eliminating these routes (together with the "West Virginian"), Amtrak could have cut its losses by at least $22 million.[31]

---

[31] Note from Table 7 that in absolute terms the largest losses are in long-haul markets; however, surprisingly, there is little difference betwen short-haul and long-haul losses per passenger-mile.

A Note on Amtrak and the Energy Crisis

During the winter of 1973-1974 the nation was racked by an "energy crisis" which brought on elaborate federal controls over the allocation of petroleum distillates. Concomitantly, Amtrak reported extremely favorable traffic and revenue figures, giving rise to considerable optimism over the program's future.[32] For several reasons this optimism is not well grounded.

First, the major reason for Amtrak's success was that alternative modes of travel were severely restricted. There were, of course, limitations on gasoline production and consumption. Even more important, the great uncertainty over gasoline availability led many persons to choose against intercity driving. In view of the fact that approximately 88 percent of all intercity travel was still by automobile (see Table 6), only a small portion of these travelers needed to "switch" in order to increase rail travel markedly. Air transportation was also restricted, with scheduling cutbacks of approximately 20 percent. But if the shortage (at given prices) is temporary, or prices are eventually to be relied upon to allocate petroleum products, this advantage for Amtrak will wither away.

Even assuming significant long-term rises in fuel prices, it is difficult to imagine that rail passenger service will become significantly more "competitive" because fuel costs for the various modes are not all that important a factor in total costs. For example, in a study sponsored by Amtrak, Harbridge House estimated that a doubling of petroleum costs would raise auto costs 1.3 cents per passenger-mile, would raise bus costs 0.9 cents per passenger-mile, and would raise air transport costs 2.8 cents per passenger-mile.[33] But from the figures given in the report, we may also infer that Amtrak's cost will rise, perhaps by more than a penny per passenger-mile.[34] Such a rise would not produce much of a change in the competitive position of Amtrak. In fact, it would appear to give bus service a greater relative advantage. In short, it appears unlikely that the energy crisis will have much of a long-term rehabilitating effect on Amtrak.

Lessons of the Amtrak Experience

Perhaps the most important lesson one can learn from the Amtrak experience is that there are perfectly understandable economic reasons for the demise of rail passenger transportation and that even the federal government will encounter great difficulty (that is, great cost) in "repealing" the relevant laws of supply and demand. On the demand side, the full costs of the other modes of travel (especially

---

[32] See Albert R. Karr, "Reviving the Rails: The Energy Crisis Now Seems to Ensure the Success of Amtrak," *Wall Street Journal*, December 28, 1973.

[33] *Role of Intercity Service*, pp. IV-53 to IV-58.

[34] Ibid., p. IV-63. Bus consumption of energy per passenger-mile is only 64 percent that of rail.

air) have continued to go down, whereas the cost of rail-passenger service has remained constant or perhaps has increased. On the supply side, a regulatory climate which restrained management's flexibility in adjusting rates, introducing new services, and discontinuing uneconomic routes led to a decrease in overall service availability. What has happened to rail passenger transportation is both explainable and, what is more important, will continue unless truly significant government intervention is maintained to alter the rational behavior of consumers and producers.

A second lesson from the Amtrak experience is that what started out as a fairly good idea—that of removing rail passenger service from the existing institutional arrangement—quickly became perverted through the establishment of constraints which ruled out the set of feasible profitable alternatives. By the late 1960s it was apparent that a viable rail passenger system just could not be maintained within the existing constraints on abandonment and rates. Amtrak was to remove those restraints, allowing the discontinuance of losing routes and giving the management of the system the requisite flexibility to compete in price and service with alternative modes. Surely, if there existed the possibility of a viable rail passenger network, then the probability of finding it would be maximized by reducing these constraints.

But look at the new restraints placed on the provision of service. First, the new corporation would have to serve the routes set out in the secretary's "basic system." While profitability was one of the major criteria in selecting these routes, it was not the only one.[35] Furthermore, after the proposed system was announced, pressure forced the secretary to expand the initial basic system. Moreover, Amtrak, responding to additional pressure, expanded the system on its own.[36] Along the same lines, Congress has required Amtrak to continue expansion. For example, the latest Amtrak legislation (P.L. 93-146, November 3, 1973) commits Amtrak to initiating at least one experimental route per year, the route to be operated for at least two years. That same legislation denies Amtrak the authority to discontinue any part of the basic system until July 1, 1974 (previously the date was July 1, 1973). Finally, of potential far-reaching significance, this latest legislation gave the ICC authority over minimum Amtrak service standards.[37] Thus, while arguably each individual constraint can be "justified," in toto they appear to have limited

---

[35] The final criteria were as follows: (1) the nation's total transportation needs, (2) demand, (3) cost, (4) integrated national rail network, (5) population, (6) profitability, (7) corporate flexibility, and (8) capital improvements required. See Secretary of Transportation, *Final Report,* pp. 1-3.

[36] Amtrak's criteria for specifying the basic-system routes were: (1) market opportunity, (2) cost economics, (3) ridership, (4) physical characteristics (condition of right-of-way, for example), and (5) alternative transport modes (that is, adequacy of other transport alternatives). National Rail Passenger Corporation, *Annual Report,* 1971, pp. 6 and 7.

[37] These were issued by the ICC on December 27, 1973, as part of *Ex Parte,* no. 277 (Sub-No. 1), "Adequacy of Intercity Rail Passenger Service."

Amtrak to a narrow set of alternatives, none of which is consistent with a viable, self-supporting enterprise.

A third lesson from the Amtrak experience relates to the way the legislation was passed and the way the initial organization was set up. "Railpax" was a last-minute alternative to a bill instituting direct subsidies to the railroads. Without detracting from the yeoman service undertaken by DOT personnel in devising and mapping out the original scheme, it may be noted that with more time for planning the results might have been somewhat better. In that same vein, Railpax did not go through the conventional hearing procedure, where weak points in the legislation might have been uncovered; instead, it was introduced on the floors of the House and Senate and passed without extensive deliberation.[38]

The hasty procedure led to several shortcomings in the original legislation. First, given the constraints placed on the corporation and the expectations of Congress, it was underfinanced; this became apparent almost immediately. Second, the corporation was given too little authority in negotiating with the railroads over the provision of Amtrak services. The contracts finally agreed upon are characteristically "cost-plus," with little control by Amtrak over the quality and character of the services provided.[39] Third, in view of a very short deadline for initiating service, the corporation devoted most of its efforts to getting some kind of rail passenger service underway. As is evidenced by an Amtrak contract to Harbridge House to help define Amtrak's "mission," [40] it would appear that the corporation had no (internal) coherent, well-articulated set of objectives.[41]

A final lesson from the experience concerns efficiency in political decision making. In participating in the congressional budget process, advocates of a new program nearly always have an incentive to understate its expected cost and overstate its expected benefits. Once a program is underway and turns out to cost more and have lower benefits than Congress anticipated, its advocates can always point to sizable "sunk costs." The relevant decision variable at any point in time is how much more needs to be spent to accomplish a stated objective, not how much has been spent. This is one reason why experimental programs quickly become permanent institutions. In this specific case, it would appear that the advocates of Amtrak were (and remain) much too optimistic about the future of rail passenger transport. Congress has yet to face up to the fact that to maintain a rail passenger service of the type commonly envisioned is going to require an ongoing (and perhaps increasing) subsidy from the general taxpayer.

---

[38] Some may argue that this was an advantage in keeping the proposal "clean."

[39] See National Rail Passenger Corporation, *Annual Report,* 1971, pp. 3-5, for a discussion of Amtrak's initial experiences negotiating with the railroads, and Appendix I for a standard Amtrak-railroad contract.

[40] *Role of Intercity Service.*

[41] See National Rail Passenger Corporation, *Annual Report,* 1971, pp. 1-36.

THREE BACK-OF-AN-ENVELOPE
EVALUATIONS OF THE INTERSTATE
HIGHWAY SYSTEM

Herbert Mohring

The way in which a competitive market—for widgets, say—reaches long-run equilibrium can be visualized as follows: In the short run, market forces see to it that the output level established is the level which equates the price of a widget with the short-run marginal cost of producing it. The revenues derived from selling at this marginal-cost price have implicit in them an accounting profit—a rent—to the fixed factors employed in widget production. If the rents generated by additional fixed factors would exceed the cost of supplying their services, it would be in someone's interest to expand industry capacity. Expansion would continue to a point of long-run equilibrium where the rent generated by an additional unit of capacity would equal its cost. In this long-run equilibrium, widgets would be provided at minimum total cost. Total costs are minimized if the cost of an additional unit of capacity services equals the value of the variable inputs that would be saved by employing that additional unit to produce the equilibrium level of output.

Society would do well to seek to replicate these workings of competitive markets in supplying highway services and many other commodities which, for whatever reasons, it has chosen to provide collectively. That is to say, society would do well to set marginal-cost prices for these services and to invest in additional capacity for their provision if and only if the rent generated by a marginal unit of capacity would exceed the cost of providing that unit's services. One way of evaluating the interstate highway system is to answer the question, "How well has provision of the system replicated the workings of competitive markets?"

This paper begins by providing a partial and very rough answer to this question. Specifically, inferences about whether marginal capacity costs exceed marginal savings in variable inputs are drawn from system cost and use data. The paper then examines the efficiency implications of (1) design changes made in the late 1960s to reduce the severity of accidents and of (2) federal financing of 90 percent of the system's capital costs.

Cost and Time Savings Benefits

Table 1 contains data on interstate highway system capital costs and on the use made of the system. These data, together with estimates of maintenance costs provided by Federal Highway Administration personnel [1] and various assumptions on the interest rate of relevance in valuing highway investments, lead to Table 2. Here it is shown that, depending on the portion of the system considered and the interest rate assumed, system costs range between 1.06 and 4.46 cents per vehicle-mile of use.

Tables 3 and 4 provide perspective for these cost data. Table 3 indicates, for example, that if the relevant interest rate were 5 percent and if the occupants of the average vehicle using the rural portion of the interstate system valued their travel time at $1 an hour, then use of the interstate must save them at least 0.73 minutes per mile if time-savings alone are to justify the cost (1.23 cents per mile) incurred on their behalf. Table 4 is based on the additional assumptions that the average speed for trips [2] on the rural components of the system is sixty mph while that for urban components is forty-five mph. It indicates that, if a 5 percent interest rate and a $1 per hour value of travel time are relevant, the rural portion of the system would yield an average time-savings return less than its average cost if the average trip on the rural portion could have been completed on an alternate road at a speed of more than 34.6 mph. Similarly, if $3 an hour and 20 percent are relevant, the average time-savings return to the urban portion of the system would be less than its average cost if, in the absence of the system, trips now using the urban portion could be completed at more than 28.4 mph.

Unfortunately, the numbers in Tables 2-4 permit neither the conclusion that the interstate system has been a roaring success nor that it has been a roaring failure. If a value of travel time in the $2-3 an hour range [3] and a 10 percent interest rate are relevant, realized average speeds of less than thirty-six to forty-one mph on alternative routes would be required for the rural portion of the 1973 interstate system to have a time-savings benefit/total cost ratio greater than one. Such speeds seem a trifle low, although diversion to alternative routes of vehicles that now use the interstate would probably reduce the speeds attainable on these routes—perhaps reduce them considerably. Also, while time-savings are by far the largest benefits of the interstate system, it has led to vehicle operating and

---

[1] From a special study prepared for the 1972 National Highway Needs Report. "Maintenance" is not defined in the table from which these figures were obtained. However, similar figures provided by Minnesota Highway Department personnel for primary roads in that state include not only repairs to bridges, road surfaces, and the like, but also such things as mowing, snowplowing, and traffic services. I therefore assume that the United States data in Table 2 also involve these activities.

[2] This is the average speed for an entire trip, not the average speed for that portion of it which is completed on the interstate system.

[3] Work by Beesley and Lisco suggests that the ratio of an individual's value of travel time to his equivalent hourly wage increases from zero for the lowest income group to about 50 percent at about $10,000 a year and above. Applying the relationships, travel time value = 0.5 × income for incomes in excess of $10,000 and travel-time value = (income)^2/$20,000 for incomes of $10,000 or less to 1970 census data on the distribution of family incomes yields an average value equivalent to $2.35. If the average private-passenger-vehicle occupancy rate is on the order of 1.25, a value of time per vehicle-hour of just under $3 would be implied.

Table 1
INTERSTATE HIGHWAY SYSTEM COST AND USE DATA, 1972-1973

Miles of System Completed	Million Vehicle-Miles Traveled, 1972		Capital Outlays on Completed System, 1973 ($ millions)	
	Total	Per route mile	Total	Per route mile
Rural 28,612	98,392	3.439	21,137	0.739
Urban 6,848	100,433	14.666	19,083	2.787
Total 35,460	198,825	5.607	40,220	1.134

Source: U.S. Department of Transportation, Federal Highway Administration, *Highway Statistics: 1972,* and *Quarterly Report on the Federal-Aid Highway Program,* December 31, 1973. The breakdown of total capital outlays into urban and rural components was estimated by Federal Highway Administration personnel.

Table 2
INTERSTATE SYSTEM COSTS PER VEHICLE-MILE, 1972-1973

Interest Rate (percent)	Cost Per Route-Mile			Total Cost Per Vehicle-Mile (in cents)
	Capital	Maintenance	Total	
Rural				
5	$ 36,950	$ 5,490 [a]	$ 42,440	1.23
10	73,900		79,390	2.31
20	147,800		153,290	4.46
Urban				
5	139,850	15,010 [b]	4,860	1.06
10	279,700		294,710	2.01
20	559,400		574,410	3.92
Total				
5	56,700	7,330 [c]	64,030	1.14
10	113,400		120,730	2.15
20	226,800		234,130	4.18

[a] Estimated annual maintenance cost per mile for a four-lane rural expressway.

[b] Estimated annual maintenance cost per mile for an urban expressway with six or more lanes.

[c] Weighted (by number of miles completed) averages of urban and rural figures.

accident cost-savings as well. Then, too, Tables 3 and 4 do not take into account the benefits the system affords present users of alternative routes by reducing volume/capacity ratios and hence increasing speeds on these routes.[4]

---

[4] Given the nature of this analysis and the techniques now used to price highways, I think it appropriate to include gains to users of alternate routes as net benefits of interstate construction. But I am not certain about this. Taking account of the equivalent of such nonuser benefits would not be appropriate in dealing with what seems to be the most nearly similar

Table 3

MINUTES SAVED PER TRIP-MILE REQUIRED TO EQUATE AVERAGE COST OF INTERSTATE HIGHWAY SYSTEM WITH VALUE OF TIME SAVED THROUGH ITS USE

Interest Rate (percent)	Value of Travel Time ($/vehicle-hour)		
	$1	$2	$3
Rural			
5	0.73 min./mi.	0.37 min./mi.	0.25 min./mi.
10	1.39	0.69	0.46
20	2.68	1.34	0.89
Urban			
5	0.64	0.32	0.21
10	1.21	0.60	0.40
20	2.35	1.18	0.78
Total			
5	0.68	0.34	0.23
10	1.29	0.66	0.43
20	2.51	1.25	0.84

Table 4

AVERAGE TRIP SPEED ON ALTERNATIVE ROUTES ABOVE WHICH VALUE OF TIME SAVED FALLS SHORT OF AVERAGE COST OF INTERSTATE HIGHWAY SYSTEM [a]

Interest Rate (percent)	Value of Time ($/vehicle-hour)		
	$1	$2	$3
Rural			
5	34.6 mph	43.8 mph	48.0 mph
10	25.1	35.5	41.1
20	16.3	25.6	31.8
Urban			
5	30.4	36.4	39.0
10	23.6	31.1	34.7
20	16.3	23.9	28.4

[a] Assumptions: The average speed of trips using rural and urban portions of the interstate system are, respectively, 60 and 45 miles per hour.

competitive-market problem. That is, suppose that a technological improvement leads to (1) a reduction in the cost of producing widgets, (2) a consequent decline in their price and expansion of their output, and (3) a downward shift in the demand schedule and hence reduction in both the price and output of a substitute commodity, gizmos. Consumers would benefit from both the widget and the gizmo price reductions. However, the latter benefit would be precisely offset by a loss in rents earned by gizmo producers. As a result, determining the net benefit of the improvement requires referring only to the widget market.

168

The figures in Tables 3 and 4 pertaining to the urban portion of the interstate system seem rather more favorable than those pertaining to the rural portion. Again at 10 percent and $2-3 an hour, if speeds on alternative routes are less than thirty-one to thirty-five mph, the urban interstate system pays for itself in user time-savings alone. It seems unreasonable to suppose that any significant number of trips taken entirely on urban street networks is accomplished at average speeds in excess of thirty mph. It seems even more unreasonable to suppose that trip speeds in excess of thirty mph would be common if trips now taken on the interstate system were diverted to the regular street network. And, of course, accident and vehicle operating cost-savings of interstate users as well as savings to present street network users are ignored in these tables.

I am left, then, with two tentative conclusions: (1) The benefit/cost ratio exceeds one for both the urban and rural portions of the interstate system, and (2) the urban benefit/cost ratio is greater—perhaps considerably greater—than the rural ratio.

Benefits and Costs of Safety-Related Design Changes

In 1967 or thereabouts, three costly changes in interstate system design standards were made in the interest of reducing the severity of accidents resulting from vehicles running off the road. First, light standards, signs, and similar structures were to be made frangible—that is, they were to be designed to give way on impact rather than to withstand it. Second, to reduce the frequency with which vehicles rolled over on leaving the road, grades on cuts and fills were to be changed from one foot vertical/three feet horizontal to one foot vertical/six feet horizontal. Third, major structures were to be built wide enough to carry not just the basic roadways but also paved shoulders of the standard width. According to the Minnesota Highway Commissioner at that time, making these changes on the uncompleted portions of the system in that state would result in a 13 percent increase in their cost.

Limited inquiry suggests that systematic cost/effectiveness studies played no part in the promulgation of these new design standards. Back-of-an-envelope calculations do not rule out the possibility that these changes were the most cost/effective way of reducing accidents. However, they do suggest that cost/effectiveness studies would be in order before additional expensive safety-related changes in design standards are made.

The death rate from motor-vehicle accidents equaled 4.80 per 100 million motor-vehicle miles in the United States during 1970. The corresponding rate on the completed portion of the interstate system was 2.91 while the rate on all other highways was 5.49.[5] The National Safety Council has reported that 24.3 percent

---

[5] U.S. Department of Transportation, Federal Highway Administration, *Fatal and Injury Accident Rates . . . 1971.*

of all automotive-vehicle fatalities involved running off the road while an additional 7.9 percent involved hitting a fixed object in the road [6] (including, I presume, such objects as immediately adjacent bridge railings). Let us suppose that these ratios apply equally to interstate and non-interstate travel. Then the interstate death rate from fixed-object collisions and running off the road would have equaled $2.91 \times (0.243 + 0.079) = 0.94$ per 100 million vehicle-miles.

If the proportionate increase in total construction costs that applied in Minnesota applies in other states, funds sufficient to build 100 miles of freeway under post-1967 standards could be used to build 113 miles under pre-1967 standards. Let us suppose, to make computations simple, that each of these hypothetical additional thirteen miles of freeway would divert the same amount of traffic from other roads as would each of the 100 miles actually incorporated in the interstate system. The fatal-accident rate applicable to these additional diverted travelers would decline from 5.49 to 2.91 per 100 million vehicle-miles. It may now be asked: What reduction in accident rates on the 100 miles of freeway with higher safety standards would be required to save the same number of lives? That is, what is the value of X for which $13 \times (5.49 - 2.91) = 100 \ X$? The answer is: $X = 0.34$. This reduction amounts to 36 percent $(0.34/0.94)$ of the interstate death rate from fixed-object collisions, plus running off the road, if that rate is, in fact, 0.94 per 100 million vehicle-miles.

Whether the improved design standards have resulted in an accident rate reduction of this magnitude can now be checked and could likely have been predicted from detailed study of accident records at the time the new standards were promulgated. If such a reduction in accident rates has not resulted, more lives as well as vehicle-operating and travel-time costs could be saved in the future by reverting to the old standards and using the resources saved to build more freeways.

Another way of addressing the same problem would be to determine the cost of saving lives through the design changes under examination and then to ask, "Are lives worth it?" or, more easily answered, "Are there other, cheaper ways of saving lives?" From Table 2, at 5 percent, the average annual capital cost of the portion of the interstate system that had been completed by 1972 was $56,700. A 13 percent increase in this cost would amount to $7,370. From Table 1, each mile of the interstate system carried an average of 5.607 million vehicle-miles a year. Hence, an average of $100/5.607 = 17.83$ miles of interstate were required to carry 100 million vehicle-miles. If the safety improvements eliminated all of the assumed 0.94 deaths per 100 million miles resulting from the causes under investigation, the cost per life saved would be $7,370 \times 17.83/0.94 = \$140,000$. The corresponding figures for 10 and 20 percent interest rates are, respectively, $280,000 and $559,000. Whether the average life saved is worth $140,000-$559,000 is, of course, moot. But it does see plausible to conjecture

[6] National Safety Council, *Accident Facts: 1971.*

that cheaper ways of saving lives—for example, kidney transplants, open heart surgery—do exist.

Possible Waste from 90 Percent Subsidies of Capital Costs

Many federal grants-in-aid to state and local governments involve contributions to the capital costs of facilities. The state or local government assumes the full cost of operating and maintaining these facilities once they have been completed. If operating and maintenance dollars cost a governmental unit $1 each while capital dollars cost 50 cents each (some Federal Highway Administration programs), 33 cents each (Urban Mass Transportation Administration programs), or 10 cents each (the interstate highway system), an incentive exists for the inefficient substitution of capital dollars for maintenance dol'ars. With those highway programs that involve 50 percent subsidies, the total cost of eligible projects generally appears to exceed a state's maximum allocation of subsidy funds. Under these circumstances, the state would be inefficient if it treated capital dollars as really costing only 50 cents. This consideration does not, however, apply to the interstate system. The system is fixed. Capital dollars that a state would save by treating them as worth more than 10 cents each would disappear into the Federal Highway Trust Fund, never to be seen by the state again.

The efficiency costs of the interstate system's 10-cent capital dollars depend on the technological possibilities for substituting capital for maintenance dollars, on the extent to which the Bureau of Public Roads acquiesces in the states' using capital dollars as if they cost only 10 cents each, and on a number of other factors on which information is unavailable. Again, however, some back-of-an-envelope calculations suggest the orders of magnitude that might be involved.

Suppose that a Cobb-Douglas production function, $Q = aK^b M^{1-b}$, applies to the provision of highway capacity, where Q refers to capacity, K to initial capital cost, and M to annual maintenance outlays. Suppose also that a highway department strives to minimize its annual cost, $B = rsK + M$, of providing Q_o units of capacity where r is the relevant interest rate for valuing capital expenditures in the state and s is the cost to the state of a subsidized capital dollar (to repeat, 10 cents for the interstate system). If the highway department succeeds in this objective, it can be shown that the true annual cost of Q_o units of capacity, $B = rK + M$, equals

$$B = (rs/b)^b (1 - b)^{b-1} (1 - b + b/s) Q_o/a . \tag{1}$$

The minimum cost of providing the same amount of capacity is

$$B' = (r/b)^b (1 - b)^{b-1} Q_o/a . \tag{2}$$

The ratio of B to B'—that is, the ratio of the actual cost of capacity to the minimum cost—equals

$$B/B' = s^b (1 - b + b/s) . \tag{3}$$

171

From Table 2, if the relevant interest rate for a state is 5 percent and capital dollars cost 10 cents each, the average annual cost to the state for one mile of interstate highway is $5,670 for capital and $7,330 for maintenance—a total of $13,000. For the Cobb-Douglas production function, the exponent, b, in equations (1)-(3) can be shown to equal the share of capital in total costs—$5,670/$13,000 = 0.44. Inserting this number and $s = 0.1$ into equation (3) yields 1.80 as the value of B/B'. The corresponding figures for 10 and 20 percent interest rates are 1.60 and 1.37, respectively.

The Cobb-Douglas production function implies a unitary elasticity of substitution between capital and variable inputs. This elasticity is probably higher than that which applies to highways particularly if, as appears to be the case, the maintenance figures cited above include such things as grass cutting and snowplowing. A reduction in the assumed elasticity of substitution would reduce B/B'. Still, the possibility that the actual costs of the interstate system are close to double its minimum possible costs would seem to justify fairly careful scrutiny of highway design procedures. After all, 37-80 percent of the interstate system's capital cost is a very large sum of money.

SUMMARY OF DISCUSSION

The discussion which followed these papers was subdued, perhaps reflecting general audience agreement with the analyses presented.

A few technical points were raised. First, on Professor Eckert's paper, a comment was made that the "clustering" of flight schedules might actually be greater under a system where airport/airway resources are price rationed. It was also pointed out that in markets where the U.S. trunk carriers have negotiated multi-carrier agreements to reduce capacity the "clustering" phenomenon has been accentuated.

Professor Hilton was asked whether it was not premature to judge UMTA a failure. After all, the program is relatively new, and if automobile travelers were charged their true marginal costs then mass transit would appear much more promising. Professor Hilton responded to the effect that the existing program is so misdirected and its performance so bad that, even making allowances for newness and certain "second-best" arguments, an assessment of failure is eminently appropriate.

Two points were raised on the paper by Professor Miller. First, what if Amtrak became profitable? Would that not tempt Congress to take a similar approach to railroad freight transportation? In response, it was suggested that Congress is unlikely to allow Amtrak to become profitable, preferring to distribute any rents that might accrue (through expanded service, for example). Another questioner suggested that it may be premature to judge Amtrak a failure and asked whether it would have been appropriate to judge the local service air carriers' subsidy program so soon after it was initiated in the 1940s. Professor Miller answered that he does not necessarily consider the local service subsidy program a "success" and pointed out further that a key difference between the two is that air service at that time was a rapidly expanding industry, whereas passenger rail service over the past several decades has been in a secular decline.

Regarding Professor Mohring's paper on the interstate highway system, a few questioners contrasted his findings with the slightly different results of previous researchers. Perhaps the most perceptive comment of the session was that, compared with other federal transportation programs, the interstate highway system would appear to have been a resounding success.

PART FIVE

RESPONSES BY TRANSPORTATION POLICY MAKERS

INTRODUCTION

A dialogue fails to have much substance if only one side speaks. Several government officials were invited to respond to the previously circulated papers contained in parts one through four of this volume.

First, Dr. John W. Snow, deputy assistant secretary for policy and international affairs of the Department of Transportation—a lawyer as well as an economist—spoke on the need for regulatory reform and also answered critics of the department's proposed Transportation Improvement Act (TIA). Dr. Snow argued that the major inefficiencies of ICC regulation can be addressed by restricting the commission's power to delay rate decreases (so long as the new rate exceeds "variable cost"), by liberalizing the standards for railroad abandonment, and by constraining the anticompetitive activities of railroad rate bureaus. As one of the authors of the TIA, Dr. Snow argued that the Nixon administration's proposal deals adequately with the problem and should receive broad support from the academic community. Also, as he made plain, the Nixon administration views the TIA as only a first step toward more fundamental regulatory reform, and further steps will follow.

A. Daniel O'Neal, the youngest commissioner of the ICC, presented a contrary pro-regulation view. In his address Commissioner O'Neal criticized the rhetoric of deregulation enthusiasts as short-sighted and, on certain points, fallacious. In general, according to Commissioner O'Neal, the academic critic of regulation focuses too much on narrowly defined economic efficiency goals, neglecting social goals. Commissioner O'Neal did, however, see a need for some reforms that would improve regulation, not constrain it.

Dr. Gary L. Seevers, member of the Council of Economic Advisers (CEA), discussed the process of regulatory reform, especially the CEA's role in the Nixon administration's two major efforts (TRMA and TIA). He suggested that through continual efforts an idea which at one time seems "radical" (an idea such as deregulation) may gain respectability. Dr. Seevers sees the council as exerting such efforts on behalf of surface transportation regulatory reform. Moreover, he believes that the recent secular increase in the number of economists in government and in the degree of their influence will continue, making deregulation of transportation an even more viable long-run goal.

Finally, Roy Pulsifer, assistant director of the CAB's Bureau of Operating Rights, presented a CAB perspective on the question of regulatory reform. Mr. Pulsifer noted briefly that—despite the arguments of academicians calling for the deregulation of the airlines—he could detect no political support for the idea and thus sees no prospect for such a change at this time. He went on to comment on the present financial status of the industry and to review major current CAB actions.

THE TRANSPORTATION IMPROVEMENT ACT OF 1974

John W. Snow

This is an important time in the history of transportation and especially in the history of the railroad industry. Some change has already taken place. The direction of change in the future is the critical question we now face. Much of our concern recently has been focused on proposals advanced for the resolution of the problems facing the bankrupt Northeastern railroads. The carriers' financial condition created a serious threat that rail service over a seventeen-state area might be sharply curtailed.

The economic and social costs resulting from the shutdown of these railroads would be intolerable. Equally intolerable, however, would have been a resolution of the problem which saddled the American taxpayers with an unreasonably high cost and which did nothing to ensure that a streamlined and viable private-sector railroad would emerge.

Legislation to resolve the bankrupt carriers' problems and create a new system in the Northeast proceeded through Congress with great speed, and the Regional Rail Reorganization Act of 1973 was signed by the President on January 2, 1974. While the act departs in several important respects from the legislation which the department proposed, and while the legislation which emerged does not in all respects represent the department's preferred position, we do consider the act an essentially sound attempt to avert a transportation and economic crisis of major proportions. The procedures provided in the act will, in time, strengthen the private-sector role of the nation's railroads in the Northeast and Midwest sections of the country. It must be regarded, therefore, as a major step away from nationalization.

Now, as the job of implementing the legislative mandate to restore the Northeast lines begins, we must turn our attention to assuring that we have a healthy, sound and progressive national rail system—and that we avoid future Penn Centrals.

The Need for Regulatory Reform

There can be no mistake about the fact that the railroad industry in the United States is deeply troubled. For the industry, net profits as a percent of equity are less than 1 percent. Many railroads cannot generate sufficient earnings to make needed improvements in track, roadbed and facilities, while funds from outside sources are not available to many railroads for these purposes. As a consequence, a substantial part of the total rail industry in the U.S. is in a state of deterioration. The railroad industry's share of total intercity freight ton-miles and the average revenue per ton-mile have been declining. The industry, furthermore, is burdened by miles of uneconomic lines which are a financial drain and add substantially to operating costs. At the same time, parts of the railroad system are operating at or close to capacity, and these segments must be upgraded and expanded if the industry is to make its contribution to the national transportation system.

A major cause of the railroad industry's problems has been an outmoded and excessively restrictive federal regulatory policy. Existing regulatory policy has seriously hampered the railroads' ability to adapt to changing economic and competitive conditions in the transportation industry. It has discouraged abandonment of uneconomic rail lines and has hindered the industry in developing new services, in responding to competitive conditions in transportation, and in attracting the traffic on which railroads have a competitive advantage.

Our basic regulatory policy towards the railroad industry has changed very little since 1887 when the Interstate Commerce Act was adopted and the Interstate Commerce Commission formed. In the intervening period, the competitive position of the railroad industry has changed dramatically with the rise of alternative modes of transportation—pipelines, trucks, barges and air. Whatever monopoly position railroads may have enjoyed in 1887, today they face intense competition from other modes of transportation. This is clearly revealed by their loss of total intercity market shares to the other regulated modes. Thus, while the basic competitive conditions in transportation have changed dramatically, federal regulatory policy towards the railroad industry has not. There is a need not only to unshackle the Northeast railroads from constricting regulations which are in part responsible for their present difficulties but also to provide a solution to problems which have become endemic in the whole railroad industry.

An efficient rail system is a great national asset. Removal of outmoded regulatory restraints is an essential condition for restoring the economic health of the rail system and enabling it to provide the efficient low-cost service of which it is capable.

The Transportation Improvement Act of 1974

For the past year or so, we have been preparing a legislative proposal to amend the Interstate Commerce Act to achieve needed reform of regulatory restraints on our railroads. On February 13, 1974, the Department of Transportation transmitted to Congress the product of these labors, the proposed Transportation

Improvement Act of 1974. The bill makes a number of significant amendments to the Interstate Commerce Act. Taken together, these amendments will substantially improve the regulatory climate under which railroads operate. Among the more important provisions of the bill are the following:

(1) Abandonment procedures would be speeded up and standards would provide that, in order to require operation, the cost of that operation would have to be covered by the revenues earned.

(2) Railroads would be given greater freedom to increase or decrease their rates and to improve the range of services offered. Rates below variable cost would be eliminated.

(3) Governments would be required to pay the same rates as other shippers.

(4) Antitrust immunity would be eliminated on agreements relating to single-line rates, or on rates in which the carrier agreeing does not participate. Prompt action by carrier rate bureaus would be required.

(5) When railroads abandon lines, a more relaxed entry standard would apply for motor or water carriers who apply for authority to provide needed service.

(6) Discriminatory state and local taxation of rail assets would be eliminated.

(7) Delays would be reduced in the processing of state approval of intrastate rates that correspond to changes in interstate rates.

Regulatory change is particularly important in the areas of rail abandonments and pricing, and I will focus my detailed comments on these aspects of the department's regulatory reform legislation.

The Problem of Excess Railroad Capacity

Excess capacity is a major problem with the railroad industry. By reducing excess capacity and eliminating uneconomic low-density lines, the railroad industry could lower per-unit operating cost and remove a heavy financial drain. However, the detrimental effects associated with the operation of uneconomic lines are not limited to the railroad industry. It is clear that motor carriers are better suited to handling much of the short-haul traffic which now moves on low-density rail branch lines, while railroads have a cost advantage in long-haul markets. The abandonment of uneconomic low-density rail lines would enable railroads to concentrate their efforts in providing those services in which they have a relative advantage while giving trucking service a further opportunity to develop in markets where it would have the relative advantage.

The bill is designed to speed up the regulatory processes for abandonment applications by providing an explicit and appropriate economic standard for determining when an abandonment is justified. Under the bill, railroads would be permitted to abandon lines where the costs of operating the line exceed the revenues attributable to the line.

While the bill would expedite consideration of rail abandonments, it would not result in an abrupt loss of rail service upon enactment—quite the contrary in fact. The bill requires a series of steps before an abandonment, and basically no abandonment may occur under the new procedures before one year has passed from the date of enactment. In the case of protested abandonment, the various procedures under the bill could delay abandonments for up to as long as two years and six months. Thus, while the bill is designed to speed up the regulatory process for abandonments, it fully protects shippers and communities against the abrupt loss of rail service.

Because our abandonment provisions are likely to result in some additional traffic for truck carriers, it is important to consider the energy-consumption and air-pollution effects of the bill. Generally abandonment candidates will be low-density short-branch lines. Our analysis shows that there is greater energy efficiency in carrying freight by truck, rather than by rail, for distances less than ten miles and shipment sizes less than 130-140 tons.

Because exhaust emissions for each mode vary directly with gallons of fuel consumed per mile, the rail/truck preference for emissions would generally be the same as that for fuel consumption. Although the branch-line abandonments envisioned will result in some increase in truck traffic, the transportation of the freight now carried on most of the lines to be abandoned will become more energy efficient and will cause less pollution than at present.

The Need for Efficient, Competitive Pricing

Another major objective of the bill is to encourage more competitive and efficient pricing of rail services. This would assist the rails in attracting traffic for which they are the low-cost mode. Thus, we anticipate that the overall effect of this bill will be to improve the energy efficiency of freight transportation and to reduce its exhaust emissions.

Of course, it must be recognized that under some circumstances an uneconomic rail line may be the most efficient mode of transportation available to shippers. To cover situations of this sort, the bill provides a mechanism whereby a state or local government or other interested party could subsidize railroad operations to assure the continuation of uneconomic service for which a special need exists. We also recognize that liberalizing abandonments would result in some loss of rail service to various shippers. In order to assure that these shippers will have an effective and efficient alternative mode of transportation without any hiatus in service, the bill provides for liberalized entry by motor and water carriers seeking to provide substitute service.

Regulatory change in railroad rate making is critical in any attempt to improve the economic position of the railroad industry and to enable it to operate efficiently. The current system of rate regulation severely limits an individual railroad's freedom to establish rates. As a consequence, the system has created serious rigidity and distortions in the railroad rate structure. It has hindered the railroad industry in providing new services and has prevented it from responding effectively to the needs of changing transportation demand. In particular, it has prevented railroads from attracting traffic for which they have a comparative advantage. Greater flexibility in rate making is essential if the performance of the railroad industry and the entire transportation system is to be improved. Serious inefficiency results when low-cost carriers are impeded or prevented from reducing rates to reflect greater efficiency. The department recognizes the need to introduce greater flexibility in the rate structure and our legislation contains various proposals designed to achieve this objective.

The bill provides that a rate decrease may not be suspended on the ground that it is unjustly or unreasonably low. Under today's practice, rates may be suspended on the ground that they are too low even though the rate may be compensatory. By removing this ground for suspension, the bill would encourage railroads to reduce rates on traffic where they have a cost advantage.

The bill also modifies the existing law on suspension of rate changes by providing that a proposed rate increase may not be suspended as being unjustly or unreasonably high if it is below the applicable class rate. On rate decreases, the bill provides that a rate may not be suspended on the ground that it is unreasonably or unjustly low. All the other grounds for suspension which exist in the act today under sections 2, 3 and 4 would remain. The changes in the suspension provisions of the act should encourage railroads to reduce rates on traffic where they have a cost advantage while increasing rates where railroads' net income will be improved.

The bill also provides new procedures for rates in the development of a new service involving a capital expenditure of $500,000 or more. This provision is designed to reduce the time, expense, delay and uncertainty involved in the introduction of new services, and thereby to encourage experimentation and the introduction of service innovations.

The bill also directs the ICC to raise all rates which are below variable cost to the variable cost level. The railroad industry loses approximately $450-$500 million annually handling traffic at rates below variable cost. Economic theory tells us that firms will not price at rates below variable cost: such conduct is irrational. Conduct which is irrational and beyond the pale in an unregulated industry apparently can and does persist in a regulated industry such as the railroad industry. Undoubtedly, the regulatory system, including the present outmoded accounting methods prescribed by the commission, have contributed to this result. In any event, such rates create a serious financial drain on the carriers and result in a misallocation of resources, both within transportation and in the economy at large.

The present regulatory process has also resulted in the rates of one mode being held high to protect another mode, causing a misallocation of resources, increasing the total cost to shippers and ultimately consumers, and adversely affecting the financial condition of the more efficient mode. Section 15a of the Interstate Commerce Act was amended in 1958 to allow carriers greater rate-making freedom to meet the competition of carriers in the other modes. While the amendment was a step in the right direction, the full benefits of greater intermodal competition have not been realized because the amendment has been interpreted to allow the ICC to hold the rates for one mode above the rates for another mode in order to protect the mode with the lower rates. The bill meets this problem by prohibiting such a course of action. This prohibition should lead to more competitive and cost-related intermodal pricing and introduce greater rate flexibility into transportation rate making. The net result should be a more economic division of traffic.

The bill also seeks to introduce greater flexibility into the rate-making process by modifying the present escrow provisions of the act. At present, a carrier may be required to put funds resulting from rate changes under investigation in escrow only after the seven-month suspension period runs. The bill provides that where rate increases have not been suspended or where rate decreases have been suspended, the carriers must keep account of all amounts received from the increase or the suspension of the decrease during a seven-month period or until a prior ICC order issues, at which time the carrier would settle any overages with shippers. These changes in the escrow provisions should provide additional incentives for contested rate cases to be disposed of more promptly.

Along with these various changes in the area of rate making, the bill makes a number of changes with respect to rate bureau practices. Under section 5a of the Interstate Commerce Act, carriers subject to the ICC's jurisdiction are permitted to act collectively in establishing rates and charges for transportation services, and such concerted action when taken pursuant to an agreement approved by the commission is immune from the antitrust laws.

Rate bureaus are the vehicles through which carriers make decisions on the rates which the member lines shall charge, whether these rates are single-line rates or rates for joint-line movements. Although rate bureaus provide a number of valuable services to their members and to the shipping public, they also dampen competitive forces in the rate-making process and discourage pricing flexibility and service innovation. As a result, they have interferred with the establishment of rates based on the cost of the most efficient carrier, and have provided a mechanism through which carriers seek to set and hold rates above a competitive level.

The bill prohibits railroad rate bureaus from voting on single-line movements and limits consideration of joint-line rates to those railroads which actually participate in the joint movement, except for scale or group rates. The bill also prohibits rail rate bureaus from taking any action to suspend rates established independently, while prohibiting motor-carrier or freight-forwarder rate bureaus from protesting a rate filed by independent action unless the protest is supported by facts showing that the rate appears to be less than the variable cost of rendering the service.

Thus, on single-line rates, individual railroads will have complete freedom to propose rates based on the cost of the most direct routing, while on joint rates the influence of carriers not participating in the joint movement will be reduced. Scale rates—rates established in cents per hundred pounds for specified distances—are excepted from this provision because these rates are designed for large inter- and intra-regional flows where traffic tends to move over all carriers.

The bill also requires all rate bureaus to dispose of proposed rate changes within 120 days from the time a rate change is proposed to the bureau. In addition, the bill requires all rate bureaus to maintain and make available for public inspection records of the votes of members. These provisions are designed to bring about speedier rate-bureau treatment of proposed rate changes and to encourage greater initiative by individual carriers in making rate changes.

While the antitrust immunity for joint rates is retained, the proposed legislative change for single-line rate agreements would exert a competitive influence on joint rates because carrier territories overlap and single-line rates are often competitive with joint-line rates.

Through these various proposals dealing with rates and rate bureaus we hope to create substantially more rate-making flexibility to correct the present distortions in the rate structure and to encourage railroads to introduce new services and attract traffic on which they have a comparative advantage. The basic thrust of the proposals is to place greater reliance on competitive market forces in rate making. I am confident that this will result in a more economic division of traffic, a lower overall freight bill, improved service, and lower cost to the ultimate consumer.

The bill also provides for needed changes in the present cost-accounting and revenue-accounting system employed by the ICC. The commission's cost system relies on broad averages rather than on the specific experience of individual carriers. Moreover, the accounting system from which the cost data are derived is based on outmoded classifications and on specifications that no longer relate to the carrier's actual financial transactions. In addition, the accounting procedures used are not adequate to resolve the complex cost-accounting problems which characterize modern transportation firms.

The development of improved cost- and revenue-accounting procedures is absolutely essential for the improved regulation of transportation. The bill would require the ICC jointly with the secretary of transportation to study and recommend uniform cost-accounting and revenue-accounting methods for rail carriers, and to issue regulations prescribing those new methods within two years of the date of enactment of the bill.

The ICC has pending proceedings dealing with the issue of developing an improved uniform cost-accounting system. These include Docket 34012, *Rules to Govern the Assembling and Presenting of Cost Evidence,* and Docket 34013 (Sub-No. 1), *Cost Standards in Intermodal Rate Proceedings.* The proceeding in Docket 34013 was instituted by an order of the commission dated April 16, 1962, and the commission's decision was issued in 1970 (337 ICC 298). In February 1971, the commission issued a new order reopening the case. The department has participated in the main proceeding since 1968. Both the timing and outcome of the reopened proceeding are uncertain. In the sub-proceeding, which was initiated in early 1969 after the Supreme Court's 1968 decision in the Ingot Molds case, the administrative law judge issued an initial decision on May 7, 1973. In brief, the bill would give direction and priority to the ICC's efforts to develop an improved uniform cost-accounting system and would offer the best prospect for realizing this result.

Among our deliberations on the type of regulatory reform we would propose to the Congress, we were well aware that the three regulated surface modes have collaborated on the preparation of the proposed Surface Transportation Act (H.R. 5385) which received the endorsement of a House committee two years ago. There are reforms in that bill which are positive. In fact, there are many areas in which the TIA and the STA closely parallel each other. But it is clear that "controversial" reforms were left out of the STA—by common consent—so that the residue of reform left in the industry bill is quite modest. We think the railroad industry needs more than that now—particularly if financial assistance is to accompany the regulatory reforms as the industry has proposed.

Financial Aid for Needed Service Improvements

As I noted earlier, considerable parts of the rail plant in the United States are in a state of deterioration and the risk exists that this general deterioration of plant and service now prevalent in the East could expand to other portions of the country. At the same time, it is clear that a potential for substantial productivity gains exists in the railroad industry if improvements are made in the basic physical plant. Thus, the bill provides for $2 billion in federal loan guarantee authority to finance needed improvements in rights-of-way, terminals and other operational facilities and systems, and to finance the acquisition of rolling stock. However, these loan guarantees would be provided only where assurance exists that the capital improvements will make a genuine improvement to the overall efficiency

186

of the rail system. In other words, the aid would help encourage needed long-term building of the existing rail system.

Another basic problem in the railroad industry is the almost chronic shortage of freight cars. There are many reasons for the shortage. A key factor has been the low rate of freight-car utilization. If we could improve utilization by 20 percent, the annual need for new cars would be reduced by approximately 10,000 to 15,000 cars. Increased utilization could save the railroads as much as $300 million annually in new car purchases. An effective system of car-fleet management is required in order to achieve greater utilization. We do not have a national management system at this time—it is sorely needed, and we have technology now to design and implement such a system.

To expedite and assure development of a national system, the department's bill would authorize the secretary of transportation to conduct research into the design of a national scheduling and control system for rolling stock which would be capable of locating and expediting the movement of rolling stock on a national basis.

Response to Critics

Clearly, the department's bill will not please everyone. Some critics, such as Professor Tollison, suggest that it represents only "modest" regulatory reform, and that it lacks a strong conceptual foundation. Let me deal briefly with Professor Tollison's assertions.

The regulatory reform measures in the bill have their cornerstone in the pricing area. Virtually every academic analysis of the railroad industry problems has concluded that the existing pricing structure in the railroad industry is rigid and results in substantial misallocation of resources both from the point of view of the transportation industry and from the point of view of the economy as a whole. In our deliberations on the bill, we were well aware of this. Our own analyses confirmed the need for greater pricing flexibility—for allowing wider play for market forces in transportation.

The provisions of the bill are carefully calculated to result in greater pricing flexibility in the railroad industry. My discussions with representatives of the barge-line industry and trucking industry reveal their concern that the bill creates substantially more pricing flexibility for railroads. They view the rate-making proposals as enabling the railroads to compete more effectively against them and this is the source of their hostility to these proposals.

In my discussions with the railroad industry, I have encountered serious concern on the pricing effects of the changes which the bill makes in rate-bureau practices, concern that the restraining influences which rate bureaus exert on initiation of new rates will be lost, and that as a consequence the free play of market forces will be given wider sway.

All this concern on the part of the various modes is strong evidence that the bill makes more than "modest" regulatory changes.

Professor Tollison's view that the bill lacks theoretical or conceptual foundation is equally without merit. Virtually all competent economic analysis of the railroad industry indicates that a critical problem is the lack of intelligent and rational pricing—the lack of pricing flexibility which seriously interferes with an efficient division of traffic among the modes. Far from lacking appropriate theoretical foundation, the bill makes the changes in the regulatory system which both theory and empirical analysis indicate should be made.

Another criticism which we have encountered is that the bill is largely limited to the railroad industry. It is true that the primary focus of the bill is the railroads. This is so because the industry's problems are most serious and immediate and it is in the railroad industry that the consequences of the present regulatory system are producing the greatest harm. It is important to note, however, that removing regulatory restraints from the railroad industry and thereby encouraging the railroads to price more intelligently and compete more effectively will clearly provide a stimulus for intermodal competition and will thereby improve competitive conditions in the trucking and water carrier industries as well.

In addition, it should be noted that in releasing the Transportation Improvement Act, Secretary Brinegar emphasized that the department had undertaken a major regulatory research program in the trucking area designed to yield legislative proposals in the near future.

The department is firmly committed to regulatory reform in other industries, but we are also firmly committed to getting effective regulatory reform in the railroad industry now. We all stand to benefit enormously as a consequence of this commitment.

NO CLAMOR FOR DEREGULATION: SHOULD THERE BE?

A. Daniel O'Neal

The debate over deregulation of transportation, sparked partly by the Department of Transportation's latest regulatory modification proposal, appears to be warming up once again. Deregulation has become an article of faith for many economists and for them the underlying issues may seem hardly worth discussing any more. Tactics appear to hold the greatest fascination for them now. On the other end of the spectrum are most regulated carriers who, with their strong collective advocacy of continued regulation, make me more than a little uneasy. Somewhere in between these poles are the shippers and the government policy makers—including, I think, most regulators. The administration currently leans in the direction of less regulation, emphasizing "improved" regulation with the Congress. For the most part, regulators are also interested in "improved" regulation, but they lean away from less regulation.

While many economists have given a negative answer to the question of whether we should have regulation, most decision makers are still sticking to a "yes" answer and have gone on to other questions, such as: What basic shape should regulation take? What improvements should be made and through what mechanism would we derive greater benefits? In all this, it is sometimes not clear who wants to turn the clock ahead and who wants to turn it back.

Should Regulation Continue?

Today, as I see it, we are here to discuss the threshold question which most interested parties have already answered to their own satisfaction—should the government continue regulating transportation? Because some, particularly those in important policy-making positions, could change their answers, today's discussion is not totally academic.

If every part of the country were completely interchangeable with every other part and if railroads were available everywhere and we had perfect multi-modal competition in every area, we might not have regulation. If every part of the coun-

On October 15, 1974, Commissioner O'Neal publicly noted that the premise of "no clamor for deregulation" advanced by the title no longer seemed as solid as it did at the time of his February remarks before the American Enterprise Institute.

try contained as much coal as West Virginia and if transportation could be isolated from the rest of the world's problems, goals, and aspirations, most defenders of regulation would have to agree that there would be no need for regulation—at least regulation as we know it. We might, nevertheless, have to search for regulatory approaches to achieving national objectives, but policies grounded on economic transportation goals would be of little significance. But the harsh facts are that we have a highly diverse, highly competitive country where transportation is not merely an end in itself, but has a dramatic impact on the location and demographics of cities, towns and industries, and on the environment, on land and water resource use, and the efficient use of energy. Discrimination is a real world threat—one that raises its head every day.

In short, we cannot view transportation as an isolated phenomenon—it must be considered as one part of the universe of national concerns. Congress and the electorate, I believe, understand (or perhaps I should say credit) this fact of life better than many academicians. This recognition of the interrelatedness of transportation and other goals is increasing, but the idea itself is nothing new. Adam Smith in his *Wealth of Nations* acknowledged this in saying:

> When the toll upon carriages of luxury, upon coaches, post-chaises, etc. is made somewhat higher in proportion to their weight, than upon carriages of necessary use, such as carts, waggons, etc. the indolence and vanity of the rich is made to contribute in a very easy manner to the relief of the poor, by rendering cheaper the transportation of heavy goods to all the different parts of the country.

Most advocates of regulation would seem to agree with Adam Smith on this point. But, while Adam Smith, the champion of laissez faire economics, seemed to have little trouble with cross-subsidies, many latter-day economists reject this theory. As I understand the economists' theories about deregulation of transportation, many of them rest on the hypothesis that the cross-subsidies which exist in the present system are deceptive, costly (because buyers pay less than full cost), and unfair to other users. Professor Eads may have hit upon the key difference between today's economists and most public policy makers. I would express his thought as follows: To a government official, fair treatment, equity, social and economic development, service, and other social considerations must be recognized to be of greater importance than, or at least equal in importance to, the economists' goals.

A few months ago in remarks before a transportation law seminar of the Association of ICC Practitioners, I observed that, with all the growing clamor for deregulation, there were still no readily identifiable advocates of deregulation in an absolute sense. I pointed out there that most of those who advocate deregulation as an approach to transportation strongly desire that the government continue to guide its national transportation affairs under some national transportation policy. Such a policy must include some transportation objectives, even if those

190

objectives are merely to foster unfettered intermodal competition for every shipment, subject only to antitrust considerations.

Moreover, many deregulation advocates have expressed a desire, to a greater or lesser extent, for regulation in some other areas affecting transportation. And it is my fundamental belief that, though economic regulation of surface transportation may not be necessary to achieve such objectives, transportation regulation, if it is to continue, must accommodate and even further such national concerns as: (1) increased determination to guarantee civil rights; (2) new emphasis on environmental conservation—including energy policies; (3) expanded programs for consumer protection; (4) changing policies for price stabilization; (5) new initiatives in export and import policies—and the resulting impact on the use of transportation facilities; (6) new approaches for dealing with shortages of commodity or transportation facilities; and (7) changing attitudes on needed but commercially unprofitable service (such as rail passenger service and Northeast rail freight service).

It is not my purpose here to go into the particulars of any legislation or, for that matter, to go into any reform proposals. The question today is whether regulation makes sense—not whether we do it well enough or whether there are needed reforms. We must focus on possible accomplishments and benefits attainable under regulation.

Important Functions of Regulation

Probably the most important function of regulation is to eliminate unjust discrimination. As with section 3 of the Interstate Commerce Act, such protection against discrimination flows not only toward carriers and shippers, but also toward regions and cities, and reaches in its effect the ultimate consumers and the initial producers of commodities. Potentially the regulatory body provides a protection which cannot easily be obtained through the judicial system. Where the regulatory body can institute rule-making proceedings and develop rules which anticipate and proscribe discriminatory actions (and later punish such actions), the courts by the nature of the judicial system are pretty much limited to punishment and required to act after the fact. Because of the devastating nature of discriminatory actions, justice delayed is often disastrous. I shall discuss this in more detail shortly.

Another aspect of discrimination is presented where a noncompetitive situation exists. Regulation may be the only way of preventing unreasonable rates from developing where there is no competition or no effective competition. An example occurs where captive shippers are limited to one railroad, a not infrequent condition in many parts of the country. The judicial system, again acting after the fact through antitrust laws and the like, probably would be an ineffective instrument against this sort of abuse. Furthermore, advocates of deregulation are not convincing in their claim that noncompetitive situations would end with the end of regulation. How effective have the antitrust laws been in curbing oligopoly or near-monopoly situations in U.S. industry? A glance at the U.S. auto industry, the steel industry and IBM raises some serious questions.

A second general area where regulation probably plays an important role is the area of service quality. Some argue that the need for regulating service quality arises only where regulation exists—that actually the marketplace is a much better regulator of quality than is a federal bureaucracy. It seems to me this theory is significantly weakened if one analyzes industries that are unregulated in the sense we mean it and where the quality is open to criticism. The automobile industry and the meat-processing industry are obvious examples here.

Related to the quality-of-service problem (indeed, sometimes a part of it) is the question of service availability. Transportation is important not only as a means of moving people and goods from point to point, but as an instrument of social and economic development. For example, in a pure market situation elimination of branch lines may make good sense, but where it is thought useful to maintain the vitality of agricultural areas or smaller cities, elimination of branch lines may be intolerable. If we still believe that non-transportation factors are important, what entity should make this evaluation? There would still be conflicting interests to resolve in most instances. Is a court capable of developing a consistent policy toward abandonment attempts and dealing with public and private interests not arising from regulation, and if the court is capable of doing this, should such a burden be imposed on the already overloaded judicial system? These questions would probably apply to many areas where there is at least arguably a need for regulation.

Another aspect of service availability relates to the conglomerate problem or the merger and acquisition problem and the effect that corporate reorganizations might have on the capacity of a carrier to provide transportation service. It would seem that a transportation regulatory agency having rule-making authority and the expertise to establish standards for determining the impact of mergers and acquisitions on transportation is in a better position than a court would be to administer this area.

It would appear to be difficult to use the antitrust laws to ensure that socially, economically, and environmentally desirable service is maintained. To ensure this requires action of a different nature, necessarily requiring the capacity to interpret and develop standards so that all parties affected are treated fairly and all goals have a chance of being attained.

While decisions on pure transportation grounds are clearly not satisfactory from a general policy standpoint, neither are decisions on pure antitrust grounds. It may be asked, as an example, whether significant deregulation of the motor-carrier household-goods movers could possibly produce the kind of service that would be acceptable to consumers.

National Transportation Policy

Any discussion such as today's inescapably leads to some review of the congressional mandate for ICC action—the policy statement of Congress, last amended in 1940, that applies to all parts of the Interstate Commerce Act. This congressional statement is known as the national transportation policy. The policy involves: (1) fair and impartial regulation of all modes of transportation subject to the act; (2) a recognition and preservation of the inherent advantages of each mode; (3) the promotion of safe, adequate, economical and efficient service; (4) the fostering of sound economic conditions in transportation and among the several carriers; (5) the establishment and maintenance of reasonable charges for transportation service, without unjust discriminations, undue preferences or advantages, and unfair or destructive competitive practices; (6) cooperation with the several states and their duly authorized officials; and (7) the encouragement of fair wages and equitable working conditions. Thus, all our regulation under the act must be directed to developing, coordinating, and preserving a national transportation system by water, highway, and rail, as well as by other means adequate to meet the needs of the commerce of the United States, of the Postal Service, and of the national defense. This policy controls regulation by the ICC. If deregulation is to be attempted, it is this policy and its implementation that must be studied and then modified or rescinded.

The purposes of regulation are manifold. Not only do they include objectives of the national transportation policy, but also the other concerns evidenced in congressional actions that implement the Interstate Commerce Act. And it is clear that they involve the whole universe of governmental concerns. They do not relate solely to transportation costs. They include plant dislocation, employee displacement, social costs, domestic implications of importing and exporting, environment and energy considerations, and the like. Each of these is a part of the fabric. Many different figures are cited for the cost of regulation—though none have been adequately documented and in my opinion they have little meaning. But, even if one of the larger ones (from $2 to $10 billion) were accepted, how much concern should be given to such a figure? To what extent would this be offset by other costs?

One objective of government has been economic development. Economic development is an appropriate governmental function and one with which few would argue. Once the decision for economic development as a governmental objective has been made (and it has been made by the federal government or by local governments with the support of the federal government), the pure market mechanism is not likely to be able to work its will. Direct subsidies are often used. But they create as many distortions and discrepancies and perhaps as many problems for economists as do cross-subsidies. It may be more fruitful to recognize the dynamic nature of the beast and admit that there is such a thing as developmental economics involved in transportation regulation, although direct subsidies are still a viable possibility. Congress, however, likes to use what is easiest to use at the moment and the best example of this may be the congressional attitude manifested in the Interstate Commerce Act in the late 1800s and early 1900s as opposed to the attitude manifested in the enactment of the CAB Act in 1938, which included a direct subsidy. In its most basic terms, this contrasts in the transportation field an internal versus external method of subsidization.

Overlooked Costs of Deregulation

In deciding which approach to take or whether or not one approach should be phased out, one may obtain different answers according to how the problem is viewed. An examination of the economics and goals of the transportation sector of the economy by itself may yield uncompromising support for deregulation, while a view encompassing the entire economy may produce a somewhat different result. Deregulation may create dense populations in city centers and social and economic dislocation. Land use and population density are matters which cannot be ignored. There is no question that transportation has a vital impact on location and the disturbing pattern of past successes and failures may be attributable to the fact that we do not know enough about the economics of land use nor do we have sufficient policy guidelines in this area. We know even less about land use and related goals than we do about the economics of transportation. The market almost never works well for land use, and transportation policy and land use have a very close relationship. If you deregulate transportation you must recognize that the deregulation will have an effect on land use. On the basis of past experience it may be predicted that this effect will be generally negative.

One argument often used to support the need for deregulation is that there is tremendous underutilization of transportation facilities (particularly in the railroad industry) and a tremendous amount of excess capacity. But even assuming that deregulation will improve utilization (and this is well worth disputing, absent the careful research necessary to reach conclusions), we still have an obligation to look at the larger world and measure the impact of deregulation on other capacities—the capacity of communities and shippers, for instance. Will plants be required to close up or move? Will whole communities be returned to nonproductivity and unemployment?

If deregulation brings lower transportation rates for high-density areas, resulting in the benefits of improved railroad utilization in those areas, must we not as a nation set off those benefits against the grave economic costs of deregulation—including not only the cost to the private shipper but also the public costs which may result from unsatisfactory land use causing greater population density in certain areas, and suddenly requiring more police, firemen, public transportation, sewers, and garbage collection? Such a problem might not exist if all parts of the

194

country were fungible—if Douglas fir trees with a diameter of eight feet grew in all parts of the country, or if meat were produced in every part of the country. But as we all know, this is far from the case.

There also seems to be an assumption on the part of many deregulators that carriers and especially railroads are ubiquitous and are competitive with one another in all places. Granted that railroads might be made more competitive with better utilization of trucks for piggyback, ubiquity and uniform competitiveness do not apply. If the railroads did take advantage of the opportunities which exist for using trucks in collection and distribution, and therefore became more ubiquitous, regulation should not prove to be a significant hindrance. In fact, regulation might still be required as a force to help balance competition and avoid the establishment of monopolistic situations.

The theory seems to also assume the ability of each consumer to exercise complete judgment. He is assumed to have complete sovereignty over satisfying his own desires. Anyone should be able to spend whatever he has, the way he sees fit, and whatever he does is okay. Of course, Congress has never accepted this idea and the community (through Congress and through local and state governmental actions) has submitted its judgment for the judgments of individuals in numerous areas, including, of course, education, where it has become compulsory, and perhaps this will also be true shortly in health care. We have been and, in many areas, continue to be unwilling to pay the social price of allowing the exercise of unfettered judgment. The government has substituted its judgment over the marketplace in this same respect in the area of transportation, and it has done this for many years. This has not been as acceptable to everyone as some other interventions by the government, so what we have seen in the past few years is an effort to achieve a re-evaluation of the government's posture toward transportation regulation.

There is no question that there are transportation subsidies. It has been argued, for example, that the shipment of western lettuce is subsidized while hardware transportation pays more than it should. Theoretically, if this imbalance were eliminated, you would buy more hardware and less lettuce. But as most of you know, when the railroads attempted to make major rate readjustments on agricultural commodities with ICC acquiescence in the 1920s, the country experienced a classic case of congressional intervention—not based on the narrow confines of transportation economics, but based on the overriding real-world problem of an agricultural depression. Congressional action took the form of the Hoch-Smith resolution, clarifying doubts about whether regulators should consider nontransportation factors. The resolution did help preserve then-existing rate relationships. Again Congress used the tools available to it, just as it did in a much different way when a pragmatic approach was taken in underfunding Amtrak to get it started, with full congressional cognizance of the fact that additional funds would be necessary to its later survival.

This, incidentally, suggests another social reason for moving traffic at less than resource cost—the reason being the need to redistribute income. The lower prices that occur on food help low-income or moderate-income groups. Higher rates on high-value commodities may take something away from the rich and from industry, but they help keep food moving at lower prices.

What about the idea that transportation should stand on its own feet and let other factors adjust to it? Why not just let prices be raised for inelastic market situations, and lowered to meet competition for elastic situations? Once again, if we remove transportation from the other considerations of the world and view it in isolation free from any consideration of public costs, we might be inclined to conclude that it would be fine to let transportation just fend for itself. But what about those public costs?

Should people move to high-density areas for better transportation? Why not let everybody move to or near New York where there is a better chance that they would get good transportation service? An obvious reason for not encouraging such action is that such encouragement ignores public costs. What are the community costs for handling such an influx? One might ask how many businesses could afford to function in the resulting environment. Could the twin towers of the Trade Buildings in New York attract any users if everybody had to pay fully for all the costs of being in that city? For instance, the garbage costs, the police-protection costs, the costs of constructing transit and road transportation facilities? Could New York exist? At present there is a feeling increasingly prevalent among people in and out of New York that New York is intolerable because of its high social cost, meaning that the costs to the private industrial sector are so much below the total public costs that it is a great burden on New York's present and future population just to meet those public costs.

Additional Reasons for Continued Regulation

Even apart from arguments that relate to the achievement of national objectives unrelated or only indirectly related to the transportation market, there are sound reasons for the continued regulation of transportation. I alluded to some of them earlier, stressing the problems of discrimination. That this is a problem is borne out by the ICC's experience with regulation. In many respects the nature of the competitor does not change depending upon whether regulation does or does not exist.

One basic purpose of the original Act to Regulate Commerce was to assure that all those who required transportation service would obtain service to the extent that it was then available. This concentration on the primacy of meeting service needs can be found in the subsequent major amendments to the act in 1935, 1940 and 1942, which brought new modes of transport under regulation. A major error by present-day detractors of regulation is their losing sight of this principle and their substituting "assurance of profitability" for "assurance of service."

While in 1887 the railroads may have had mixed feelings about regulation, the subsequent major amendments to part I and the addition of the other parts of the act, if not enthusiastically promoted by the interested carrier groups, were at least not vigorously opposed by them. The lack of opposition was prompted by what the carrier groups saw as provisions advantageous to their own selfish interests, largely the likelihood of assuring profitability and possibly increasing profits. Thus, the carrier groups favored controls over cutthroat rate reductions and limitations on free entry. The restrictions on competition—the legalization of semi-monopolistic positions—were the *quid pro quo* for the imposition of a quasi-public utility status on the regulated carrier. And what did that status involve? First and foremost, it required the provision of a transportation service with all that the word "transportation" connotes.

As a quasi-public utility the carrier is obligated to satisfy the public's need for transportation in several ways: (1) it must provide transportation service; (2) it must provide service equally to all who apply under reasonably comparable conditions; and (3) it must provide service at fair, reasonable and nondiscriminatory rates equally for all shippers and travelers. The proponents of deregulation frequently contend that achievement of these worthwhile ends no longer requires regulatory constraints although these constraints may have been necessary in the early days of railroad monopoly. They say that the increased competition from other forms of transport will itself assure that the public will be provided with all the service it requires at just and reasonable rates and with equality for all. Unfortunately, the ICC's experience in its harsh role as enforcer does not support this rosy view. The cases which we are and have been making with regularity still disclose a predilection on the part of common carriers of all modes to discriminate in the furnishing of their services and to discriminate in the application of their charges so that certain shippers or communities are favored and others are discriminated against. In short, the mandate calling for equality in service and equality in price is not universally carried out. The failure to carry it out, of course, is prompted by claims of necessity rather than whim, but nevertheless shippers and travelers still complain regularly and vehemently that they are being victimized both by unequal service and unequal rates. The discrimination and favoritism practiced are not of the flagrant and crude varieties known to the early railroad barons; they have been replaced by subtle and sophisticated devices. But the undesirable effect on the public interest remains substantially the same.

The basic adverse effects of discrimination on the quality and availability of service can be found in practically every serious enforcement action undertaken by the ICC under the authority of long-standing provisions of the act. For example, the recent contempt-of-court case concluded against the Greyhound companies, in which fines of $600,000 were imposed, illustrated a strong and concerted effort over a ten-year span to deny to a significant segment of the traveling public the service which could be available from a competitive carrier to and from the Pacific

Northwest area. Moreover, Greyhound had been found guilty of similar anti-competitive practices at other times in the recent past in different areas of the country, practices all of which would, if successful, have denied to the passenger services to which he was entitled. In addition to the monetary fines that were levied, injunctions were obtained to assure the company's good conduct in the future.

The theme of assuring each shipper equal availability to his fair share of the transportation plant is the basis for many other ICC activities. The many civil forfeiture cases either voluntarily settled by the railroads or the subject of court suit for violations of ICC service orders are, as the name implies, designed to make critical rail equipment (and thus rail service) available on as equitable a basis as possible. Theoretically, as the deregulators would have it, the normal play of competitive pressures would mean that the "best" use of equipment naturally would be practiced by the carriers. Yet we find, time after time, that wasteful or discriminatory use of freight cars is the rule, or that favoritism is practiced in allowing certain shippers excessive periods of time for the payment of transportation charges, or that rate concessions or rebates are extended to preferred shippers. These practices frequently mean that other shippers are being discriminated against and possibly placed in such a weakened competitive position that they are precluded from a market and thus, for all practical purposes, being denied their right to transportation service. It should be obvious that the removal of regulatory restraints would not automatically eliminate these abuses. Unfortunately, in this imperfect world, in an industry affected by the public interest, the big stick of heavy penalties may be the only way to keep these adverse effects on the public interest within reasonable bounds.

The same attempt to assure continued service is evident in the many ICC proceedings. A particular proceeding might involve a clear-cut failure of a licensed carrier to serve specific shippers or points or areas which his certificate of public convenience and necessity obligates him to serve. Or it might involve his failure to handle shipments which he considers undesirable because he believes them to be unprofitable. Frequently, no other carrier is available or interested in providing the service required by the particular segment of the shipping public. It is difficult to see how the elimination of the certification process sought by some of the deregulators would help those thousands of small businesses whose traffic is not particularly heavy or particularly attractive from a profit standpoint when compared with that of other and more affluent shippers. While ICC efforts on behalf of these small businesses may be far from perfect, I am unaware of any practical remedy available to them now or proposed for the future which would secure the relief they need.

In addition to placing too much faith in the ameliorating effects of competition, those favoring deregulation frequently overlook the poor management practices of many carriers. Many deregulators place all the blame for the sad state of many carriers on the "outmoded" restraints placed on them by regulatory laws.

Now admittedly the Northeastern area has more than its share of difficult operating problems, but this is not to say that the shortsightedness (if not the venality) of the former Penn Central management did not have a significant part to play in the wreck of the Penn Central nor that the unwise and costly management decisions which ICC investigations constantly turn up have not had a significant effect on the viability and profitability of many other carriers. After all, the Delaware and Hudson and many large motor carriers all operating under full regulation have returned a profit operating alongside the Penn Central. The Southern roads and the Western roads, under regulatory controls similar to those in the Northeast, regularly produce satisfactory returns. Without claiming perfection in the provisions of the act or in the ICC's administration of the act, we can say that our experience has shown that poor management frequently is the principal cause of the serious bind that many carriers find themselves in.

Regulation Can Be Improved

Regulation, overall, is far from perfect or complete. Too frequently the investigations of violations, although technically supportable, are carrier welfare cases rathere than public interest cases. An investigator may discover a number of shipments of unauthorized commodities or transportation to unauthorized points. He often expects extreme penalties to be imposed even though there is no evidence that the service by other carriers has been endangered. In such a case the only evidence may be theoretical loss of revenue to authorized carriers who may or may not be interested in providing service to the shippers involved. Technical (or sometimes inadvertent) violations may be uncovered and made the subject of full-scale investigations. These investigations can represent regulation only for the sake of regulation—a practice the ICC constantly attempts to discourage. We encourage efforts to uncover serious economic assaults on the public's right to the best available transportation service at fair, equally applied, and reasonable charges. Under regulation, we must continue these efforts but they can only be successful with a practical regulatory law as their foundation, and this law must be subject to constant scrutiny.

At present it would appear that there is a communications gap between deregulation advocates and the chief policy makers (in this case, primarily Congress). The policy makers are concerned about shifts in policy that might upset the existing tangled web of relationships, thereby creating unacceptably high nontransportation costs. If deregulation can save as much as the deregulators claim, but will result in greater losses elsewhere, members of Congress know they will not find solace in debate on the floor. It will be too late for that then. Until the course of possible deregulation is charted better than it has been thus far, the proper attention of Congress will be directed toward improving the existing system or making adjustments where the penalties will be small or the direction will be reversible.

It is important to keep in mind here that the ICC to its credit has not held a hard-and-fast line against all attempts at deregulation. In the past the ICC has recommended to Congress that it be given authority to deregulate entry requirements where it appears that the particular operating-rights regulation being enforced accomplishes no public purpose. Perhaps this recommendation could be revised and amplified to provide the agency with the specific authority to attempt selected deregulation on a pilot basis. If this were done, the agency could monitor deregulation experiments and document their consequences. It could thereby contribute the actual results of experience under such experiments to the theoretical dialogue between those favoring and those opposed to regulation.

During the last few years there have been calls for abolition of the ICC which have engendered more heat than light to the regulatory reform dialogue. Now that this cry has subsided—perhaps mooted by the passage of time and events that have made the need for at least some form of transportation regulation evident to most of those who would have to be convinced—it may be time to put aside also the bogey of "deregulation" as well as the bogey of "abolition" and concentrate on the proper form of regulation and on carrying out improved regulation for the future. It is only with a redirected emphasis upon regulatory reform within the context of a full review of regulatory objectives that we can expect progress in tailoring regulation to our nation's needs for today and tomorrow.

PROSPECTS FOR REGULATORY REFORM

Gary L. Seevers

As Professor Eads described it so well yesterday afternoon, the fight for deregulation of transportation has been the story of a few brave but lonely economists stubbornly attacking the American economy's largest legal cartel. The audience that must hear their message is, unfortunately, unaware of the fight or what it is all about. Many of the members of that audience are simply apathetic about the outcome. Protected by a powerful coalition of regulators and the "regulated," the cartel is thus far intact, even if a little apprehensive. Eads warned us to expect a long and frustrating siege rather than a quick and glorious victory.

This is not a cheerful story. Sieges are won by numbers and resources, not by bravery and brains. Eads predicts that economists will win, in the long run, only if we use our brains to increase the numbers of our supporters. I believe that he is right.

When we as economists engage in the study of political economy, it is essential that we not confuse the economic case with the political strategy. Political realities sometimes change quickly, and require changes in strategy. The economic case does not. Most economists support the economic merits of deregulation. Several of the members of this audience understand the economic case extremely well and have helped develop it. I shall not indulge in an exercise of convincing the committed. And anyone who is uncommitted at this time would not be convinced by another restatement of the arguments.

Instead, I want to discuss some aspects of the process by which deregulation can be achieved. First, I want to describe the role of the Council of Economic Advisers in the deregulation story. Second, I want to discuss some of the lessons that we have learned about how economic policy is made and how it is implemented.

CEA's Role in Deregulation Initiatives

The CEA has enjoyed a closer association with the academic and research community than any other governmental agency that participates actively in the policy-formulation process. The Council's personnel come from the academic community on an interim basis and we are made up purely of economists. Many other agencies have good economists and more of them than the council has. Our uniqueness is that we are all economists and we are a way station between the economic community and the makers of public policy.

The conceptualization of the waste and inflexibility that regulation causes in the transportation industry entered the economic policy arena largely through academicians who were induced to serve a term in government. This fact is important because deregulation is not the sort of idea that is likely to arise from practitioners, bureaucrats, or others involved closely with political processes. Deregulation is an idea that comes to life only to those who have seen a particular form of an abstract ideal—resource allocation in a free and essentially competitive economy.

As I said, this is simply not the sort of idea that naturally occurs to practitioners and policy makers. Their daily environment does not encourage or perhaps even permit speculation or conceptualization of such abstract ideals. They tend to think in terms of incremental improvements in the status quo. Their goal tends to be relative comfort and not absolute bliss.

This goal of relative comfort introduces a degree of caution and conservatism into the policy-making process that is not without its advantages, but it also underscores the importance of an agency in which longer perspectives and less "practical" thoughts are encouraged. Looking back over past economic reports one can find periodic references to transportation and the need for regulatory reform. Both the 1966 and 1969 reports discuss the problem with some specificity. However, it was really in the 1970s that momentum toward deregulation was achieved. Strong personal support and hard work by the council and its staff were instrumental in getting the proposed Transportation Regulatory Modernization Act presented before the 92d Congress in 1972.

It would not be accurate to assert that the idea of deregulation or the qualified version of it in the 1972 proposal enjoyed immediate or widespread support even within the federal government. To many it seemed a radical and dangerous proposal. In bureaucracies, however, time does tend to confer respectability. The CEA has continued to support and advocate deregulation. As a consequence, the idea no longer frightens as many people as it did at one time.

Lessons for Policy Development and Implementation

I am convinced that policy is implemented when the right people know what they want and are adequately prepared to argue for what they want and when these people are in positions in which they have the power to make their case effectively. Agricultural policy and international monetary policy are both important recent examples of this.

For some time economists have pretty much shared a consensus on what ought to be done in these areas. But it was not until the right set of circumstances or the optimum crisis (depending upon how one views the matter) occurred that reforms were possible.

Given this view of the policy process, where do we stand with respect to deregulation of transportation?

Will those who give transportation deregulation an important place in their list of goals be in positions from which they can effectively argue their case when and if the proper circumstances arise? Deregulation today has an important place in the transportation policy of the Nixon administration. This place is clearly recognizable in the transportation message that President Nixon sent to the Congress on February 13, 1974—as well as in the Transportation Improvement Act that was submitted to Congress the same week. Deregulation now has broad support within the Nixon administration.

I think that this will continue to be the case regardless of partisan fortunes in the future. Although the number of formally trained economists in policy-making positions is certainly at a record level, I see no evidence that this is a peak of an "economist in government" cycle.

As long as economists are in positions to speak, I believe that the case for deregulation will be made—regardless of the political party that controls the Old Executive Office Building. Congressional and congressional staff tenure rivals academic tenure. Getting modern economists into the right places on the Hill appears to take a longer time than getting them into the right places in the executive branch, but I think progress is being made there too.

This leaves us with the question of the arrival of the proper circumstances or the "optimum crisis." As you know, the CEA is trying to get out of the business of predicting the future with precision, and I am certainly not going to predict the quarter or even the year when the Federal Energy Office will move into the office space made available by the trimming back of the ICC. However, I think that it is useful to raise the question because it bears directly on some of the peculiarities of the deregulation tactics and this is the topic with which I want to conclude my comments.

In speculating on the "optimum crisis" it is important to keep in mind our earlier discussion of the nature and origin of the deregulation idea. At the limit, deregulation is an almost completely new way of doing things. Normally one system does not replace another system in an orderly and timely way as the consequence of incremental changes in the status quo. Obsolete systems tend to be replaced only after they have become so obsolete that their shortcomings are evident to even the least perceptive observers.

As Professor Nelson and others have pointed out, the policy of the regulatory agencies does evolve by response to the changing needs of their constituencies—however slowly—over time. One cannot depend upon irate truck drivers or even epidemic bankruptcies to bring about deregulation.

Successful deregulation will require the policy maker to do three things. He must keep the goal of deregulation firmly in mind. He must keep reminding himself that the marginal or incremental adjustments practitioners are likely to make in the status quo will not necessarily lead to that long-run goal. And he must, therefore, evaluate incremental changes not only by short-term standards but also by their consistency with long-run goals.

A CAB PERSPECTIVE ON AIRLINE REGULATION

Roy Pulsifer

I want to begin with the standard disclaimer that I do not speak for the Civil Aeronautics Board. On the other hand, I am an official of the CAB, and everything I say will, I hope, be consistent with the board's thinking.

Regulation or Deregulation

The question of regulation or deregulation for the airlines can be summed up quite succinctly. Economic regulation, in its present form, began with the enactment of the Civil Aeronautics Act of 1938. This legislation was reenacted in 1958 without substantive change. Moreover, Congress has approved approximately thirty amendments affecting title IV, the section of the act dealing with economic regulation, and none of these—not one—indicates any movement toward deregulation. In other words, there has been no chipping away at the basic commitment to regulation. One could argue, in fact, that a little cement has been added here and there. I see no effective pressure for deregulation in air transportation, none whatsoever. If the present situation is an accurate guide to the future, the Civil Aeronautics Board will continue to regulate the airlines indefinitely. So much for deregulation. For the remainder of my comments I would like to mention two ironies and then give you a very brief rundown on the state of the industry and major regulatory problems.

The first irony is that in 1938 about nineteen carriers received grandfather authority by act of Congress. And, through the years, because of merger, bankruptcy and for other reasons, this group of trunk carriers has been reduced to ten. Starting about 1965, the CAB enlarged the role of local-service carriers which became, in essence, very small trunk carriers. The irony is that in 1938 we had nineteen nonspecialist carriers and today we have eighteen, the board having kept constant (or brought back to constancy) the number of carriers operating in the system.

The second irony is as follows. The domestic forty-eight states generated over 120 billion revenue passenger-miles in 1972 as compared to one-half billion in 1938. The airline fleet in 1938 consisted of about 250 DC-3s and other similar

Editor's note: It should be noted that Mr. Pulsifer spoke extemporaneously as a last-minute substitute for another official of the Civil Aeronautics Board. Mr. Pulsifer's willingness to do this was much appreciated.

planes, more or less. And the CAB's staff, which quickly grew in number to about 500, was charged with regulating this industry. Today the unregulated component of the interstate system, the commuter/air-taxi carriers, make up an industry about the same size as the original grandfather carriers—the fleet is roughly equivalent, as is the volume of traffic generated. But the CAB's present staff of some 700 is not economically regulating these commuter operations, and the board has determined, as a matter of policy, that they should not be regulated.

State of the Industry

Of obvious recent concern to the industry and the CAB is the fuel-allocation program. The only previous time that the supply side of air transportation was similarly restrained was during World War II.

In November 1973, the carriers were cut back about 10 percent on the fuel that they were then getting, and in January they were told that a further 15 percent cut would be required, making their operations about 25 percent under what they would otherwise have been. The fuel allocation was later increased to some extent, but as of mid-February 1974 the trunk carriers were offering a level of service some 15 percent less than they would otherwise have offered, and the local-service carriers were providing about 10 percent less service.

During this energy crisis, fuel costs rose dramatically, with domestic increases averaging about 50 percent. This, of course, has led to considerable pressure for fare increases. While because the restraint on capacity load factors went up and thus presumably carriers were able to realize higher earnings, a recent CAB staff study has indicated that only about three dollars of every ten in cost savings are brought through to net profit.

Overall, the financial performance of the airlines represents a very mixed bag. For example, Eastern is experiencing very serious operating losses. American is also experiencing operating losses, but the trends suggest a pull-out. Pan American continues a five-year trend of net losses, but the gap is narrowing. In any case, these three trunk carriers are performing poorly.

The balance of the industry is doing quite well. Continental is marginally profitable, the only middle-sized carrier that is doing relatively poorly. On the other hand, Delta, Western, National, and Northwest are all earning quite high levels of profit. While the rate of return earned by TWA and United does not meet the CAB's standard of 12 percent on total investment, it is at least acceptable and most airlines are paying dividends.

Recent Regulatory Activities

There are two major areas of regulation to which the CAB is currently devoting special attention. First, on the question of new routes, the board is being very

206

cautious. By and large, the CAB is not hearing applications for new route authority. However, now under consideration are a few route transfer cases, under which one carrier proposes to trade routes with another. There are also several applications involving interchanges—that is, through-plane operations over the routes of two carriers, a type of authority that was last employed domestically about twenty-five years ago. On the other hand, there are a fair number of deletion cases involving small communities where low traffic generators are being stricken from the certificated system. Paradoxically, while constraining route entry domestically, the CAB is going forward with the biggest route case of all time on the international side— the transatlantic case, which involves the sixteen domestic co-terminals now served by Pan American and TWA, and, in addition, a large number of cities in the Southeast and the Southwest that at present do not receive transatlantic service. All the trunk carriers, except United, are in the case and are vigorously prosecuting their applications. That proceeding will go to hearing this summer and should be wound up in about two and one-half years.

Finally, I will note that the board is concluding the last major phase of the domestic passenger fare investigation. That investigation will determine the fare taper—that is, the price of air transportation in relation to the distance traveled— and whether the fare should be "cost-based" or "cost-related." [1]

---

[1] Editor's note: This decision, CAB Order 74-3-82, was issued on March 18, 1974, and found that, in general, fares should be "cost-based," not simply "cost-related." However, the board did reject several proposals for a "zone of reasonableness" approach to price competition.

SUMMARY OF DISCUSSION

In the discussion which followed these presentations, a number of questions were directed to the two regulatory agency representatives on the panel (Commissioner O'Neal and Mr. Pulsifer). For example, one member of the audience questioned Mr. Pulsifer as to why the CAB renders decisions which, in the face of seemingly overwhelming evidence, simply do not make economic sense. Mr. Pulsifer replied forthrightly that the CAB's congressional directive is contained in the Federal Aviation Act's section 102, "Declaration of Policy," and that the board's responsibility is one of carrying out that directive to the best of its ability. If that policy directive contains goals inconsistent with maximizing economic efficiency, then perhaps economists might be well advised to present their case to Congress rather than blame the CAB for inept and inefficient management of the industry.

A question directed to Commissioner O'Neal requested ICC justification for the constraints placed on rate decreases. Commissioner O'Neal responded by asking anyone to cite to him recent cases where the ICC has in fact held up rate decreases when the new rates were above variable cost. In fact, he said, many rate decreases are approved where the new rate arguably is below variable cost. As for the rate-bureau problem, Commissioner O'Neal noted, carriers can petition independently whenever a rate decrease is disapproved in bureau proceedings.

Two comments were made on this response. First, Dr. Snow suggested that if indeed it is ICC policy to approve rate decreases so long as the new rate exceeds variable cost, then the commission should not object to (and should, in fact, support) that provision in the TIA. Another commentator, however, questioned the validity of Commissioner O'Neal's assertion on the ICC's receptive attitude toward rate decreases. This observer stated that inflation had done much to ameliorate the observed problems with ICC constraints on rate floors. He chastized the commission for not tabulating and making publicly available summary information on the number, kind, and significance of ICC rate disapprovals. If the commission did make this summary information publicly available, then all could have a better grasp of the degree to which the ICC "protects consumers" or "protects competitors."

Some of the academicians in the audience appeared exasperated at the assertions of some policy makers that economists have not done a credible job in presenting a good case for deregulation. Their response was to ask, "What, conceivably, would constitute conclusive evidence?" After all, it was argued, look at the work that has been done on the unregulated California intrastate air carriers (for example, by William A. Jordan). Look at the unregulated commuters. What about the innumerable studies by academicians showing the inefficiencies of ICC regulation? Are not the constraints on trucking entry so blatant that their effects are obvious? Some voiced a view that there are few real-world examples of deregulated transport markets (thanks to the regulators) and that when economists analyze those that remain, regulators respond that such examples "are not comparable." Moreover, why should the burden be on the deregulation advocates? Since unregulated competition is the "natural" state of affairs, does it not seem reasonable to require regulators periodically to justify their existence?

The regulator representatives on the panel and in the audience answered that they are not alone in their skepticism over economists' alleged proof of the inferiority of regulation. Some equally competent experts tend to disagree. Moreover, Congress has not at all been persuaded by the arguments of "deregulators," as witness the eighty-seven years of ICC regulation and the thirty-six years of CAB regulation. However, most of the regulator representatives did concede that academicians and their analyses of regulatory inefficiencies have served a "policing" function. That is, whenever economists bring to light blatant regulatory inefficiencies, pressures by the administration and by Congress force regulators toward "self-reform."

Finally, there was some discussion of and general agreement over the need for more efficient communication among those involved in transportation policy making. For example, the emotionally charged term "discrimination" means one thing to an economist and quite another thing to a lawyer. Such semantic differences often lead to debates that shed much heat but little light. Also, what is the decision calculus of regulatory commissions? In reaching decisions, how much do they weigh economic efficiency? Equity? National interest? Is their implicit policy the same as that stated explicitly? Or is the explicit policy, especially that expressed in individual decisions, merely a "justification" for actions decided on other grounds? Is their policy internally consistent? Across modes? Over time? This led some members of the audience to conclude that more work needs to be done on the behavior of regulatory commissions as well as on effects of their decisions.

PART
SIX

EPILOGUE

OPPORTUNITIES FOR ACADEMICIANS TO INFLUENCE TRANSPORTATION POLICY

John W. Barnum

Talking to this group about transportation policy would be very much like preaching to the choir and besides, my deacon, the secretary of transportation, says that we will not be unveiling our transportation policy statement until March 5, at our House Appropriations Committee hearings. Chairman McFall has been waiting for this day, and we are going to be ready. I would, however, like to offer a couple of observations on one of the topics that I understand to be among the principal issues before you, namely the interface between the university community and government in transportation.

In thinking about this issue I go back to an experience I had in the General Motors monopoly case, brought by the Antitrust Division against General Motors for having "monopolized" the locomotive industry. We have today in this country some ten steam locomotives, as against about 30,000 diesel-electrics. There was a time, of course, thirty years ago, when the figures were quite the reverse. General Motors attained its "monopoly" position in diesel-electrics in substantial part because it came up with a better idea, and it marketed it in a way that was consistent with modern automobile marketing practices. It was the classic Model-T all over again. General Motors made one locomotive, and it was black, whereas many of the railroads at that time were still each designing their own favorite steam locomotive to be manufactured by Baldwin or Lima or Alco or some other manufacturer.

That is the "mechanical" explanation of how General Motors got there. The reason I think the story is pertinent to your mission, however, is this: I remember going to interview Martin W. Clement, who had been president of the Pennsylvania Railroad during the period that General Motors had captured the locomotive market. Mr. Clement was a potential witness at the trial, and I asked him how it had come to pass that General Motors acquired such a large market share in the locomotive industry—an industry that was already occupied by substantial competing companies. (To be sure, each producer had its favorite clients, but by and large it was quite a competitive industry.) His answer was more philosophical than the dollars-and-cents explanation I have just given you. It went like this: You know, at the turn of the century, the best students in the universities, when they graduated, would go into civil engineering. This was what they studied, and in large part it was they who went out and built the railroads. During the first two or three decades of this century, railroading was the great industry of this country. But by the 1930s, and certainly by the 1940s, the good people in the universities were no longer studying civil engineering. By now, they were more interested in mechanical engineering, and they were going into the great new glamor fields of the automobile industry. So, of course, when steam locomotion tumbled, here was a company, General Motors (that had already proven itself in the automotive field), which seized upon the idea of the diesel engine. It made one engine, and it was black, and it knocked the pants off the people who had been building steam locomotives for decades and who, as late as 1949, were saying there will always be steam locomotives.

Since the 1930s and 1940s, of course, the technical people studying in the universities have gone on to other fields. Space is the obvious example; computer science is another. What I ask of you is this: As you think about the interface between the universities and government, think of how you are inspiring the people in your universities to work on transportation questions. Because, indeed, the future of transportation in this country is greatly dependent upon your students.

Along these lines, I would like to quote a short section of a very good editorial entitled "The Wasted Resource," which appeared in the *New York Times* last December:

> In every major crisis in recent American history, the nation's leadership has regularly turned to the universities for help. Today, the universities are idling. The demands on the university by Government and society have declined. Their research capacity is under-utilized and in danger of being dismantled. This is clearly a time to mobilize the universities once again to respond to the larger needs of the nation.

Mass transportation, in the words of the editorial, "must be rescued from the inefficient, unimaginative and change resistant transportation industry." The editorial goes on to recommend that, indeed, we must look more to the universities as a source of ideas, as a testing ground and, I would add, as a birthplace for the transportation leaders of the future.

We are doing something about this challenge in the Department of Transportation. Specifically, we have two programs to do something about it. First, there is the University Research Program, run out of Dr. Cannon's office, where, in the course of the last two years, we have received some 808 proposals from 200 different universities, and where we have arranged funding for 73 proposals from 54 universities.

For example, in Buffalo, the State University of New York is studying urban-transportation demands in the Buffalo area, particularly for persons without cars. Results of this study are already being distributed to the Niagara Frontier Transportation Authority, the Greater Buffalo Development Foundation, and the New

214

York State Department of Transportation. Another project is being carried out by a consortium of six colleges and universities located around the Great Lakes. These schools, in Michigan, Wisconsin, and Minnesota, are studying the transportation problems peculiar to their region—an area that obviously, by virtue of its weather conditions, has its own quite distinct transportation problems. The northern parts of these states are underdeveloped, and what this consortium is attempting to do is to identify some of the transportation options that are feasible for that part of the world.

Those are just two of the seventy-three projects we have underway. I recognize that these are, in many respects, nuts-and-bolts problems. They are discrete. They are often local. But I think that they as well as some of the more widely ranging problems that the universities have put to us (and that we are funding) could turn out to be the crucible in which you will be making the transportation leaders of the next generation.

The second DOT program is in the Urban Mass Transportation Administration, where there is funding for a number of schools working on problems specifically related to mass transportation.

Whatever may be the popular image of the academic community and policy makers in government as ships passing in the night, these two programs are evidence—to me at least—of a sincere interest on our part in taking advantage of what you can do to bring to us, and to the nation as a whole, a new generation of bright people who are willing and able to address transportation problems. In short, if you can encourage your students to become enthusiastic about the crucial issues we are facing in transportation today, we will all be better for it. I urge you to focus on the opportunity you have to influence the transportation policies of the future, and to seize that opportunity.

LIST OF
CONFERENCE PARTICIPANTS

Adams, Robert T., *Federal Highway Administration*
Adkins, Roger, *Office of Management and Budget*
Banner, Paul H., *Southern Railway System*
Barnum, John W., *Under Secretary, Department of Transportation*
Boyd, J. Hayden, *Motor Vehicle Manufacturers Association*
Brooks, Robert J., *Interstate Commerce Commission*
Brown, Samuel L., *Civil Aeronautics Board*
Brown, William F., *Department of Transportation*
Brozen, Yale, *Professor, University of Chicago*
Carlin, Alan, *Environmental Protection Administration*
Carol, Arthur, *Aide to Senator William Brock*
Clearwaters, Keith, *Department of Justice*
Demory, Willard, *Civil Aeronautics Board*
De Vany, Arthur S., *Professor, Texas A&M University*
Diller, George, *Interstate Commerce Commission*
Douglas, George W., *Professor, University of North Carolina (Chapel Hill)*
Eads, George, *Professor, George Washington University*
Eastman, Samuel E., *Department of Transportation*
Eckert, Ross D., *Professor, University of Southern California*
Eldridge, Paul, *Civil Aeronautics Board*
Ericson, Ellen, *Journal of Commerce*
Fahlstrom, Paul G., *Department of Transportation*
Feulner, Edwin, *Staff of Congressman Philip Crane*
Foley, Martin E., *Interstate Commerce Commission*
Fox, Harrison, *Aide to Senator William Brock*
Gansle, James J., *Department of Transportation*
George, Jim, *Aide to Senator William Brock*
Gould, Bernard A., *Interstate Commerce Commission*
Grady, John A., *Interstate Commerce Commission*
Guth, Herbert J., *Federal Aviation Administration*
Hay, George, *Department of Justice*
Hilton, George W., *Professor, University of California (Los Angeles)*
Horton, George, *Auburn University*
Hymson, Edward, *Professor, George Mason University*
Johnson, David B., *Professor, Louisiana State University*
Jones, Wynford, *Aide to Senator William Brock*
Jordan, William A., *Professor, York University (Toronto)*

217

Kahn, Fritz, *Interstate Commerce Commission*
Karr, Albert R., *Wall Street Journal*
Klem, Richard, *Department of Transportation*
Knowles, Don, *RHD Travel Publications*
Kutzke, William A., *Department of Transportation*
Lobdell, Jared, *Professor, Pace University Graduate School*
McAdams, Alan, *Professor, Cornell University*
McCormick, William J., *Interstate Commerce Commission*
Meeker, William G., *National Transportation Safety Board*
Miller, James C., III, *Professor, Texas A&M University*
Mohring, Herbert, *Professor, University of Minnesota*
Morrissey, John E., *National Commission on Productivity*
Morton, Alexander L., *Professor, Harvard Business School*
Murphy, Russell F., *Department of Transportation*
Nelson, James C., *Professor, Washington State University*
Nupp, Byron, *Department of Transportation*
O'Neal, A. Daniel, *Commissioner, Interstate Commerce Commission*
Oppler, Edward P., *Department of Transportation*
Pfahler, Robert D., *Interstate Commerce Commission*
Pollock, Bruce, *Office of Representative Patricia Schroeder*
Pulsifer, Roy, *Civil Aeronautics Board*
Pulsipher, Allan, *Council of Economic Advisers*
Rhodes, Robert G., *Interstate Commerce Commission*
Schotta, Charles, *Department of Treasury*
Seevers, Gary L., *Member, Council of Economic Advisers*
Shea, Dick, *Department of Transportation*
Snow, John W., *Department of Transportation*
Studnicki-Ginzbert, K. W., *Canadian Transport Commission*
Tollison, Robert D., *Professor, Texas A&M University*
Trilling, Donald, *Department of Transportation*
Wechsler, A. N., *Cahners Publications*
Whitehurst, Clinton, *Professor, Clemson University*

Cover and book design: Pat Taylor